Parachute Workbook and Resource Guide

Contents

I. The Parachute Workbook

The Quick Job-Hunting Map

for
Determined
Job-Hunters & Career-Changers

*How to Create A Picture
of Your Ideal Job
or Next Career*

Introduction

I N ORDER TO HUNT FOR YOUR IDEAL JOB, or even something close to your ideal job, you must have a picture of it in your head. The clearer the picture, the easier it will be to hunt for it. The purpose of this Workbook is to guide you as you draw that picture.

We have chosen a "Flower" as a model for that picture. While such expressions as "plugging in," "turning on," and other common phrases portray you (implicitly) as a machine, you are actually much more like a Flower than a machine. That is to say, you flourish in some job-environments, but wither in others. Therefore, the purpose of putting together this Flower Picture of yourself is to help you identify what kind of a work climate you will flourish in, and thus do your very best work. Your twin goals should be to be as happy as you can be at your job, while at the same time you do your most effective work.

The small picture of our Flower model on the next page gives you an overview. That picture of the Flower, however, isn't large enough, nor does each petal have enough detail, to be really useful as a worksheet.

The actual worksheets, dealing with one petal at a time, are scattered throughout the remainder of this Workbook. You will deal with the petals in a *logical* order of learning, beginning with the ones that are easiest to fill out, and working on through to the harder ones.

The order in which you will work on the eight petals is:

1. Physical Setting
2. Spiritual or Emotional Setting
3. My Favorite Skills -- what I like to do with *Things, People* and/or *Information.*
4. My Favorite Kinds of **People** I Like to Use These Skills with
5. My Favorite Kinds of **Information** I Like to Use These Skills with
6. My Favorite Kinds of **Things** I Like to Use These Skills with
7. Outcomes: Immediate and Long-range
8. Rewards: Salary, Level and Other

And when you are done, you will put all the petals together, so that they will form one complete Flower picture of your Ideal Job. Okay? Then, get out your pen and pencil and *let's get started.*

A Picture of My Ideal Job

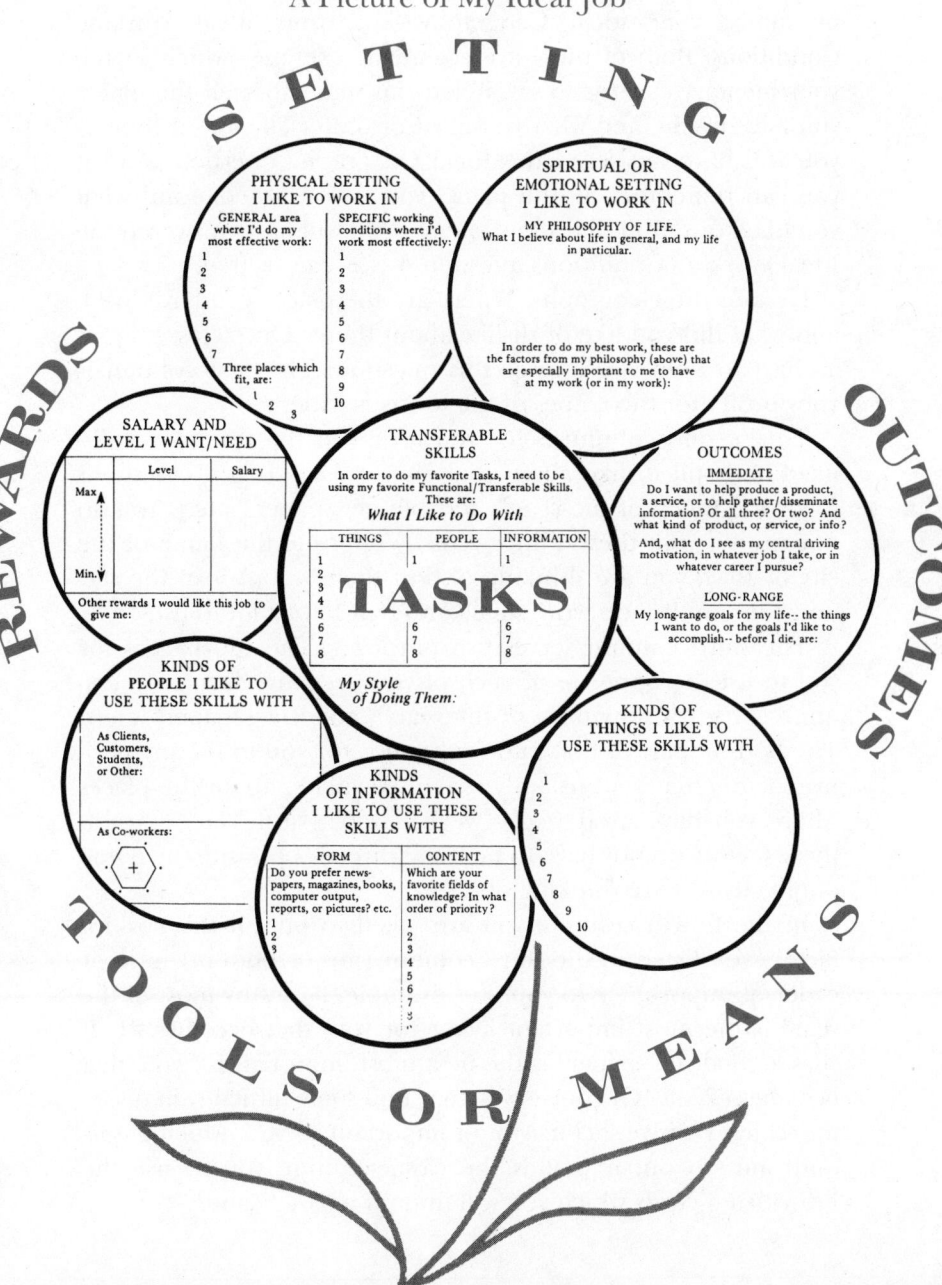

SETTING

PHYSICAL SETTING
I LIKE TO WORK IN

GENERAL area where I'd do my most effective work:
1
2
3
4
5
6
7
Three places which fit, are:
1 2 3

SPECIFIC working conditions where I'd work most effectively:
1
2
3
4
5
6
7
8
9
10

SPIRITUAL OR EMOTIONAL SETTING
I LIKE TO WORK IN

MY PHILOSOPHY OF LIFE.
What I believe about life in general, and my life in particular.

In order to do my best work, these are the factors from my philosophy (above) that are especially important to me to have at my work (or in my work):

REWARDS

SALARY AND LEVEL I WANT/NEED

	Level	Salary
Max		
Min.		

Other rewards I would like this job to give me:

TRANSFERABLE SKILLS

In order to do my favorite Tasks, I need to be using my favorite Functional/Transferable Skills. These are:
What I Like to Do With

THINGS	PEOPLE	INFORMATION
1	1	1
2		
3		
4		
5		
6	6	6
7	7	7
8	8	8

TASKS

OUTCOMES

IMMEDIATE
Do I want to help produce a product, a service, or to help gather/disseminate information? Or all three? Or two? And what kind of product, or service, or info?

And, what do I see as my central driving motivation, in whatever job I take, or in whatever career I pursue?

LONG-RANGE
My long-range goals for my life-- the things I want to do, or the goals I'd like to accomplish-- before I die, are:

OUTCOMES

KINDS OF PEOPLE I LIKE TO USE THESE SKILLS WITH

As Clients, Customers, Students, or Other:

As Co-workers:

My Style of Doing Them:

KINDS OF THINGS I LIKE TO USE THESE SKILLS WITH
1
2
3
4
5
6
7
8
9
10

KINDS OF INFORMATION I LIKE TO USE THESE SKILLS WITH

FORM	CONTENT
Do you prefer news-papers, magazines, books, computer output, reports, or pictures? etc.	Which are your favorite fields of knowledge? In what order of priority?
1	1
2	2
3	3
	4
	5
	6
	7
	8

TOOLS OR MEANS

Step One: Physical Setting

In order to fill out the petal dealing with The Physical Setting I Like to Work In (pages *14–15*), you will need to think about two questions: your ideal Geography, and your ideal Working Conditions. Both of these are essentially exercises which search your memory. That is to say, if you can remember all the places you have lived -- and what you liked or didn't like about them -- you will have answered the Ideal Geography question. And if you can remember all the places you have worked -- and what you liked or didn't like about them -- you will have answered the Ideal Working Conditions question. It's as easy as that.

First, to the Geography. Where are the places you have lived, and what did you like or dislike about them? On pages *12–13* is a chart to help you answer this question. The first column is (obviously) for the names of the towns or cities.

The second column is for you to list all the things you disliked and still dislike about that city or town (e.g., "cloudy or foggy too much of the year," "terrible newspaper," etc.). You do not need to put these things directly opposite the name of the city or town you are thinking of. Put them *anywhere* in the second column. But do write small! You may have a lot to list.

The third column serves two purposes. The top part is for you to list the **opposite** of each of your negative factors in column 2 (e.g., "sunny most of the year," "good newspaper," etc.). The bottom part of that same column is for you to list any positive factors that you instantly remember liking about the places where you have lived (e.g., "we had a big yard," etc.). Again, these factors do not have to be listed directly opposite the name of the city you are thinking of.

In the fourth column, you are asked to put all the positive factors you listed in the third column (top or bottom) in their order of importance to you. For example, if "sunny most of the year" is the most important factor for you, that becomes #1. If "has a good newspaper" is the next most important for you, that becomes #2, etc. Of course, you may find some difficulty in deciding which Positive factor is most important to you, which is second, and so on; if that is the case, we urge you to use the Prioritizing Grids which you will find on pages *17* and *18*.

The fifth column requires your friends to help you. You read to them the list of Positive factors that you have arranged, in order, in the fourth column, and see what cities or towns they can think of, that have these characteristics. Don't stumble over two factors that seem contradictory, like "sunny all year round" and "skiing nearby." There's usually an answer (like, "Palm Springs with the tram up Mt. San Jacinto to the snow"). When your friends are through suggesting places, pick the one you like best, next best, and third best, and put them on the bottom left side of petal #1 on page *14*. If you don't know enough about them, put your three favorites in any order, and write away to their Chambers of Commerce, to find out more about them. The library can also help!

The last three columns are only to be used if you have a wife, husband, or partner, and you are doing joint decision-making about where you eventually want to move to. In that case, your partner will need to photocopy the Geography chart (before you fill it out, obviously) and do their own first five columns. If your preferred geographical areas turn out to be identical, then you are done with the chart. But if they don't, then go on to column #6 and copy your partner's positive factors from his or her column #4.

Now, on to column #7. Merge together, there, your "Ranking of My Positives" and your partner's ranking. Your factors, obviously, are numbered 1, 2, 3, 4, 5, etc., while your partner's are numbered a, b, c, d, e, etc. You will notice that column #7 asks you first to list your partner's top priority, then your top one, then your partner's second priority, then your second one, etc.

When done, move on to column #8. It involves exactly the same procedure as column #5. Show column #7 to all your friends and ask them what cities or towns they think of, when they read this (combined) list of factors. Again, don't be put off by apparently contradictory factors. There's usually some place, somewhere, that can give you both factors.

Incidentally, you may have looked at this chart and sort of shrugged your shoulders, because you already know your geographical destination, and by name. It's either where you already are, or some place you both *have to* move to, or some place you both would love to move to. Nonetheless, try filling out columns #1 through #4, anyway. It helps a lot if you know which characteristics you like best -- or you *each* like best -- in that city or town, and in what order. When this is done, fill out the left hand side of petal #1 on page *14*, please. Then, on to Working Conditions.

(continued on page 16)

My/Our Geographical

Decision Making for Just You

Column 1 Names of Places I Have Lived	Column 2 From the Past: Negatives	Column 3 Translating the Nega- tives into Positives	Column 4 Ranking of My Positives
	Factors I Disliked and Still Dislike about That Place		1.
			2.
			3.
			4.
			5.
			6.
			7.
			8.
			9.
			10.
		Factors I Liked and Still Like about That Place	11.
			12.
			13.
			14.
			15.

Preferences

	Decision Making for You and a Partner		
Column 5 Places Which Fit These Criteria	Column 6 Ranking of His/Her Preferences	Column 7 Combining Our Two Lists (Columns 4 & 6)	Column 8 Places Which Fit These Criteria
	a.	a. 1.	
	b.	b. 2.	
	c.	c. 3.	
	d.	d. 4.	
	e.	e. 5.	
	f.	f. 6.	
	g.	g. 7.	
	h.	h. 8.	
	i.	i. 9.	
	j.	j. 10.	
	k.	k. 11.	
	l.	l. 12.	
	m.	m. 13.	
	n.	n. 14.	
	o.	o. 15.	

How to Prioritize Your Lists of Anything
(*A Digression*)

Here is a method for taking (say) ten items, and figuring out which one is most important to you, which is next most important, etc.

• Insert the items to be prioritized, in any order, in Section A. Then compare two items at a time, circling the one you prefer -- between the two -- in Section B. Which one is more important to you? State the question any way you want to: In the case of geographical factors, you might ask, "If I were being offered two jobs, one in an area that had factor #1, but not factor #2; the other in an area that had factor #2, but not factor #1, all other things being equal, which job would I take?" *Circle it.* Then go on to the next pair, etc.

• When you are all done, count up the number of times each number got circled, all told. Enter these totals on the TIMES line in Section C. Then notice the number of times each item was circled ("Times" = "Times Circled"). This determines the item's ranking. Most circled = #1, next most circled = #2, etc. Enter this ranking on the RANK line in Section C. If two items are circled the same number of times, look back in Section B to see -- when those two were compared there -- which one you preferred. Give that one an extra half point. List the items, now in their proper rank, in Section D.

Each time you use this grid, make a photocopy of it, and fill in the photocopy rather than the original. You will need to photocopy this grid many times as you go through this map.

Working Conditions

Now that you have filled out the General Geographical half of the Physical Settings petal, on to the other half: Working Conditions.

You use the same method as you did for Geography. In fact you can make up a chart where you copy the first four columns (only) of the Geography Chart. The only change you will need to make is to relabel column #1 as "Names of Places I Have Worked." Here name all the companies, or all the jobs you have ever held.

(continued on page 19)

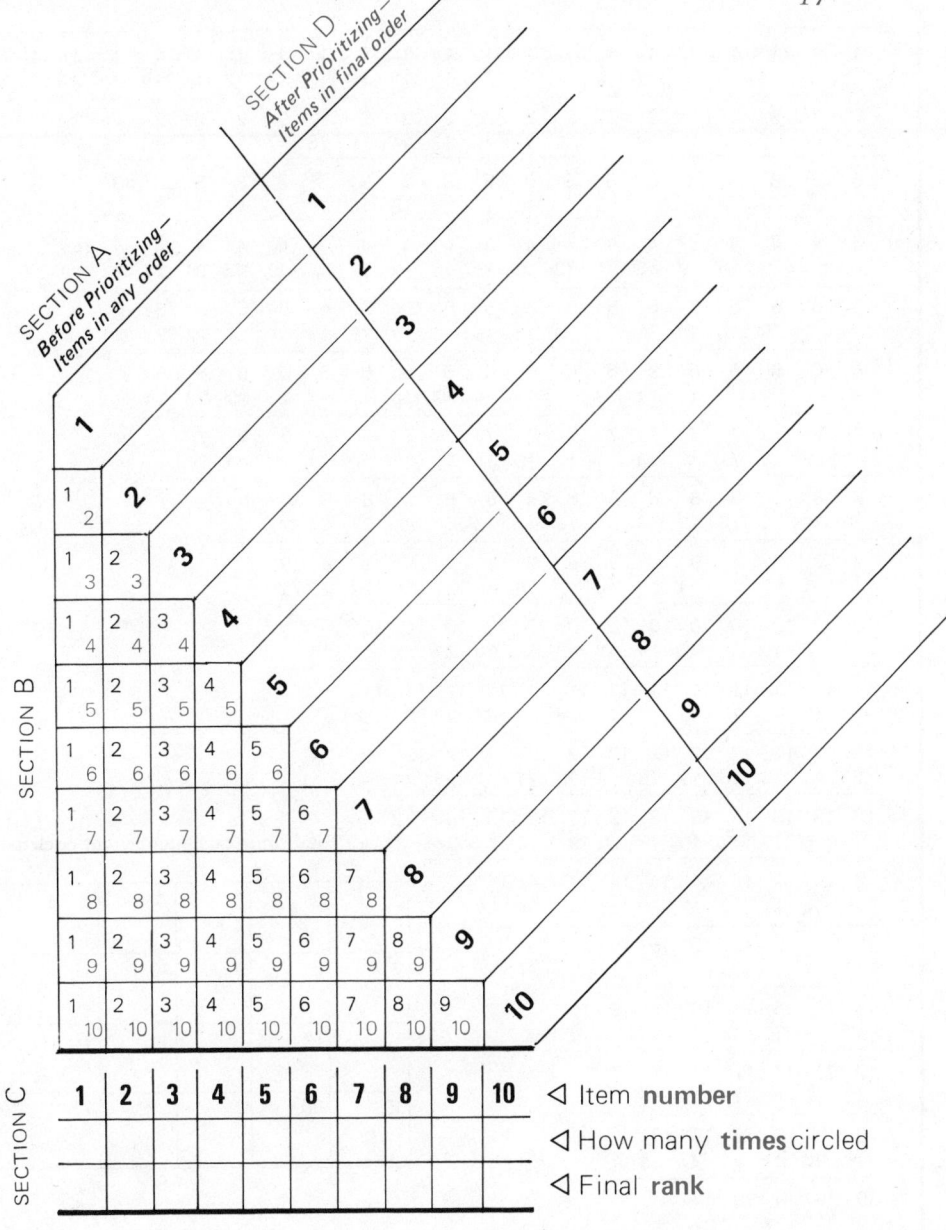

SECTION D—
After Prioritizing—
Items in final order

SECTION A—
Before Prioritizing—
Items in any order

SECTION B

SECTION C

◁ Item **number**

◁ How many **times** circled

◁ Final **rank**

Prioritizing Grid
for 10 Items

```
1  1  1  1  1  1  1  1  1  1  1  1  1  1  1  1  1  1  1  1  1  1  1
  2  3  4  5  6  7  8  9 10 11 12 13 14 15 16 17 18 19 20 21 22 23 24

2  2  2  2  2  2  2  2  2  2  2  2  2  2  2  2  2  2  2  2  2  2
  3  4  5  6  7  8  9 10 11 12 13 14 15 16 17 18 19 20 21 22 23 24

3  3  3  3  3  3  3  3  3  3  3  3  3  3  3  3  3  3  3  3  3
  4  5  6  7  8  9 10 11 12 13 14 15 16 17 18 19 20 21 22 23 24

4  4  4  4  4  4  4  4  4  4  4  4  4  4  4  4  4  4  4  4
  5  6  7  8  9 10 11 12 13 14 15 16 17 18 19 20 21 22 23 24

5  5  5  5  5  5  5  5  5  5  5  5  5  5  5  5  5  5  5
  6  7  8  9 10 11 12 13 14 15 16 17 18 19 20 21 22 23 24

6  6  6  6  6  6  6  6  6  6  6  6  6  6  6  6  6  6
  7  8  9 10 11 12 13 14 15 16 17 18 19 20 21 22 23 24

7  7  7  7  7  7  7  7  7  7  7  7  7  7  7  7  7
  8  9 10 11 12 13 14 15 16 17 18 19 20 21 22 23 24

8  8  8  8  8  8  8  8  8  8  8  8  8  8  8  8
  9 10 11 12 13 14 15 16 17 18 19 20 21 22 23 24

9  9  9  9  9  9  9  9  9  9  9  9  9  9  9
 10 11 12 13 14 15 16 17 18 19 20 21 22 23 24

10 10 10 10 10 10 10 10 10 10 10 10 10 10
 11 12 13 14 15 16 17 18 19 20 21 22 23 24

11 11 11 11 11 11 11 11 11 11 11 11 11
 12 13 14 15 16 17 18 19 20 21 22 23 24

12 12 12 12 12 12 12 12 12 12 12 12
 13 14 15 16 17 18 19 20 21 22 23 24

13 13 13 13 13 13 13 13 13 13 13
 14 15 16 17 18 19 20 21 22 23 24

14 14 14 14 14 14 14 14 14 14
 15 16 17 18 19 20 21 22 23 24

15 15 15 15 15 15 15 15 15
 16 17 18 19 20 21 22 23 24

16 16 16 16 16 16 16 16
 17 18 19 20 21 22 23 24

17 17 17 17 17 17 17
 18 19 20 21 22 23 24

18 18 18 18 18 18
 19 20 21 22 23 24

19 19 19 19 19
 20 21 22 23 24

20 20 20 20
 21 22 23 24

21 21 21
 22 23 24

22 22
 23 24

23
 24
```

Total times each number got circled

1	2	3	4	5	6
7	8	9	10	11	12
13	14	15	16	17	18
19	20	21	22	23	24

Prioritizing Grid
for 24 Items

Each time you use this grid, make a photocopy of it, and fill in the photocopy rather than the original. (You will need to photocopy this grid many times as you go through this process.)

Column #2, now, is "Factors I Disliked and Still Dislike About That Job." Examples would be "no windows," "a boss that over-supervised me," "had to come in too early," etc.

Columns #3 and #4 remain the same. List, and then prioritize, the positive factors about the working conditions you like best. Remember, these are also the working conditions under which you can do your best and most effective work. When you're done, list them on the right hand side of petal #1 on page *14*.

And voila! The first petal is all finished.

Step Two: Spiritual or Emotional Setting

Every job or career has not merely a physical setting, but a spiritual or emotional one also: the realm of things we cannot see. For example, a man once phoned me to ask what he should do about a crooked contract his firm had just executed. I asked him who drew it up. He said, "I did." I asked him why. He said, "My boss told me it was that, or I'd lose my job."

You need to think out, as part of your picture of your Ideal Job, what is important to you in life -- in the area of things we cannot see: values, principles, what you are willing to stand up for, and what you are not willing to stand up for, what you care about.

The most useful way to do this is to take a piece of blank paper (or two) and write out on it your *philosophy about life*: which typically might include some statement of why you think we are here on earth, what it is that you believe we are supposed to do while we are here, what you think is important in life and what is not important, and which values of our society you agree with, and which ones you disagree with. As a suggested framework only, you might want to choose from among these elements (you *don't* have to use them all):

- Behavior: how you think we should behave in this world
- Beliefs: what your strongest beliefs are
- Choice: what you think about its nature and importance
- Community: what ways we belong to each other, and what you think our responsibility is to each other
- Compassion: what you think is its importance, and how it should be manifested in our daily life

(continued on page 22)

The Second Petal

Spiritual or Emotional Setting I Like to Work In

MY PHILOSOPHY OF LIFE.

What I believe about life in general,
and my life in particular:
(key ideas here)

In order to do my best work,
these are the factors from my philosophy (above) that are especially important to me
to have at my work (or in my work):

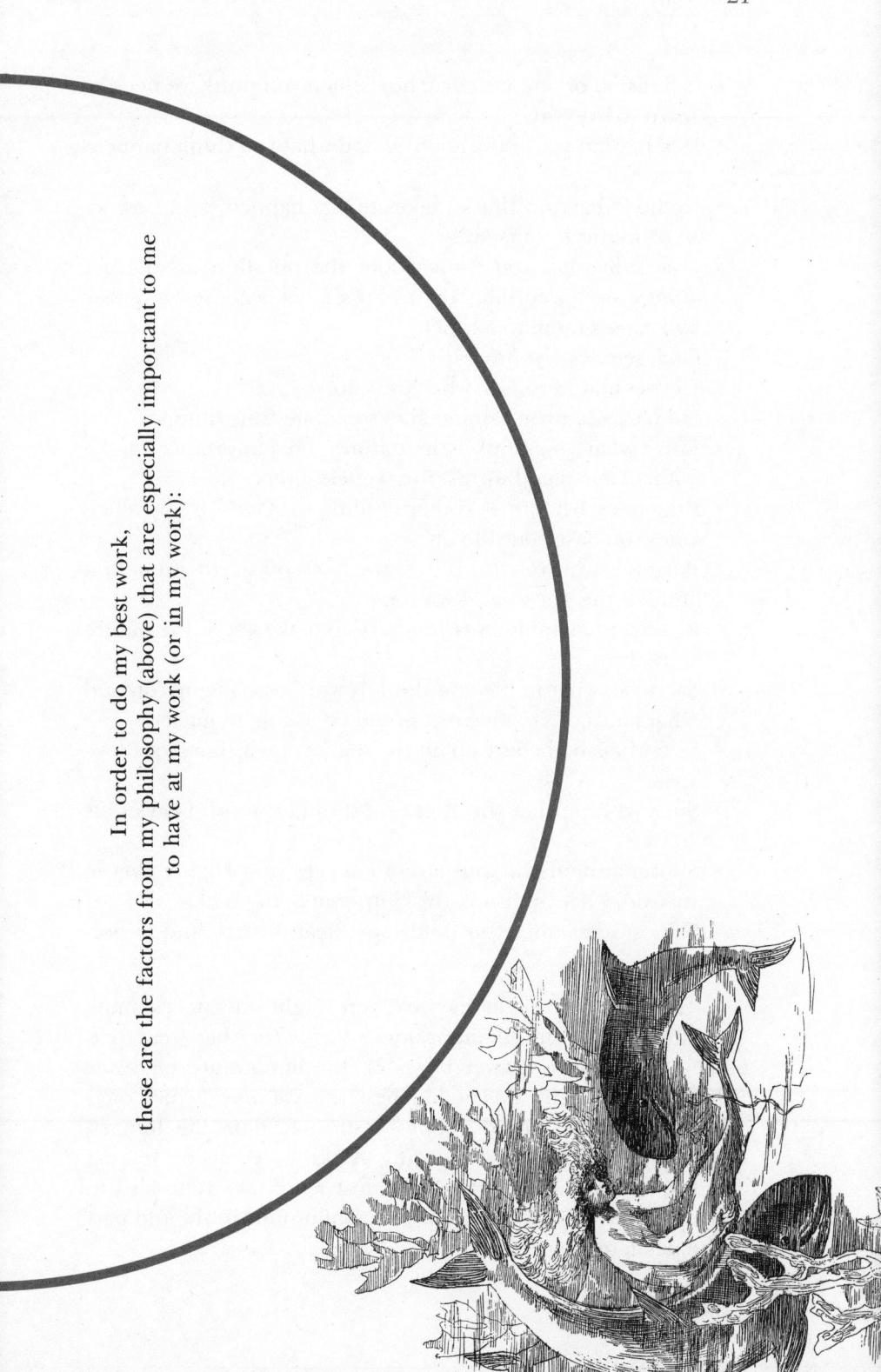

- Confusion or ambivalence: how much you think we need to learn to live with
- Death: what you think about it and what you think happens after it
- Events: what you think makes things happen, and how we explain this to ourselves
- Free will: what you think about the question of whether things are 'preordained to happen' or whether our free will causes them to happen
- God: see *Supreme Being*
- Heroes and heroines: who yours are
- Human: what you think makes someone truly 'human'
- Love: what you think is its nature and importance, along with all its related words: forgiveness, grace, etc.
- Principles: what ones you are willing to stand up for, which ones you base your life on
- Purpose: why you think we are here on earth, what you think is the purpose of your life
- Reality: what comments you have to make about the nature of reality
- Sacrifice: what in life you think is worth sacrificing for, and what kinds of sacrifice you would be willing to make
- Self: what you believe about the self, ego, selfishness, selflessness
- Stewardship: what you think we should do with God's gifts to us
- Supreme Being: if you have a concept of a Higher Power, or God, what you think this Supreme Being is like
- Values: what ones you hold most dear, sacred, and important

To help you in this latter area, you might want to examine your thoughts about the importance of *truth* (in what areas, particularly, does truth matter to you?), the importance of *beauty* (what kinds of beauty do you like best?), *moral issues* (which ones are you most concerned about -- justice, feeding the hungry, helping the homeless, comforting AIDS sufferers, or what?), and the importance of *love*. Don't just *write*; take time also to *think!* Jot down the key ideas of your philosophy in the top part of the petal, on pages *20–21*.

When you are done writing your philosophy of life, the bottom part of this petal asks you to lift out of that philosophy any factors which are especially important to you at your future place of work, or in your future work. For example, your philosophy of life might have reminded you, "I have to work in a place where I am never asked to do anything dishonest." Or: "I want to be among loving, supportive co-workers, and not among people who are always backbiting or gossiping about everyone." Whatever occurs to you, after studying your philosophy, put this stuff down, in the bottom part of that petal.

And, voila! The second petal is all finished.

Step Three: My Favorite Transferable Skills

Now, you know what it is you're going to do here. You are going to figure out what skills you use when you are enjoying yourself the most -- either in your work, or in your home, or when you are doing some hobby or recreation. These skills, no matter where you used them in the past, are transferable now to other jobs or careers.

There are two ways to identify your transferable skills. "Quick, but Superficial" and "Slow, but Absolutely Thorough." Let's look at "Quick, but Superficial" first.

The Party Exercise:
What Skills You Have and
Most Enjoy Using

As John L. Holland has taught us all, skills may be thought of as dividing into six clusters or families. To see which ones you are *attracted to*, try this exercise.

On the next page is an aerial view of a room in which a two-day (!) party is taking place. At this party, people with the same or similar interests have (for some reason) all gathered in the same corner of the room.

R for "Realistic"

I for "Investigative"

C for "Conventional"

A for "Artistic"

E for "Enterprising"

S for "Social"

The Party

People who have athletic or mechanical ability, prefer to work with objects, machines, tools, plants, or animals, or to be outdoors.

People who like to observe, learn, investigate, analyze, evaluate, or solve problems.

People who like to work with data, have clerical or numerical ability, carrying things out in detail or following through on others's instructions.

People who have artistic, innovating or intuitional abilities, and like to work in unstructured situations, using their imagination or creativity.

People who like to work with people -- influencing, persuading or performing or leading or managing for organizational goals or for economic gain.

People who like to work with people-- to inform, enlighten. help, train, develop, or cure them, or are skilled with words.

(1) Which corner of the room would you instinctively be drawn to, as the group of people you would most enjoy being with for the longest time? (Leave aside any question of shyness, or whether you would have to talk with them.) Write the letter for that corner here:

☐

(2) After fifteen minutes, everyone in the corner you have chosen leaves for another party crosstown, except you. Of the groups that still remain now, which corner or group would you be drawn to the most, as the people you would most enjoy being with for the longest time? Write the letter for that corner here:

☐

(3) After fifteen minutes, this group too leaves for another party, except you. Of the corners, and groups, which remain now, which one would you most enjoy being with for the longest time? Write the letter for that corner here:

☐

*(If you want to explore this further, see Holland, John L., "Self-Directed Search, 1985 Revision." This is a self-marking test which you can use to discover your "Holland code" and what occupations you might **start** your research with. Psychological Assessment Resources, Inc., Box 998, Odessa, FL 33556.)*

Now, on to "Slow but Absolutely Thorough."

In order to find out this information, it will be necessary for you to write out seven (7) stories of some enjoyable and satisfying experiences or accomplishments which you have done in your life. Which stories should you choose? Ah, that's a good question. Not necessarily the ones which occur to you right off the top of your head. Sometimes you have to dig deeper.

To guard yourself against impulsively choosing stories which may not tell you much about your skills, it is helpful to construct a basic outline of your life, for yourself, first. One way to do this is through a Memory Net.

The Memory Net

That Net is on the next two pages. You should take at least three hours (with some hard thinking, as well as writing) to fill it in.

In the first column of the Memory Net are the years of your life, divided into five-year periods (cross out the years before your birth, of course). Some of you will be able to remember what activities you were doing during each of these five-year periods, just from seeing the dates. Use this column, then, to jog your memory, and fill in the rest of the Net.

The second column is for those of you who don't remember things by Dates, but by what job you were holding down, or what school you were attending, or organizations you were involved with, or people who were influential upon your life, etc. Use this column, then (with whatever title you want to put on it), to jog your memory -- fill it in, and then fill in the rest of the Net.

The third column is for those of you who don't remember things by either Years or Jobs, but by where you were living at the time. Use this column, then, to jog your memory -- fill it in, and then fill in the rest of the Net.

Once you've tackled the first three columns, as you go across the rest of the Memory Net you will generally find it pays to fill in

(continued on page 28)

the three Activities columns first (columns 4, 6, and 8), and then go back to the Accomplishments columns (5, 7, and 9). That is to say, once you remember what you were *doing* (activities) in the way of Leisure, Learning, or Labor (Work), you will then find it easier to think of specific accomplishments in your Leisure or your Learning or your Labor. Put down titles only, or a few words to jog your memory, rather than attempting any more detailed description of your accomplishments, at this time.

Once you have the Net all filled in, you are ready to choose and write your stories. You will need at least seven sheets of paper. On each of these sheets you are (eventually) going to write one of your stories -- picked from the Memory Net. Then you will analyze each story, one by one, to see what skills you were using, in that story.

For the time being, you start by writing **just one** of those stories. Look over your Memory Net, and most particularly at columns 5, 7, and 9. Look at your accomplishments. Whether they were early in your life, or more recently, whether they were in your leisure life, or your learning life, or your labor/work life, does not matter.

Just be sure also that it deals in turn with TASK, TOOLS or MEANS, and OUTCOME or RESULT. See the example that follows:

1. A TASK. Something you wanted to do, just because it was fun or would give you a sense of adventure or a sense of accomplishment. Normally there was a problem that you were trying to solve, or a challenge you were trying to overcome, or something you were trying to master or produce or create.

2. TOOLS or MEANS. You used something to help you do the task, solve the problem, overcome the challenge. Either you had certain *Things* to help you -- objects, materials, tools or equipment, or you had other *People* to help you, or you got a hold of some vital *Information*. Tell us what tools or means you used, and how you used them.

3. AN OUTCOME or RESULT. You were able to finish the task or solve the problem, overcome the challenge, master a process, or produce or create something. You had a sense of pride, even if no one else knew what it was you had accomplished.

Once you have selected your first story, write it out in detail -- but keep it comparatively brief -- two or three paragraphs at most. Be sure that it is *a story* you tell -- that is, that it moves step by step. It may help if you pretend that you are telling it to a small whining child who keeps asking, "An' then whadja do?" "An' then whadja do?"

When you are done, label that sheet "#1."

THIS WON'T DO.
TOO BRIEF.

SAMPLE

"The Halloween Experience. I won a prize on Halloween for dressing up as a horse."

THIS WILL DO.

SAMPLE

"My Halloween Experience When I Was Seven Years Old. Details:

When I was seven, I decided I wanted to go out on Halloween dressed as a horse. I wanted to be the front end of the horse, and I talked a friend of mine into being the back end of the horse. But, at the last moment he backed out, and I was faced with the prospect of not being able to go out on Halloween. At this point, I decided to figure out some way of getting dressed up as the whole horse, myself. I took a fruit basket, and tied some string to both sides of the basket's rim, so that I could tie the basket around my rear end. This filled me out enough so that the costume fit me, by myself. I then fixed some strong thread to the tail so that I could make it wag by moving my hands. When Halloween came I not only went out and had a ball, but I won a prize as well."

Identifying Your Skills

Once this first story is written, you are ready to identify what skills you used, in that story. The list of skills you are to use is found on pages *32–37*. The skills resemble a series of typewriter keys. You go down each column vertically. As you look at each key, you ask yourself, "Did I use this skill **in this story**? (story #1)." If you did, you color in the little box *right under* that key which has the number 1 in it (color right *over* the "1"). We suggest you use a **red** pen, pencil, or crayon, to do this coloring in. Keep going down each column, in turn, on each of the following six pages.

When you are done with all the skills keys, for Things, People, and Information, you have finished with story #1. You now know what skills you used while you were doing this first enjoyable achievement, that you have selected to analyze.

However, "one swallow doth not a summer make," and the fact that you used certain skills in this one accomplishment doesn't yet tell you much. What you want to look for are patterns, i.e., which skills keep getting used, again and again, in accomplishment after accomplishment, story after story. It is *the patterns* that are meaningful for choosing your future job or career.

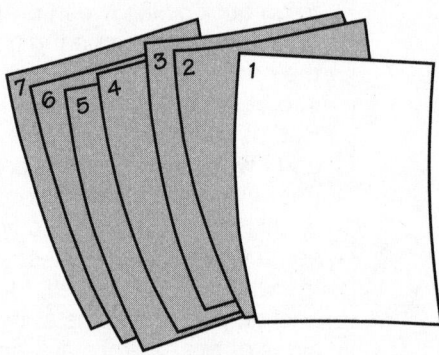

So now it is time to take a second sheet of paper, label it "#2", and look over the Memory Net to see which achievements you want to pick for your second story. Once you have selected it, and written it out in detail, you go back to the Skills Keys and again ask yourself, "Did I use this skill **in this story**? (story #2)." And, again, if you did, you color in the little box right under that key that has the number 2 in it (color right over the "2"). Again, use the red pen, pencil, or crayon. Continue through the six Skill Pages.

Take a third sheet of paper and repeat the process, and so, continue on through sheet (and story) #7. When you are done, look over the Skill Pages to see which skills stand out (i.e., which ones have *the little boxes* under them colored in the most).

Choosing Your Favorites from Among All Your Transferable Skills

You must now choose your favorites, from the Skill Pages you just filled out. How you make that choice is entirely up to you. Here are two different methods for doing this:

a) **The Top Ten.** Look at all the Skill Pages you just filled out, and put a big check mark by your ten favorite skills -- never mind whether they are with Things, People, or Information. It could turn out, for example, that eight of your favorite skills are with Things, and one with People and one with Information. On a sheet of scratch paper, list all ten and then rearrange them so that they end up being listed *in their order of importance to you.* You can do this prioritizing either by guess and by gosh, **or** by using the Prioritizing Grid on page *18*. What you want to end up with is a *prioritized list* -- on which the skill that is most important to you is listed first, the skill that is next most important to you is listed second, next most important is third, next most important is fourth, and so on.

b) Alternative Method: **Eight, Eight, and Eight.** Look at the Skill Pages and pick your eight favorites off *each diagram*: your eight favorite Skills with Things, your eight favorite Skills with People, and your eight favorite Skills with Information. Put *each* eight in order, again either by guessing, or by using the Prioritizing Grid three times. You will end up with three lists: your eight favorite Skills with Things, *in order of priority for you;* your eight favorite Skills with People, *in order of priority for you;* your eight favorite Skills with Information, *in order of priority for you.*

Optional: Restating Skills in Your Own Language

Now (*and only now*) that you have a list of your favorite skills -- either The Top Ten or the Eight, Eight, and Eight -- you *may* want to restate them in other language than was on the Skills diagrams, language that is more uniquely and personally yours.

(continued on page 38)

My transferable skills dealing with

THINGS

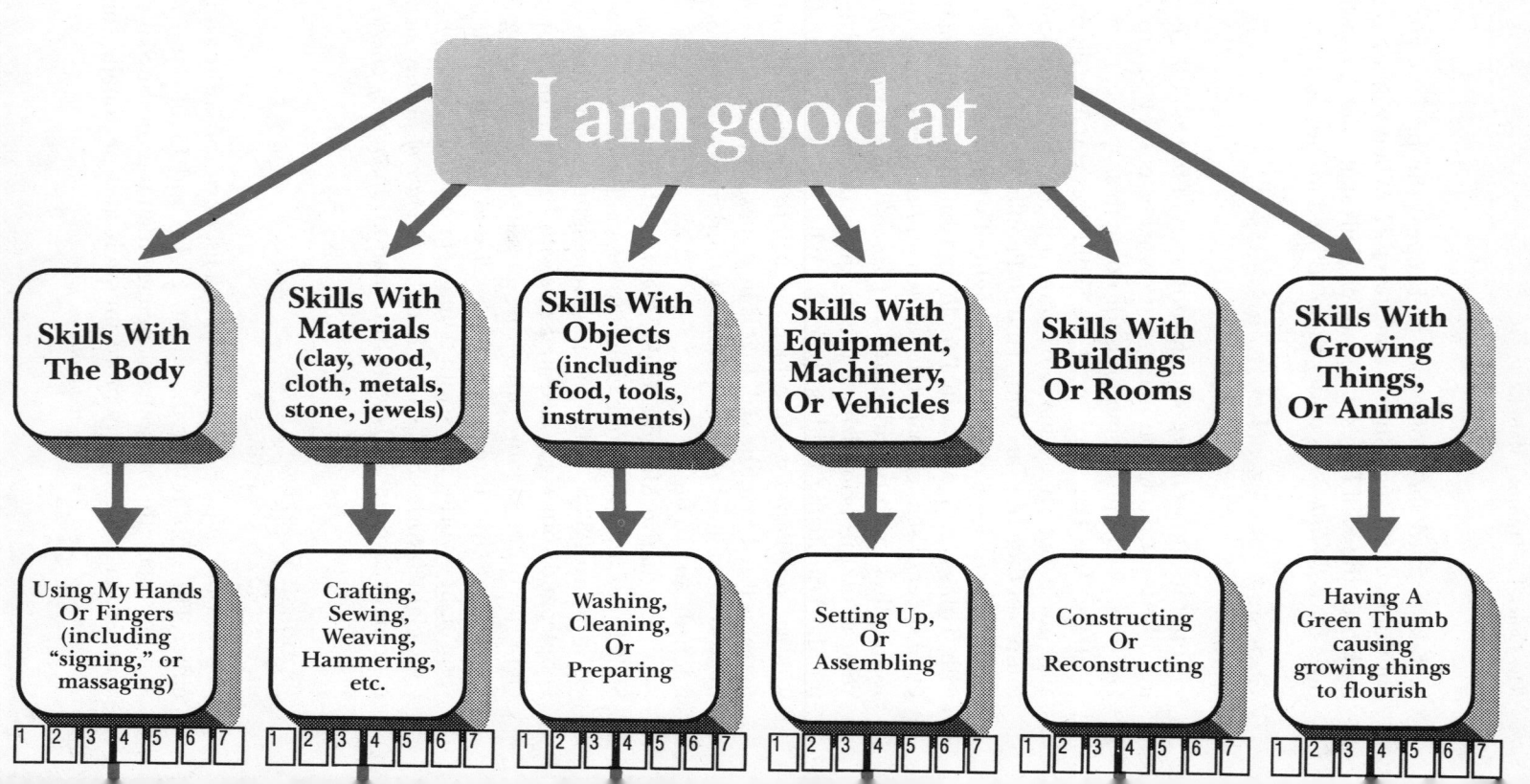

I am good at

Skills With The Body

Skills With Materials (clay, wood, cloth, metals, stone, jewels)

Skills With Objects (including food, tools, instruments)

Skills With Equipment, Machinery, Or Vehicles

Skills With Buildings Or Rooms

Skills With Growing Things, Or Animals

Using My Hands Or Fingers (including "signing," or massaging)

Crafting, Sewing, Weaving, Hammering, etc.

Washing, Cleaning, Or Preparing

Setting Up, Or Assembling

Constructing Or Reconstructing

Having A Green Thumb causing growing things to flourish

1 2 3 4 5 6 7   1 2 3 4 5 6 7   1 2 3 4 5 6 7   1 2 3 4 5 6 7   1 2 3 4 5 6 7   1 2 3 4 5 6 7

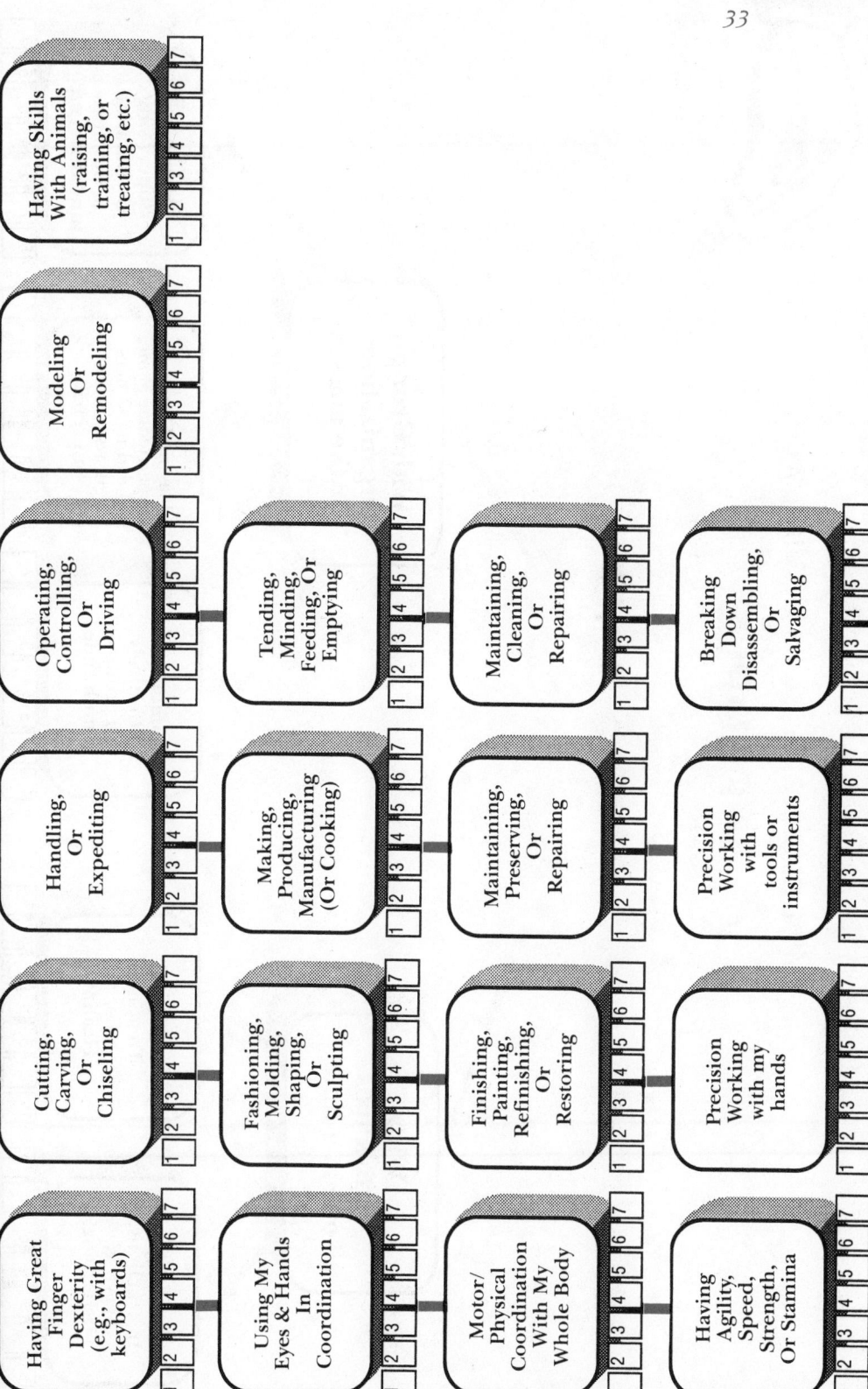

Having Skills With Animals (raising, training, or treating, etc.)
1 2 3 4 5 6 7

Modeling Or Remodeling
1 2 3 4 5 6 7

Operating, Controlling, Or Driving
1 2 3 4 5 6 7

Handling, Or Expediting
1 2 3 4 5 6 7

Cutting, Carving, Or Chiseling
1 2 3 4 5 6 7

Having Great Finger Dexterity (e.g., with keyboards)
1 2 3 4 5 6 7

Tending, Minding, Feeding, Or Emptying
1 2 3 4 5 6 7

Making, Producing, Manufacturing (Or Cooking)
1 2 3 4 5 6 7

Fashioning, Molding, Shaping, Or Sculpting
1 2 3 4 5 6 7

Using My Eyes & Hands In Coordination
1 2 3 4 5 6 7

Maintaining, Cleaning, Or Repairing
1 2 3 4 5 6 7

Maintaining, Preserving, Or Repairing
1 2 3 4 5 6 7

Finishing, Painting, Refinishing, Or Restoring
1 2 3 4 5 6 7

Motor/ Physical Coordination With My Whole Body
1 2 3 4 5 6 7

Breaking Down Disassembling, Or Salvaging
1 2 3 4 5 6 7

Precision Working with tools or instruments
1 2 3 4 5 6 7

Precision Working with my hands
1 2 3 4 5 6 7

Having Agility, Speed, Strength, Or Stamina
1 2 3 4 5 6 7

My transferable skills dealing with

PEOPLE

I am good at

With Individuals one at a time

With Groups, Organizations, or the masses

Taking Instructions, Serving, Or Helping

1	2	3	4	5	6	7

Diagnosing, Treating, Or Healing

1	2	3	4	5	6	7

Communicating Effectively to a group or a multitude

1	2	3	4	5	6	7

Playing Games, or a particular game, Leading Others in recreation or exercise

1	2	3	4	5	6	7

Managing, Supervising, Or Running (a business, fund drive, etc.)

1	2	3	4	5	6	7

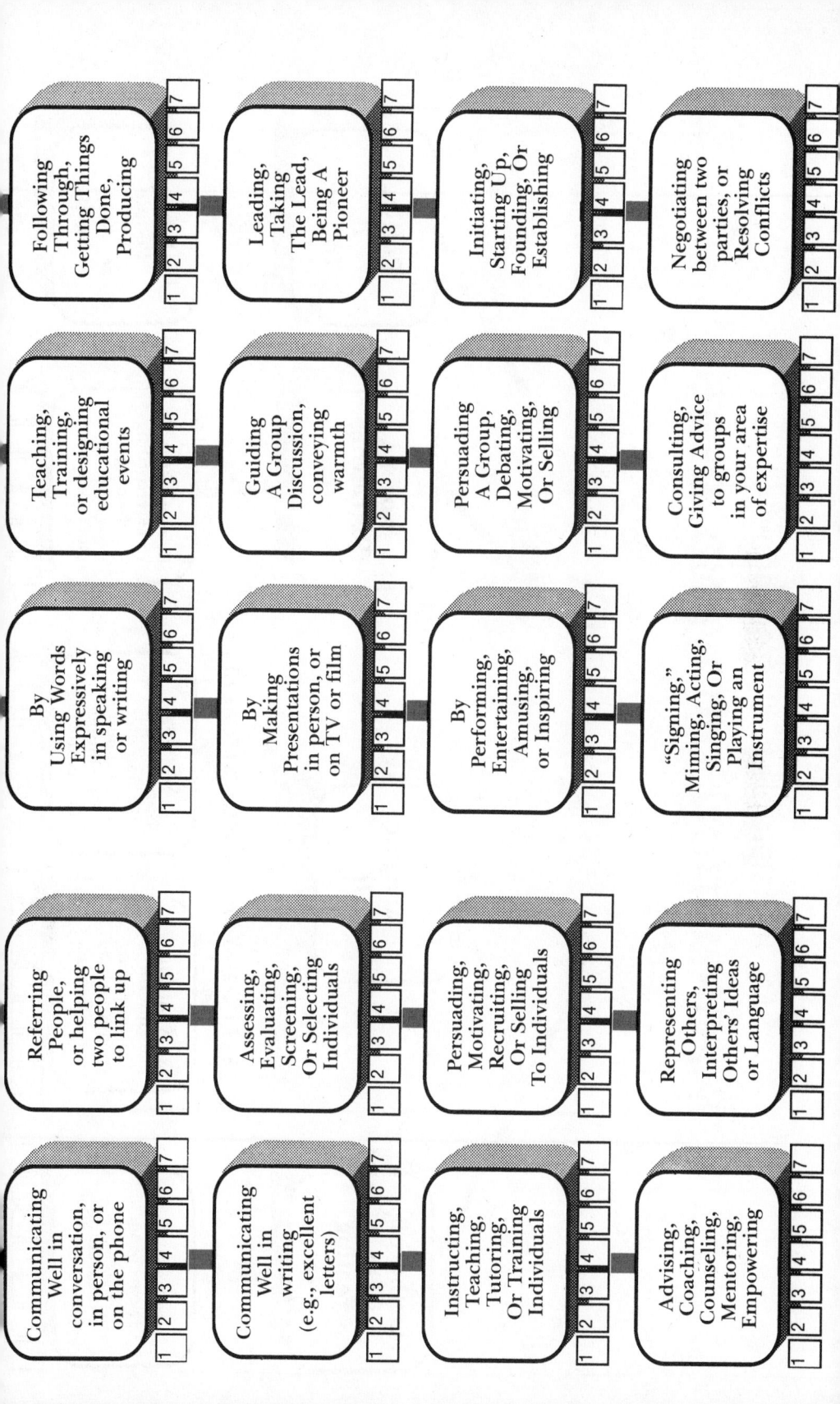

My transferable skills dealing with

INFORMATION, DATA, AND IDEAS

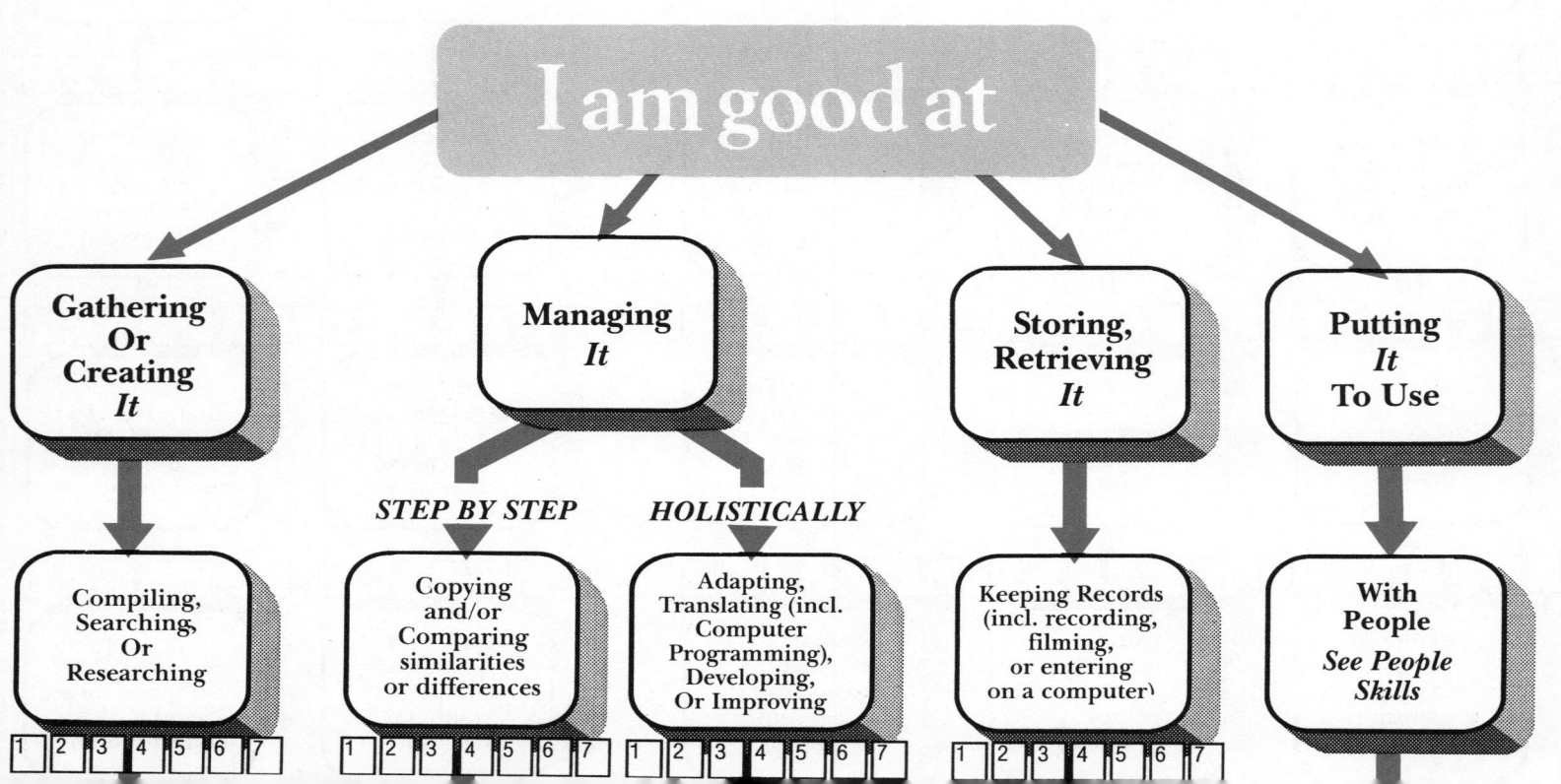

Gathering Information By Interviewing Or Observing People						
1	2	3	4	5	6	7

Computing, Working with Numbers, Doing Accounting						
1	2	3	4	5	6	7

Visualizing, Drawing, Painting, Dramatizing, Creating Videos, Or Software						
1	2	3	4	5	6	7

Storing Or Filing (in file cabinets, microfiche, video, audio, or computer)						
1	2	3	4	5	6	7

With Things
See Skills with Things

Gathering Information By Studying Or Observing Things						
1	2	3	4	5	6	7

Analyzing, breaking down into its parts						
1	2	3	4	5	6	7

Synthesizing, combining parts into a whole						
1	2	3	4	5	6	7

Retrieving Information, Ideas, Data						
1	2	3	4	5	6	7

Having An Acute Sense Of Hearing, Smell, Taste, Or Sight						
1	2	3	4	5	6	7

Organizing, Classifying, Systematizing, and/or Prioritizing						
1	2	3	4	5	6	7

Problem Solving or seeing patterns among a mass of data						
1	2	3	4	5	6	7

Enabling Other People To Find Or Retrieve Information						
1	2	3	4	5	6	7

Imagining, Inventing, Creating, Or Designing new ideas						
1	2	3	4	5	6	7

Planning, laying out a step-by-step process for achieving a goal						
1	2	3	4	5	6	7

Deciding, Evaluating, Appraising, Or Making Recommendations						
1	2	3	4	5	6	7

Having A Superior Memory, keeping track of details						
1	2	3	4	5	6	7

The Third Petal
Tasks

In order to do my favorite Tasks,
I need to be using my favorite
Functional/Transferable Skills.
These are:

What I Like to Do With

THINGS	PEOPLE	INFORMATION
1.	1.	1.
2.	2.	2.
3.	3.	3.
4.	4.	4.

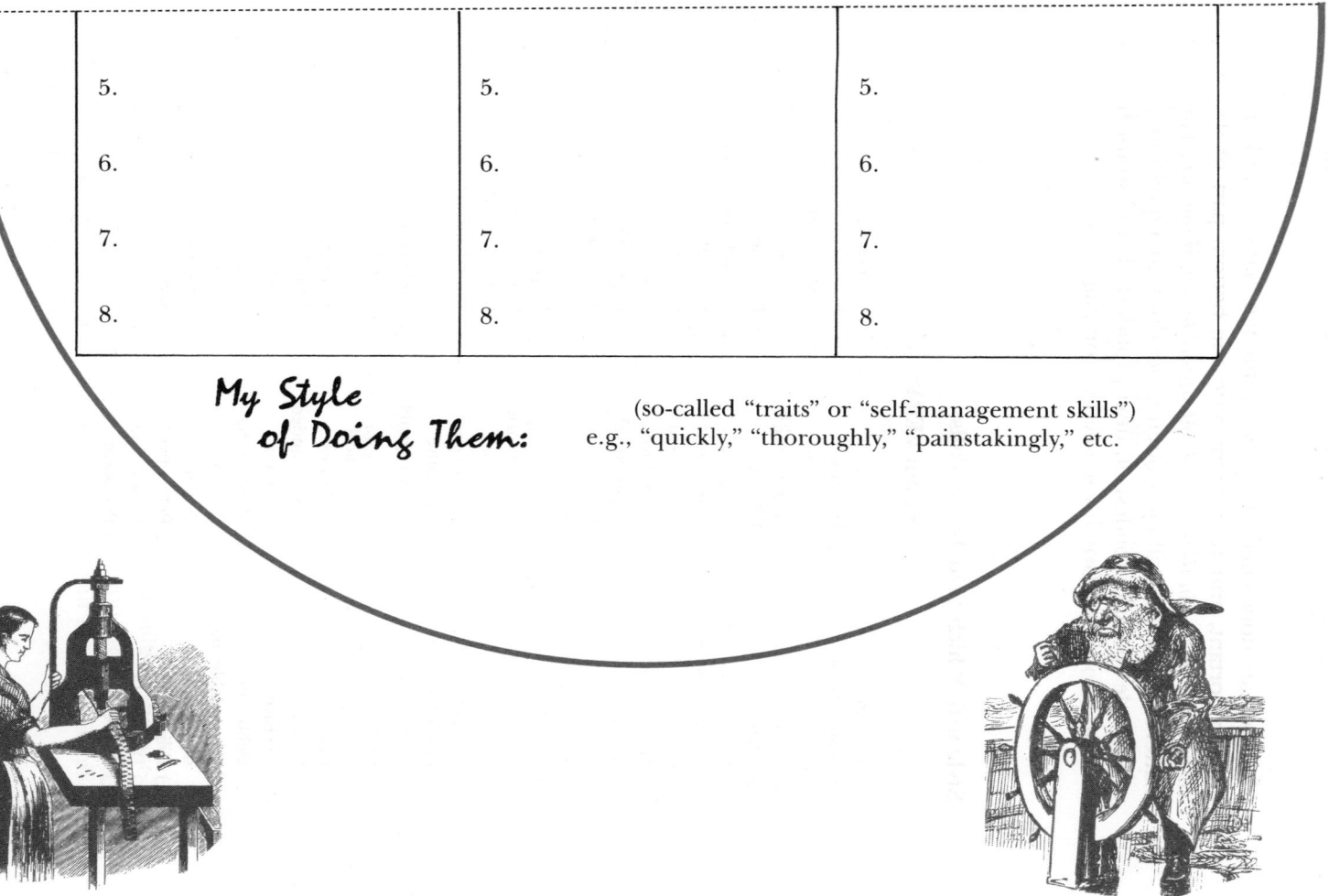

5.	5.	5.
6.	6.	6.
7.	7.	7.
8.	8.	8.

My Style of Doing Them: (so-called "traits" or "self-management skills")
e.g., "quickly," "thoroughly," "painstakingly," etc.

The Things You Like to Act Upon

These next three steps, that is, and the next three petals, are called "**Tools or Means**." Skills *always* require some tool or means. A tool or means is something you love **to handle**, or something you like **to use**, or something you like **to work on**, or **act upon**. It may be *people,* or *information,* or a *thing.*

For example, if you love to hammer things, you need both a hammer and a thing to hammer -- let us say a nail. The hammer and the nail are the tools or means that enable you to use your skill -- of hammering. And, in this case, they are *things.* Of course, you also need some knowledge concerning *how to hammer,* and that means that some *information* is also used here, as a tool or means.

On the next three petals, and in the next three steps, we will look first at People, and then at Information, and then at Things, to see which of these are your favorites.

Step Four: My Favorite People to Work With

If you checked any skills with People, as your favorites, in Step Three, it is important that you now specify *what kind of* People you prefer to work with. Let us say, for example, that you checked "teaching" as one of your favorite skills. The question now is: *What* people do you most enjoy teaching? All people? Particular age groups? If so, *which ones?* People with particular problems? If so, *which ones?* People who are working on particular issues in their life? If so, *which ones?*

Following is a list of people. Put a check mark in front of any description that describes people you particularly like (or think you would particularly like) to work with -- as clients, customers, students, or whatever, in your work. Add any others that may occur to you, which are not on the list. Then when you are done checking, pick the ten that you think are **most** important, and copy them onto petal #4, called *Tools or Means: One* (found on pages *48–49*) -- *in your order of preference. "I would most enjoy working with these people, next with these people, next with these people,"* etc. *Use the Prioritizing Grid if you need to (on page 18).*

Kinds of People I Prefer to Serve Or Try to Help:

- ☐ Men
- ☐ Women
- ☐ Individuals
- ☐ Groups of eight or less
- ☐ Groups larger than eight
- ☐ Babies
- ☐ School-age children
- ☐ Adolescents or young people
- ☐ College students
- ☐ Young adults
- ☐ People in their thirties
- ☐ The middle-aged
- ☐ The elderly
- ☐ The retired
- ☐ All people regardless of age
- ☐ Heterosexuals
- ☐ Homosexuals
- ☐ All people regardless of sex
- ☐ People of a particular cultural background
- ☐ People of a particular economic background
- ☐ People of a particular social background
- ☐ People of a particular educational background
- ☐ People of a particular philosophy or religious belief
- ☐ Certain kinds of workers (blue-collar, white collar, executives, or whatever)
- ☐ People who are poor
- ☐ People who are powerless
- ☐ People who wield power
- ☐ People who are rich
- ☐ People who are easy to work with
- ☐ People who are difficult to work with
- ☐ People in a particular place (The Armed Forces, prison, etc.)

Kinds of Problems I Like to Try to Help People With:

- ☐ Physical handicaps
- ☐ Overweight
- ☐ Mental retardation
- ☐ Pain
- ☐ Disease in General
- ☐   Hypertension
- ☐   Allergies
- ☐   Self-healing, psychic healing
- ☐   Terminal illness
- ☐   Holistic health
- ☐ Life/work planning or adjustment
- ☐ Identifying and finding meaningful work
- ☐ Job-hunting, career change, unemployment, being fired or laid off
- ☐ Illiteracy, educational needs
- ☐ Industry in-house training
- ☐ Performance problems, appraisal
- ☐   Low energy
- ☐   Nutritional problems
- ☐   Physical fitness
- ☐   Work satisfaction
- ☐   Discipline problems, self-discipline
- ☐   Stress
- ☐   Sleep disorders
- ☐ Relationships
- ☐   Personal insight, therapy
- ☐   Loneliness
- ☐   Boredom
- ☐   Complaints, grievances
- ☐   Anger
- ☐   Anxiety
- ☐   Fear

❏ Shyness
❏   Meeting people, starting
   friendships
❏ Communications, thoughts,
   feelings
❏ Love
❏   Self-acceptance and
   acceptance of others
❏   Learning how to love
❏ Marriage
❏   Competing needs
❏ Sexual education, sexual
   problems
❏   Sexual Dysfunction
❏ Pregnancy and childbirth
❏ Parenting
❏ Physical abuse
❏ Rape
❏ Divorce
❏ Death and grief

❏ Addictions
❏   Drug problems
❏   Alcoholism
❏   Smoking
❏ Mental illness
❏   Depression
❏   Psychiatric hospitalization
❏ Personal economics
❏   Financial planning
❏   Possessions
❏   Budgeting
❏   Debt bankruptcy
❏ Values
❏ Ethics
❏ Philosophy or religion
❏   Worship
❏   Stewardship
❏   Life after death
❏   Psychic phenomena

If while you are checking off these descriptions, you see any which apply to the kind of **co-workers** you would most like to have, copy them onto the bottom part of petal #4 on page *49*. (You may also find clues about your preferred co-workers, in *the Styles list* that you worked on in the previous exercise.) The following list may also help. Check off the descriptions which apply, or add any others which occur to you.

My Preferred Co-workers:

I prefer to work with what kinds of co-workers or colleagues, bosses, or subordinates?

❏ Both sexes
❏   Men primarily
❏   Women primarily
❏ People of all ages
❏   Adolescents or young people
❏   College students
❏   Young adults
❏   People in their thirties
❏   The middle-aged
❏   The elderly
❏   The retired

❑ All people regardless of sexual orientation
❑   Heterosexuals
❑   Homosexuals
❑ All people regardless of background
❑   People of a particular background
❑   People of a particular cultural background
❑   People of a particular economic background
❑   People of a particular social background
❑   People of a particular educational background
❑   People of a particular philosophy or religious belief
❑   Certain kinds of workers (blue-collar, white-collar, executives,
          or whatever)
❑   People in a particular place (the Armed Forces, prison, etc.)
❑ People who are easy to work with
❑ People who are difficult to work with

In the bottom part of petal #4, on page *49*, you will see an outline of a hexagon. This represents the Party Exercise, found on pages *23*, and *24*, and is put there to remind you that you *may* want to put down *the descriptions* from your *favorite* corners of the hexagon, as descriptions of what you would like your co-workers to be doing (true, the corners you chose were supposed to be descriptive of you, but in identifying co-workers you would like to work with, the ancient truth is that birds of a feather tend to flock together -- e.g., artistic types tend to like to work and communicate with other artistic types, not accountants in three-piece suits -- and vice versa). Within the hexagon on that petal, you will see a figure resembling a cross -- to remind you (*you* are at the center of the figure) to think out what kind of person you want *over* you as a boss (top of the figure), *beside* you as co-work-ers (middle left, of the figure), *before* you as customers, clients, students or whatever (middle right, of the figure) and *below* you, as subordinates (bottom of the figure).

When you are all done with this exercise, you will have now finished the fourth petal out of eight; the picture of your ideal job should be *starting* to get clearer. Also you can begin to see how you are cutting down the size of the job-market that you will need to explore, to a much more manageable territory. On to the next step.

(continued on page 50)

The Fourth Petal

Tools or Means: 1

Kinds of
PEOPLE *I Like To*
Use These Skills With

As Clients,
Customers,
Students, or
Other:

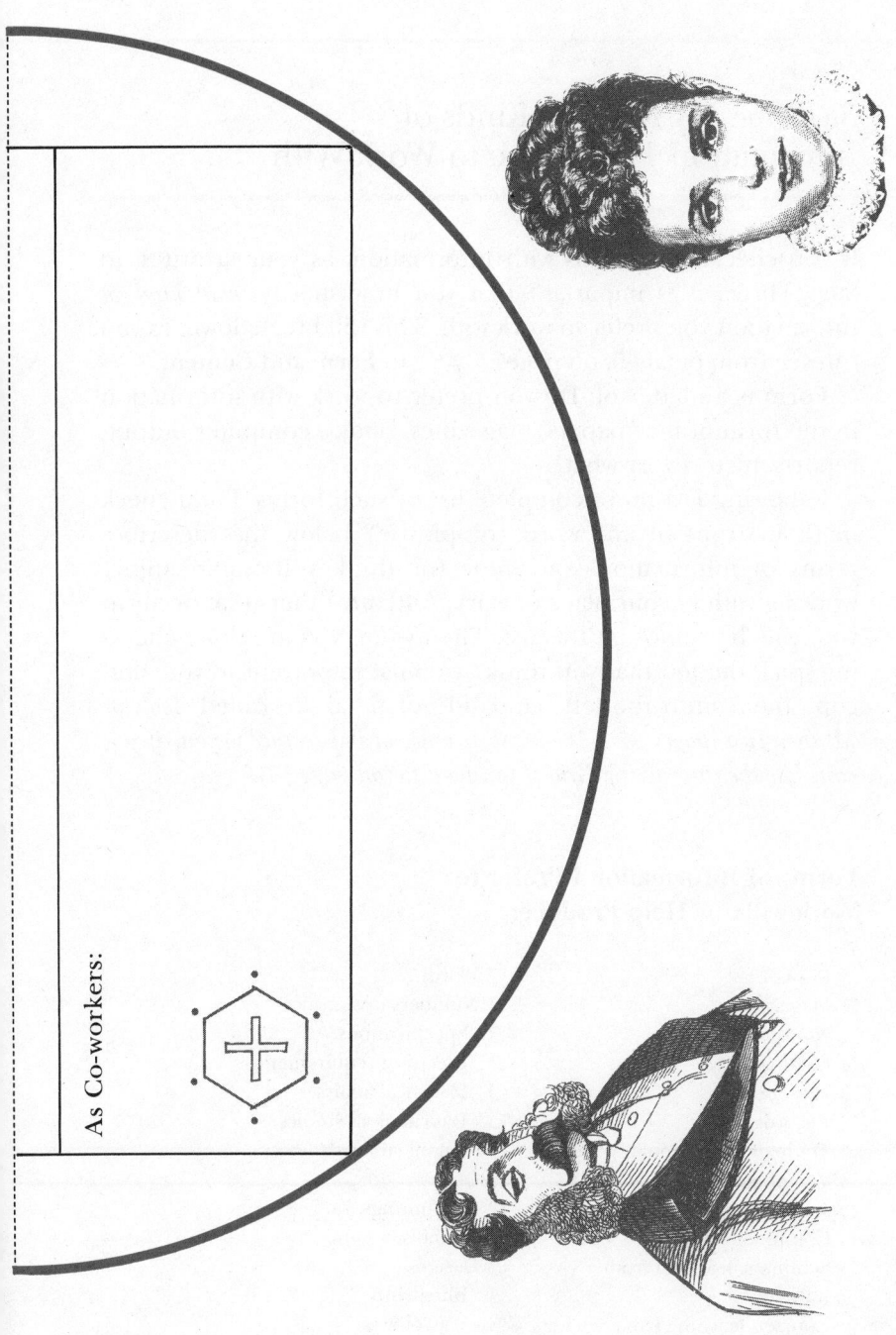

As Co-workers:

Step Five: My Favorite Kinds of Information That I Like to Work With

If you checked any skills with Information, as your favorites, in Step Three, it is important that you now specify *what kind* of Information you prefer to work with. This will break down, as you can see from petal #5, on pages *52–53*, to **Form** and **Content**.

Form is a matter of: Do you prefer to work with information in the form of newspapers, magazines, books, computer output, reports, pictures, or what?

Following is a more complete list of such forms. Put a check mark in front of any word (or phrase) below that describes forms of information you enjoy (or think you would enjoy) working with at your place of work. Add any others that occur to you, which are not on this list. Then when you are done checking, pick the ten that you think are **most** important to you, and copy them onto the left hand side of petal #5, called *Tools or Means: Two (pages 52–53) -- in their order of importance to you, if you can. Use the Prioritizing Grid if you need to (on page 18).*

Forms of Information I Prefer to Work with, or Help Produce:

❑ Books	❑ Words
❑ Magazines	❑ Numbers or statistics
❑ Newspapers	❑ Specifications
❑ Catalogs	❑ Precision requirements
❑ Handbooks	❑ Statistical analyses
❑ Records, files	❑ Data analysis studies
❑ Trade or professional literature	❑ Financial needs
❑ Videotapes	❑ Costs
❑ Audiotapes	❑ Accountings
❑ Computer printouts	❑ Symbols
❑ Seminars, learning from trainers	❑ Designs
	❑ Blueprints
❑ Courses, learning from teachers	❑ Wall-charts

- ❏ Time charts
- ❏ Schema
- ❏ Facts
- ❏ History
- ❏ Ideas
- ❏ Conceptions
- ❏ Investigations
- ❏ Opinion-collection
- ❏ Points of view
- ❏ Surveys

- ❏ Research projects, research and development projects, project reports
- ❏ Procedures
- ❏ Guidebooks
- ❏ Manuals

I Like to Collect or Deal with Information about Any of the Following:

- ❏ Principles
- ❏ Physical principles
- ❏ Spiritual principles
- ❏ Values
- ❏ Standards
- ❏ Repeating requirements
- ❏ Variables
- ❏ Frameworks
- ❏ Organizational contexts
- ❏ Boundary conditions
- ❏ Parameters
- ❏ Systems

- ❏ Programs
- ❏ Operations
- ❏ Sequences
- ❏ Methods
- ❏ Techniques
- ❏ Procedures
- ❏ Specialized procedures
- ❏ Analyses
- ❏ Data analysis studies
- ❏ Schematic analyses
- ❏ Intuitions

I Like to Help Put Information to Use in Any of the Following Practical Ways:

- ❏ Principles applications
- ❏ Recommendations
- ❏ Policy recommendations
- ❏ Goals
- ❏ Project goals
- ❏ Objectives
- ❏ Solutions
- ❏ New approaches

- ❏ Plans
- ❏ Tactical needs
- ❏ Performance characteristics
- ❏ Proficiencies
- ❏ Deficiencies
- ❏ Reporting systems
- ❏ Controls systems

(continued on page 54)

The Fifth Petal

Tools or Means: 2

Kinds of INFORMATION I Like To Use These Skills With

FORM	CONTENT
e.g., "Do you prefer to work with information in the form of newspapers, magazines, books, computer output, reports, or pictures?" etc.	Among the fields of knowledge which you know something about, which ones are your favorites? And in what order of priority?
1.	1.
2.	2.

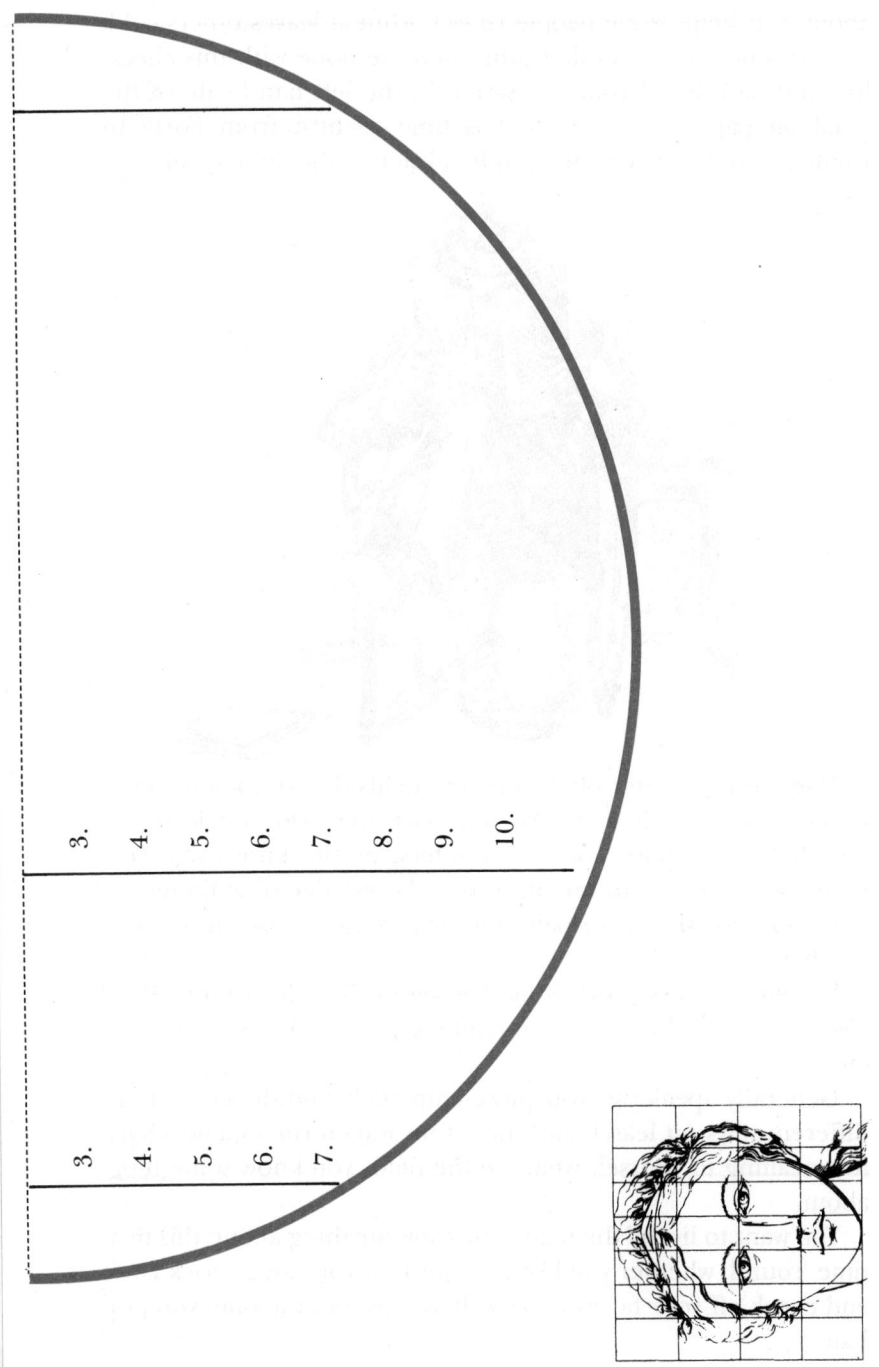

**Fields of Knowledge I Learned About on the Job, or
Just by Doing (at Home or Work)**

*e.g., How to operate a computer
How a volunteer organization works
Principles of planning and management*

Fields of Knowledge I Learned from Seminars or Workshops

*e.g., The way the brain works
Principles of art
Speed reading
Drawing*

**Fields of Knowledge I Learned About by Personal Instruction
from People or by Reading a Lot**

*e.g., How to sew
How to drive an automobile
How computers work
Principles of comparison shopping
Knowledge of antiques
Principles of outdoor survival*

You may want to look back at your Memory Net, pages *26–27*, at this point, for help in filling in the preceding chart. *And*, to further aid you, you may want to see a list, or at least a sampler, of other possible fields of knowledge, just to jog your memory. Following is such a list. Put a check mark in front of any word (or phrase) that describes possible fields of knowledge that you already are familiar with, and would enjoy getting a chance to use in your ideal job. Write in any others that occur to you, as you go down this list.

A SAMPLER OF POSSIBLE FIELDS
YOU MAY KNOW ABOUT

Primarily about People

- ❑ Sociology
- ❑ The *how to* of customer relations and service
- ❑ Principles of group dynamics
- ❑ Principles of behavioral modification
- ❑ Instructional principles and techniques

- ❑ Organization planning
- ❑ Manpower requirements analysis and planning
- ❑ Personnel administration
- ❑ Recruiting
- ❑ Performance specifications

Primarily about Things

- ❏ Physics
- ❏ Astronomy
- ❏ Chemistry
- ❏ Computer programming
- ❏ Knowledge of a particular computer and its applications
- ❏ Design engineering
- ❏ Interior decorating
- ❏ How to run a particular machine
- ❏ Horticulture
- ❏ Car repairs
- ❏ Industrial applications
- ❏ Government contracts
- ❏ Maintenance

- ❏ Financial planning and management
- ❏ Bookkeeping
- ❏ Fiscal analysis, controls, reductions and programming
- ❏ Accounting
- ❏ Taxes
- ❏ R & D program and project management
- ❏ Merchandising
- ❏ Systems analysis
- ❏ Packaging
- ❏ Distribution
- ❏ Marketing/sales

Other Fields (not easily categorized)

- ❏ Principles of art
- ❏ Cinema
- ❏ Principles of recording
- ❏ Knowledge of foreign countries (which ones?)
- ❏ Musical knowledge and taste
- ❏ Graphic arts
- ❏ Photography

- ❏ Broadcasting
- ❏ How to make videos
- ❏ Linguistics or languages
- ❏ Spanish
- ❏ Music
- ❏ Policy development
- ❏ Religion

You will *of course* want to know if you can put down some field that you are **not** yet knowledgeable about, but think you would just *love* to learn about and use in your future ideal job. Well, sure, if you are absolutely, one hundred percent, planning on studying that field in the near future. Or if you want to find a volunteer job or an apprenticeship where you could pick up knowledge of that field *on the job.* But let's not *just* talk about what you do not yet have; in addition to these **do** list knowledge *you already possess,* as well. (*In other words, don't duck the exercise.*)

When you are done listing or checking off all the fields you already know something about, *then* go back over the list and check your favorites, as well as cross out the ones you just hate. And, from among your favorites, pick the ten that you feel are **most** important to you to be able to use in your future ideal job (from both the chart *and* this list), and copy these ten onto the right hand side of the petal called *Tools or Means: Two* (pages *52–53*) *in their order of importance to you, if you can. Use the Prioritizing Grid if you need to (on page 18*).

When you are done, you are now ready to move on to:

Step Six: My Favorite Kinds of Things That I Like to Work With

If you checked any skills with Things, as your favorites, in Step Three, it is important that you now specify *what kind* of Things you prefer to work with.

Following is such a list of Things. Put a check mark in front of any word that describes *things* you particularly like (or think you would particularly like) to use, or act upon, or help produce in your work. Add any others that may occur to you, which are not on the list. Then when you are done checking, pick the ten that you think are **most** important, and copy them onto petal #6 on pages *62–63*, in your order of preference: *"I would most enjoy us-ing this thing in my ideal job; next this thing; next this thing,"* etc. Use the Prioritizing Grid if you need to (on page 18).

Things I Enjoy Working With:

Types of Material
- ❑ Paper
- ❑ Pottery
- ❑ Pewter
- ❑ Paraffin
- ❑ Papier-mâché
- ❑ Wood
- ❑ Other crafts materials
- ❑ Bronze
- ❑ Brass
- ❑ Cast iron, ironworks
- ❑ Steel
- ❑ Aluminum
- ❑ Rubber
- ❑ Plywood
- ❑ Bricks
- ❑ Cement
- ❑ Concrete, cinder-blocks
- ❑ Plastics
- ❑ Textiles
- ❑ Cloth
- ❑ Felt
- ❑ Hides
- ❑ Synthetics
- ❑ Elastic
- ❑ Crops
- ❑ Plants
- ❑ Trees

Types of Manufactured Stuff
- ❑ Machines
- ❑ Tools
- ❑ Toys
- ❑ Equipment
- ❑ Controls, gauges
- ❑ Products

❑ Housing items
- ❑ Tents
- ❑ Trailers
- ❑ Apartments
- ❑ Houses
  - ❑ Chimneys
  - ❑ Columns
  - ❑ Domes
  - ❑ Carpenter's tools
  - ❑ Paint
  - ❑ Wallpaper
  - ❑ Heating elements, furnaces
  - ❑ Carpeting
  - ❑ Fire extinguishers, fire alarms, burglar alarms
  - ❑ Household items
    - ❑ Furniture
    - ❑ Beds
    - ❑ Sheets, blankets, electric blankets
  - ❑ Laundry
  - ❑ Washing machines, dryers
  - ❑ Washday products, bleach
  - ❑ Kitchen appliances, refrigerators, microwaves, ovens, dishwashers, compactors
  - ❑ Kitchen tools
  - ❑ Dishes
  - ❑ Pots and pans
  - ❑ Can openers
  - ❑ Bathtubs
  - ❑ Soaps
  - ❑ Cosmetics
  - ❑ Toiletries
  - ❑ Drugs
  - ❑ Towels
  - ❑ Tools, power tools

❑ Old Equipment
- ❑ Clocks
- ❑ Telescopes
- ❑ Microscopes

Foods or Food Manufacturing Equipment
- Wells, cisterns
- Meats
- Breads and other baked goods
- Health foods
- Vitamins
- Dairy equipment
- Winemaking equipment

Clothing Items
- Clothing
- Raingear, umbrellas
- Spinning wheels, looms
- Sewing machines
- Patterns, safety pins, buttons, zippers
- Dyes
- Shoes

Electrical and Electronics
- Radios
- Records
- Phonographs
- Stereos
- Tape recorders
- Cameras
- Television cameras
- Television sets
- Videotape recorders
- Movie cameras, film
- Electronic devices
- Electronic games
- Lie detectors
- Radar equipment

Amusement, Recreation
- Games
- Cards
- Board games, checkers, chess, Monopoly, etc.
- Kites
- Gambling devices or machines

Musical Instruments
- Specify:

Financial Things
- Calculators
- Adding machines
- Cash registers
- Financial records
- Money

Office Related Things
- PBX switchboards
- Desks, tables
- Desktop supplies
- Pens, ink, felt-tip, ballpoint
- Pencils, black, red or other
- Typewriter
- Computers
- Copying machines, mimeograph machines, printers

Communication Things
- Telephones, answering machines
- Cellular phones
- Telegraph
- Fax machines, teleprinters
- Voice mail machines
- Ship-to-shore radio, shortwave, walkie-talkies

Printing Materials
- Printing presses, type, ink

Art Materials
- Woodcuts, engravings, lithographs
- Paintings, drawings, silk screens

Reading Materials
- Books, braille books
- Newspapers
- Magazines

☐ **Educational Materials**
☐ Transparencies

☐ **Manufacturing or Warehouse Supplies**
☐ Dollies, handtrucks
☐ Containers
☐ Bottles
☐ Cans
☐ Boxes
☐ Automatic machines
☐ Valves, switches, buttons
☐ Cranks, wheels, gears, levers
☐ Hoists, cranes

☐ **Things That Produce Light**
☐ Matches
☐ Candles
☐ Lanterns, oil lamps
☐ Light bulbs, fluorescent lights
☐ Laser beams

☐ **Energy Things**
☐ Fuel cells
☐ Batteries
☐ Transformers, electric motors, dynamos
☐ Engines, gas, diesel
☐ Windmills
☐ Waterwheels
☐ Water turbines
☐ Gas turbines
☐ Steam turbines
☐ Steam engines
☐ Dynamite
☐ Nuclear reactors

☐ **Transportation Things**
☐ Land
☐ Roads
☐ Bicycles
☐ Motorcycles
☐ Mopeds
☐ Automobiles
☐ Parking meters
☐ Traffic lights
☐ Trains
☐ Subways

☐ Air
☐ Gliders
☐ Balloons
☐ Airplanes
☐ Parachutes
☐ Sea
☐ Rivers
☐ Lakes
☐ Streams
☐ Canals
☐ Ocean
☐ Boats
☐ Steamships
☐ Other vehicles

☐ **Medical Materials or Equipment**
☐ Medicines
☐ Vaccines
☐ Anesthetics
☐ Thermometers
☐ Hearing aids
☐ Dental equipment
☐ X-ray machines
☐ False parts of the human body
☐ Spectacles, glasses, contact lenses

☐ **Gym Equipment**

☐ **Sports Equipment**
☐ Fishing rods, fishhooks, bait
☐ Traps, guns

☐ **Gardening or Farm Equipment**
☐ Garden tools
☐ Shovels
☐ Picks
☐ Rakes
☐ Lawnmowers
☐ Ploughs
☐ Threshing machines, reapers, harvesters
☐ Fertilizers
☐ Pesticides
☐ Weed killers

The Sixth Petal

Tools or Means: 3

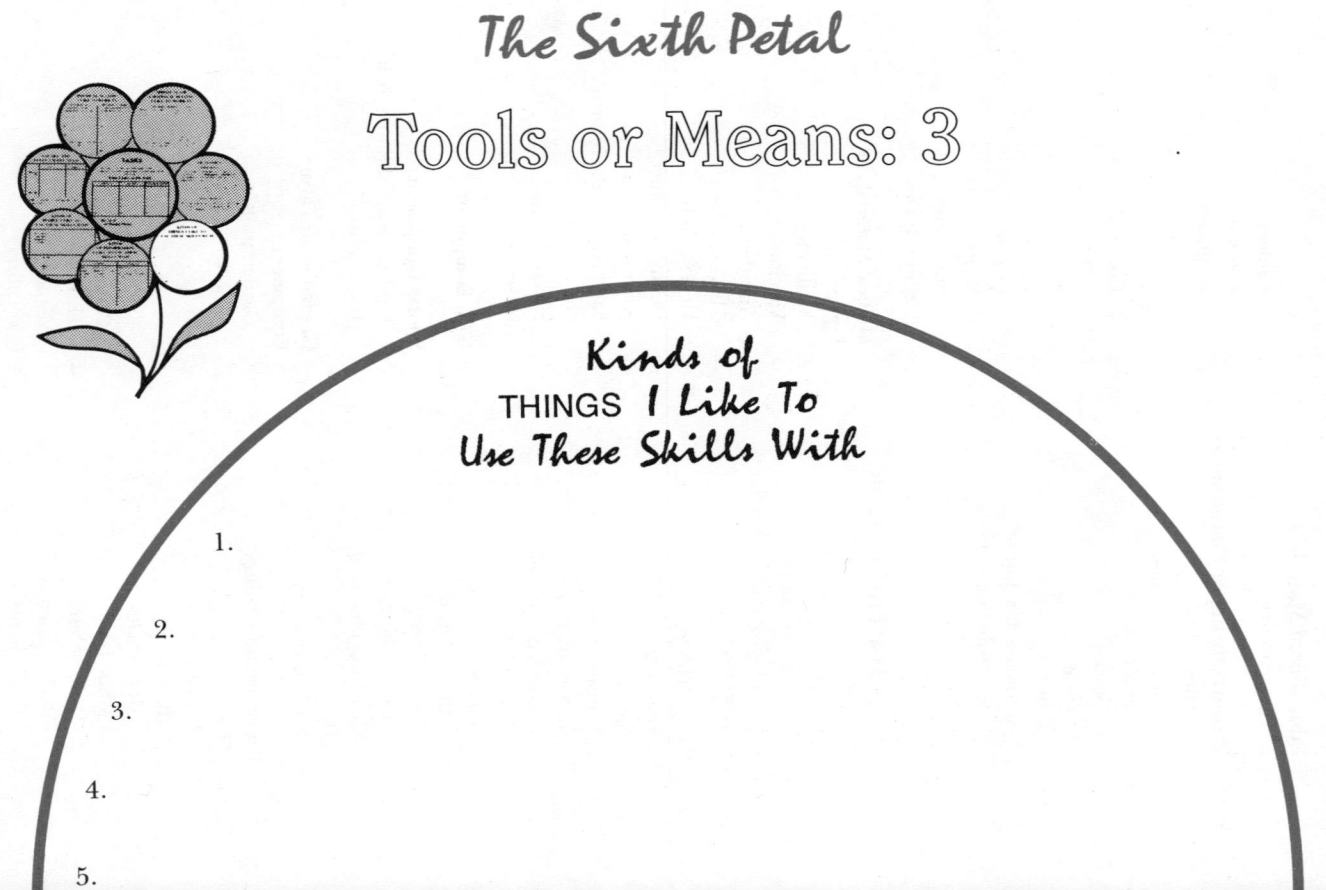

Kinds of
THINGS I Like To
Use These Skills With

1.

2.

3.

4.

5.

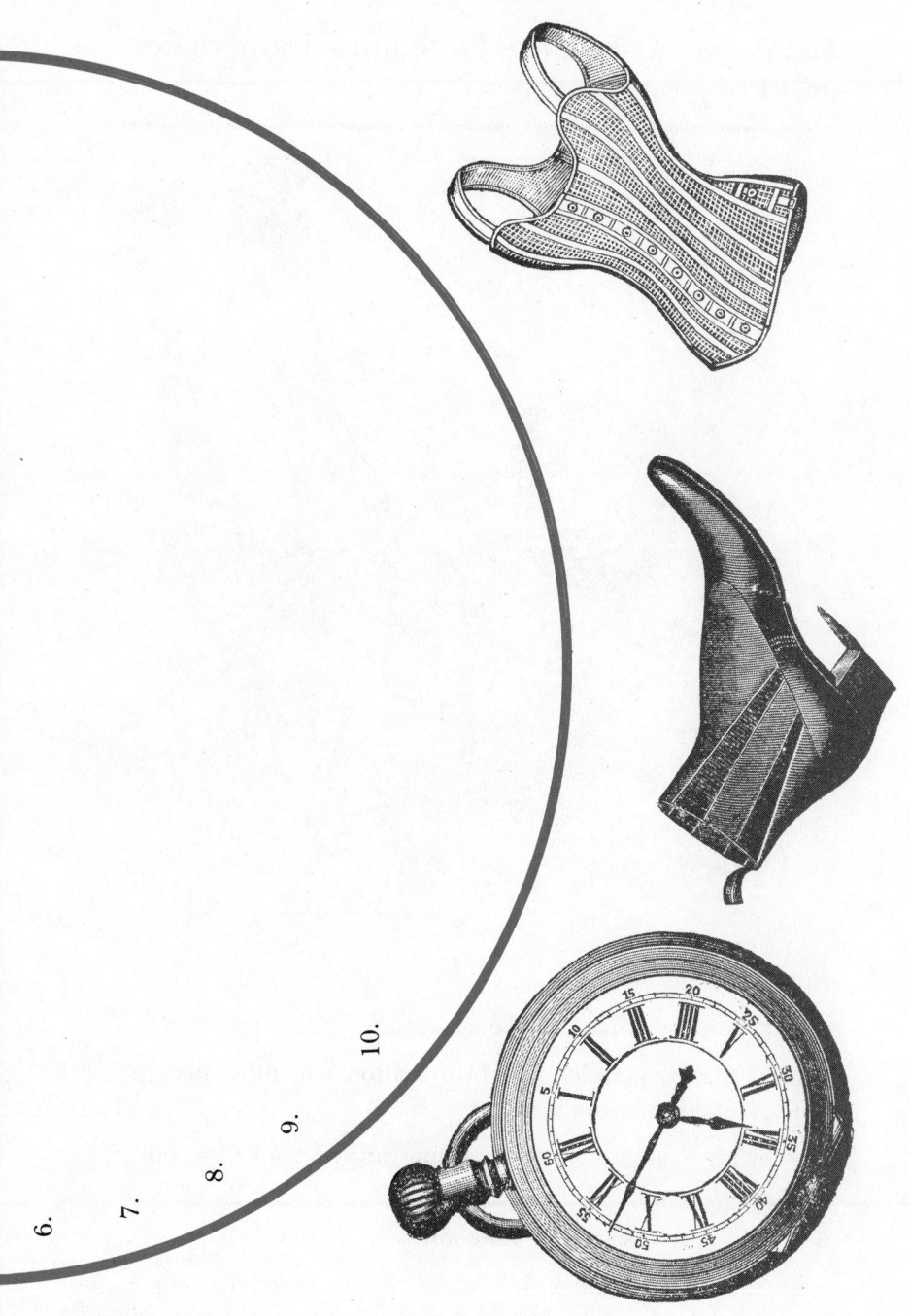

6. 7. 8. 9. 10.

Step Seven: My Favorite Outcomes, Immediate and Long-range

Now that you know:

- what your favorite skills are, and

- what **things**, **people**, and **information** you most like to use these skills on, as well as

- what physical and spiritual **setting** you do your most effective work in,

we turn to the question of **outcomes**.

In the world of work, it is not enough merely to keep busy. One must be keeping busy for some purpose. We are talking about **outcomes**, or **where does it all lead to**? In the world of work, this is often called "the bottom line." I remember some years ago sending out two of my staff to find some materials for me, and after four hours' fruitless search, one turned to the other and said, "Well let's go back. At least we tried." And the other replied, "Unfortunately, in the world of work you're not usually rewarded for *trying*, you're only rewarded for *succeeding*." So they kept on, until they found what they were looking for. This underlines the point here: generally speaking, when you set about to use your skills in the world of work, you must be aiming at some **result** -- in accordance with some **purpose** or **goal**, defined by either you or the organization (preferably *both*).

So, look on the petal on the next page. There you will see that *Outcomes* divides into two parts: **Immediate** and **Long-range**.

Immediate Results of Your Work

Immediate results, at your place of work, is a matter of: "At the work I'd most love to do, what result am I aiming at? Do I want to help produce a **product**, or do I want to help offer some **service** to people, or do I want to help gather, manage, or disseminate **information** to people? Or all three? Or two? And in what order of priority? Do I think the world basically needs me to help it have more information, or more service, or more of some product -- such as food, clothing, or shelter?"

Once you've answered that, the next question *of course* is: **what** product, or service, or information?

Well, the *what* is relatively easy to answer (I said *relatively*). If your preferred outcome is some **product** that you'd like to help produce or market, you'll probably find it identified on your *Favorite Things* petal, on page *62f.* If your preferred outcome is some **service** to people, you'll probably find it identified on your *Favorite People* petal, on page *48f.* And if your preferred outcome is some kind of **information** that you'd like to help gather, manage, or disseminate, you'll probably find it identified on your *Favorite Information* petal, on page *52f.*

Another way of looking at this subject of Immediate Outcomes is to study your seven stories, to see what central motivation seems always to be driving you, what one result you seem always to be reaching for -- above all others. Here is how to discover that:

(continued on page 68)

The Seventh Petal

Outcomes

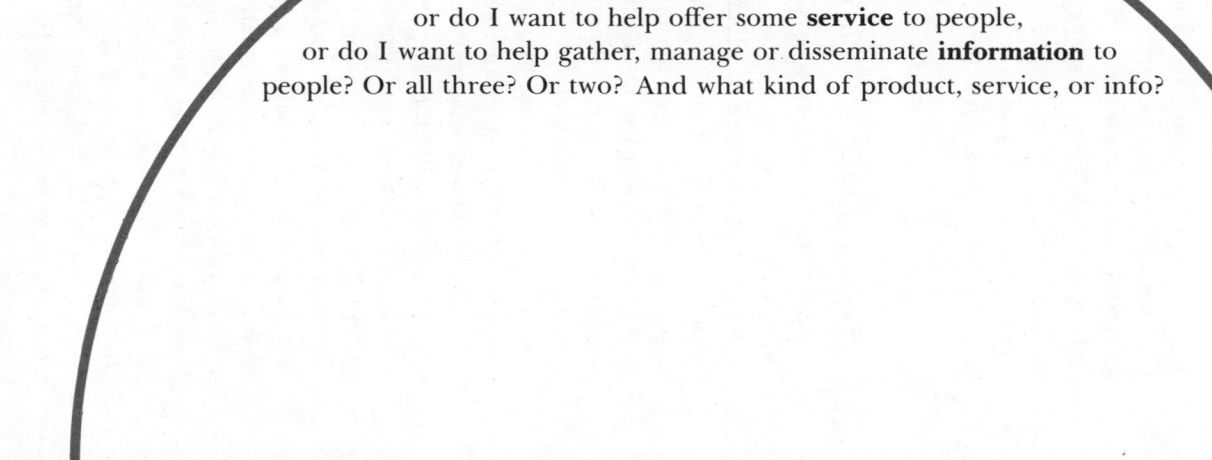

Immediate

At the work I'd most love to do,
do I want to help produce a **product**
or do I want to help offer some **service** to people,
or do I want to help gather, manage or disseminate **information** to
people? Or all three? Or two? And what kind of product, service, or info?

And, what do I see as my central driving motivation in whatever job I take, or in whatever career I pursue?

Long-range

My long-range goals for my life -- the things I want to do, or the goals
I'd like to accomplish -- before I die, are:

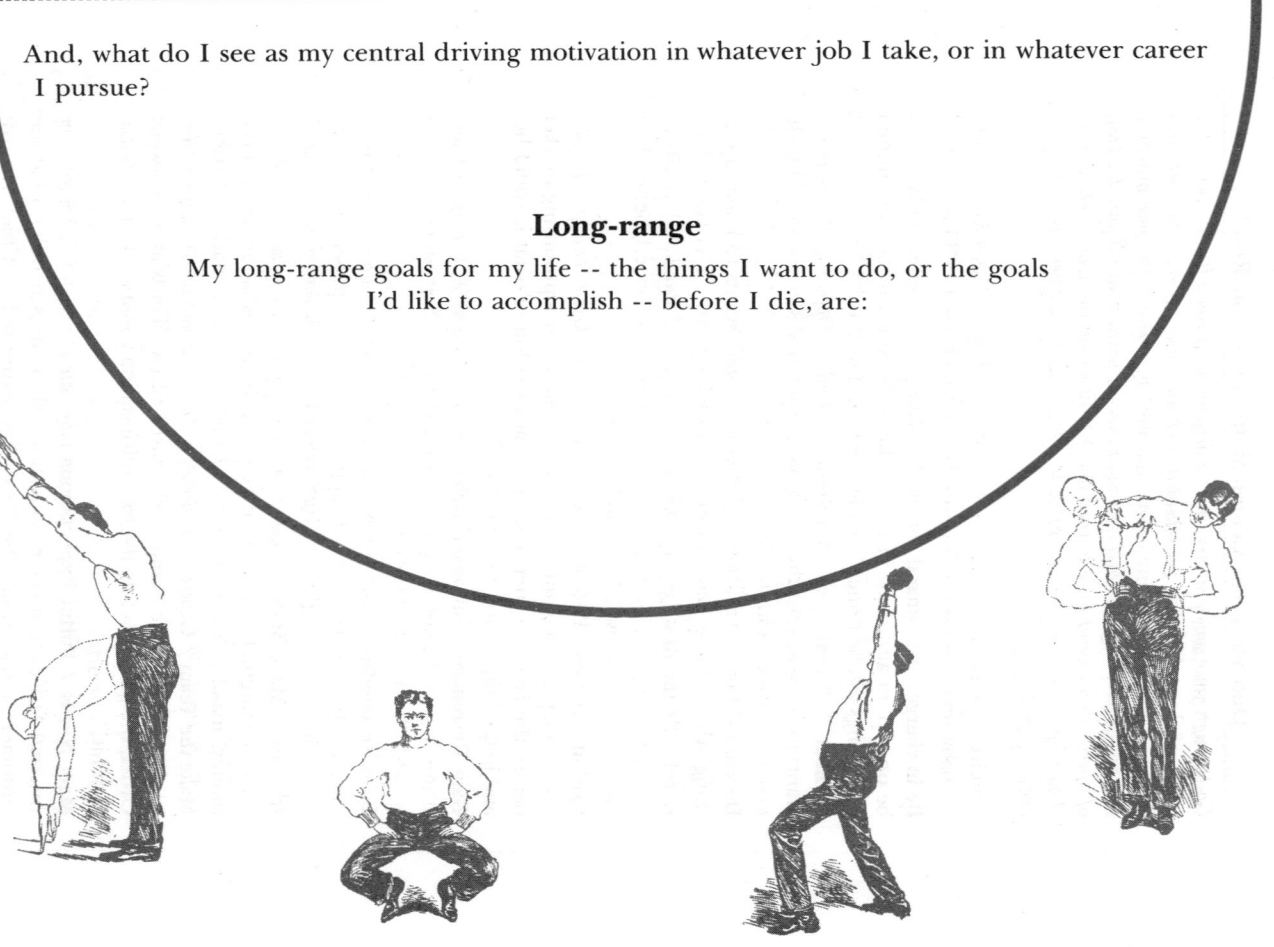

The Eighth Petal

Rewards

Salary and Level
I Want/Need

	LEVEL	SALARY
MAX		

MIN

Other rewards I would like this job to give me:

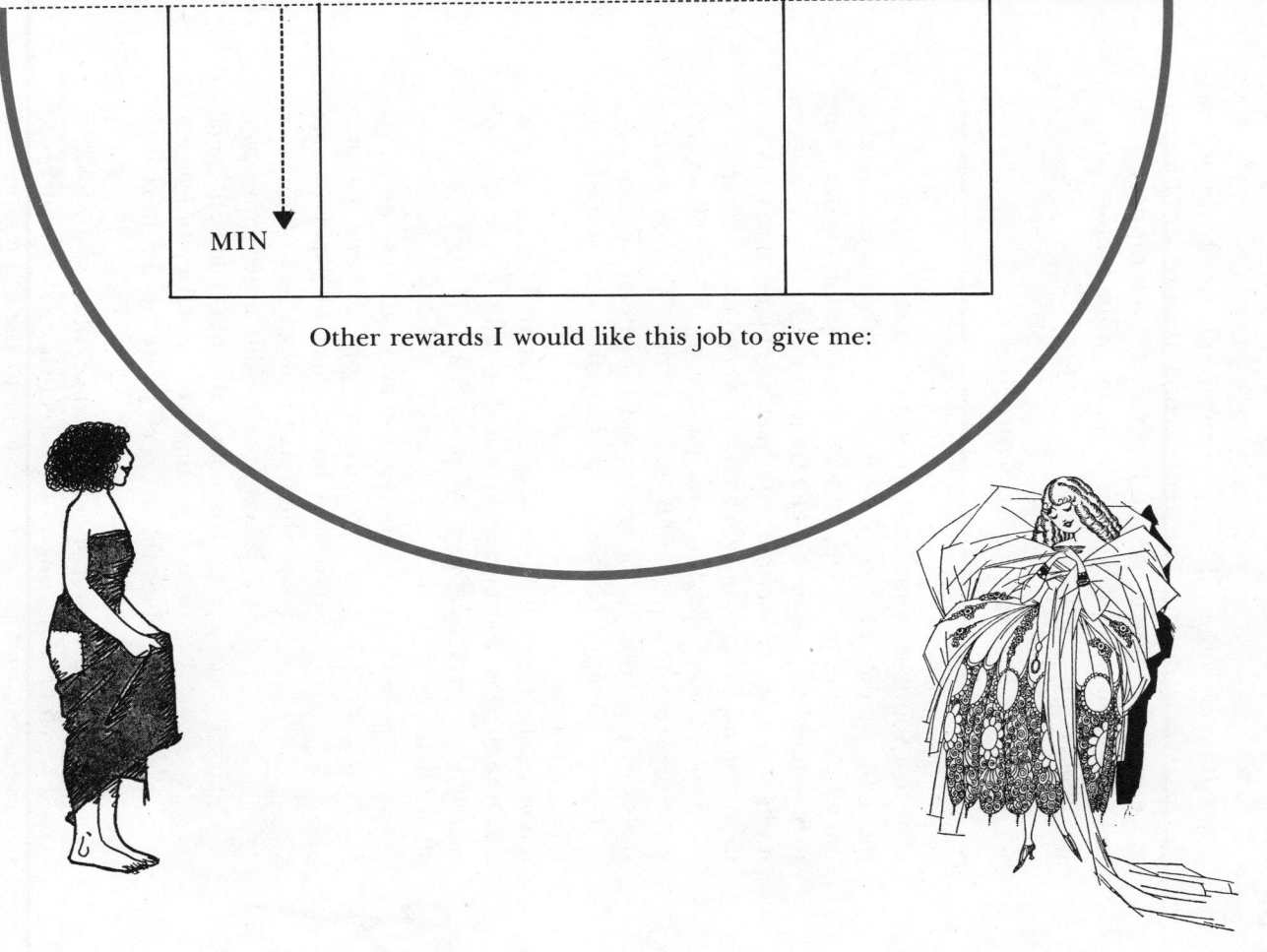

Jot down any others that may occur to you, which are not on this list. When you are done, rank them in their order of importance to you (you may use the Prioritizing Grid, on page *18*, if you wish), and then copy them in order on the bottom part of this petal.

Conclusion: Putting It All Together

Now that you have completed all of the petals, it is time to put them all together on one piece of paper. Why do you need to put all the petals together? Because, your ideal job is not going to be found lying about the countryside in eight separate pieces; it will be a unity, and so must your picture of it be, that you carry in your mind (or in your notebook) as you go job-hunting.

So, don't leave the filled-out picture of the petals as they presently are -- all separated from each other, lying on separate sheets in this booklet. Please cut out the circles of each petal and paste them, or photocopy them -- all of them -- onto one piece of paper.

Obviously, you will need a large sheet of blank paper on which to do this. You may make this sheet most easily by simply taping together nine sheets of plain 8½ × 11 inch paper as shown here:

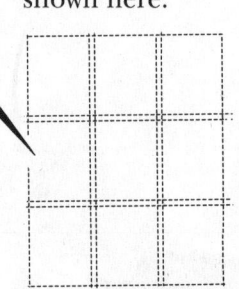

Or, if you want to avoid all this taping, you may go to any art supply or large stationery store, and buy a sheet of paper or cardboard there that is about 24 × 36 inches in size. When you have this larger paper, *please* paste (or copy) all your filled-out petals onto it, so that the overall picture resembles the Flower Picture on the next page:

This is what your Flower should look like, when you have it all pasted together: For a successful career-change, or a successful job-hunt, you **must** know the answers to these questions. You must, you must, you must *thus* have cut down the territory that you now need to go exploring.

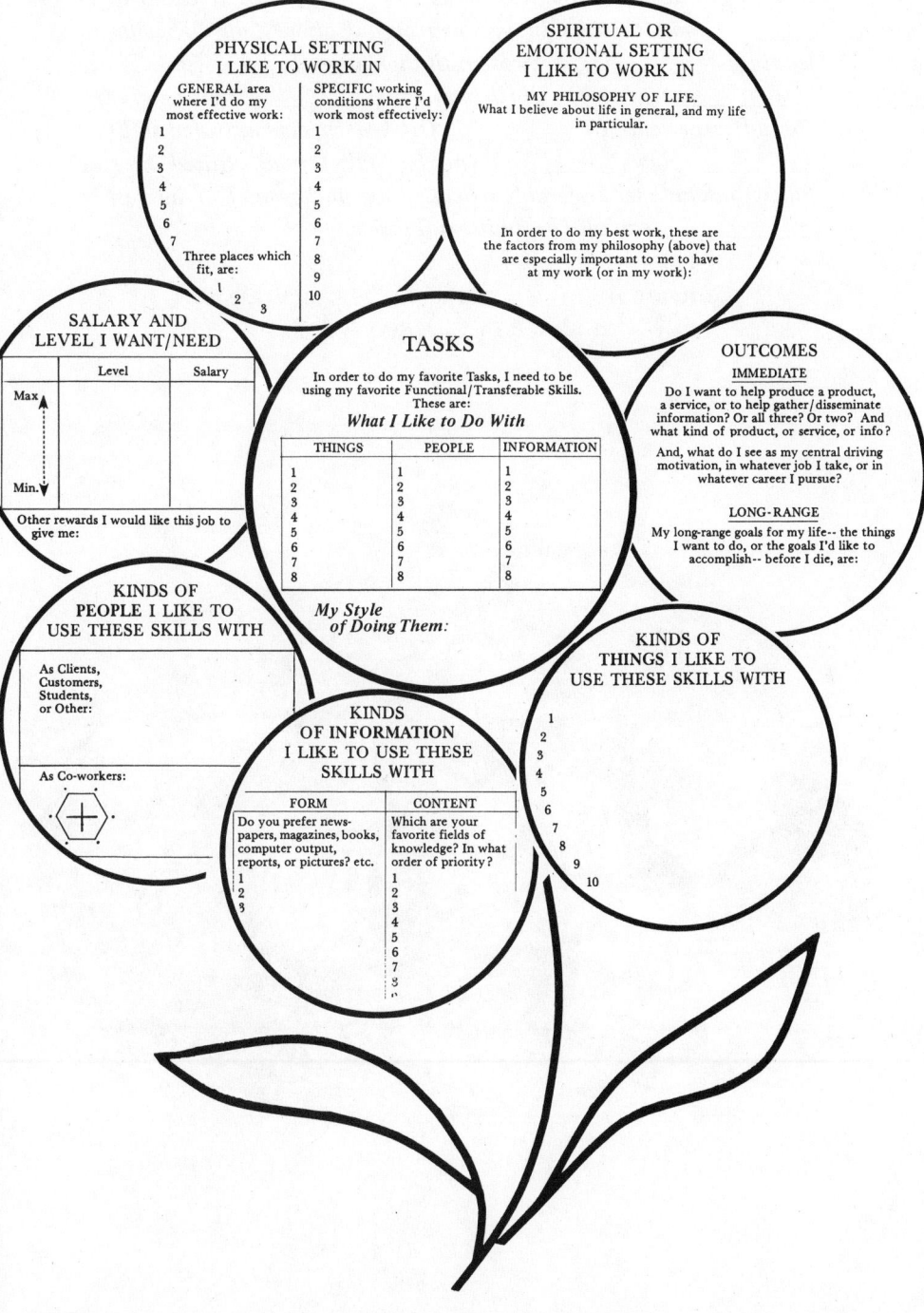

If you want some kind of written career description statement to tie it all together at the end of these exercises, here is a form you might use: *I want a post as _____ OR a challenging _____ post/position in my own organization/shop OR with (a leading) _____ firm/institution/organization (seeking to _____) where/in which/requiring _____ knowledge, OR (broad) experience in _____ OR proven/demonstrated skills in _____ plus _____ can be (fully) used/utilized to (the fullest) advantage, preferably where strong background/or interest in _____ can also be additional assets.*

**You are now ready to tackle the practical steps
outlined in Chapters 6 & 7.**

II. Options

Job-Land
John Holland's Self-Directed Search
When You Want To Start Your Own Business
Moving
Working Overseas

THE MANY PATHS THROUGH JOB-LAND

SAME CAREER BUT IN A NEW PLACE

STAYING AT YOUR PRESENT ORGANIZATION

CONTINUING IN YOUR PRESENT CAREER ←

STARTING A NEW CAREER →

JOB-LAND

STAYING WHERE YOU LIVE NOW

OR MOVING TO A NEW PLACE

R for "Realistic"

People who
have athletic or
mechanical ability,
prefer to work with
objects, machines, tools,
plants, or animals, or to
be outdoors.

I
for
"Investigative"

People who
like to observe,
learn, investigate,
analyze, evaluate,
or solve problems.

C
for
"Conventional"

People who like
to work with data, have
clerical or numerical
ability, carrying things
out in detail or
following through on
others's instructions.

People who
have artistic,
innovating or intuitional
abilities, and like to
work in unstructured
situations, using
their imagination
or creativity.

A
for
"Artistic"

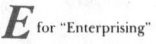

People who like to
work with people --
influencing, persuading
or performing or
leading or managing
for organizational
goals or for
economic gain.

People who
like to work
with people -- to
inform, enlighten.
help, train, develop,
or cure them, or
are skilled
with words.

E for "Enterprising"

S for "Social"

John Holland's
SDS
(The RIASEC System)

John Holland invented this system more than twenty years ago, and has continually updated it since then. It has been used by more than 15 million people, thus far.

In John's system, all jobs, careers, skills, and personality types are reduced to just six clusters or *families*: **R**ealistic, **I**nvestigative, **A**rtistic, **S**ocial, **E**nterprising, or **C**onventional. Hence, **R I A S E C.** You are asked to figure out your 'Holland Code,' which consists of three of the six letters.

The most thorough way to do this is to get your hands on a copy of John's instrument called **'The Self-Directed Search (SDS).'** The SDS is a self-marking test, which takes about 30–40 minutes. You score it yourself, and it will tell you *exactly* what your 'Holland code' is. Details about ordering a specimen set can be found at the end of this section.

If you want an immediate but not quite so accurate way of identifying your 'Holland Code' take the 'Party Exercise,' to the left (instructions on page 24). This will yield, in one minute, a quick guess at your 'Holland code.' It will consist of three letters, and look something like 'S I A'.

Once you know your 'Holland code,' whether from this Party Exercise, or from the more thorough and trustworthy *Self-Directed Search*, -- you then want to look up *what* jobs or careers match that 'code.'

The way to do this is to buy, borrow, or go to your local library to consult a copy of Holland's *Dictionary*, listed at the end of this section.

Do not use the brief Occupations Finder, that is included in the SDS Specimen Set, as an attempted substitute for Holland's 640-page-Dictionary. The Occupations Finder's list is so short, that it depresses people when they find little or nothing that matches their code.

Use the *Dictionary*, instead, and try all six 'permutations' of your code, when you look it up in that *Dictionary*. What do I mean by 'permutation?' Well, if your code is, say, S I A, then you rearrange it in every way you can, thus:

S I A	**A S I**
S A I	**A I S**
I S A	
I A S	

> *P. S. I am the inventor of the Party Exercise. I mention this because we receive many inquiries from career counselors each year as to who invented it, and how can one get permission to buy or make multiple copies of it. The answer is, that in order to avoid competing with my friend John Holland's SDS, which I don't want to do, the Party Exercise is not available separately, nor can it be reproduced by itself. It is available in a relatively cheap form, namely The Beginning Quick Job-Hunting Map, available from Ten Speed Press, Box 7123, Berkeley CA 94707, at $1.95 apiece.*

When You Want
To Start
Your Own Business

Self-Employment
Working for Yourself
Working at Home
Being An Independent Contractor
Being An Inventor
Becoming a Free-Lancer
Running A Franchise

Sure, you've thought about it, a million times. Hasn't everyone? Every time you're tied up in traffic going to or from work. You've toyed with the idea of not having to go to an office or other place of business, but of running your own business, keeping all the profits for yourself, being your own boss, making your own product or selling your own services, maybe out of your own home. It's called 'the world's fastest commute,' or 'going downstairs, instead of downtown.'[1]

Great idea! *But,* so far as you are concerned, nothing's ever come of it. Until now. Now, you're out of work, or you're fed up with your job, and you're thinking to yourself: *Maybe it's now, or never. Maybe I ought to just do it.*

WHAT KIND OF
BUSINESS
DO YOU WANT TO START?

You need to begin, of course, by deciding **what** kind of business you want to be in. Perhaps you haven't the foggiest notion.

Or, perhaps you know exactly *what,* because you've been thinking about it for *years,* and may even have been *doing* it for years -- only, in the employ of someone else. If you are now thinking about doing this on your own, whether it be business services, or consultancy, or repair work, or some kind of craft, or the making of some kind of product, or teaching, or offering of home services such as childcare or delivery by night.

---

1. Coined by Robert E. Calem in *The New York Times,* 4/18/93.

The next question you need to decide is just exactly **where** you're going to be doing it. Some self-employment ideas will require an outside place. For example, your dream may be: *I want a horse ranch, where I can raise and sell horses.* Or *I want to run a bed-and-breakfast place.* Stuff like that.

Some businesses are *independent of site.* It is possible to define a business -- given the telephone, fax machine, e-mail, and the Internet -- which could be run from a ski resort or wherever your preferred environment in the whole world is -- whether out in nature, or at your favorite vacation spot, or even in some other country. You can put them anywhere.

The only rule is, be *sure* to go talk to other people who have already done what you are contemplating *or something like it.* Pick their brains for everything they're worth. No need for you to step on the same *landmines* that they did.

WORKING OUT OF
YOUR OWN HOME

Most people, however, when starting their own businesses, prefer to begin by running them out of their home if they possibly can. They can thus save money, overhead, rent, and cut down on many other expenses.

Three hundred years ago, of course, nearly everybody worked this way. They worked at home or on their farm. Only when the industrial revolution came, did the idea of working *away from* home become the rule.

In recent times, however, the idea of working at home has been finding new life, due to congestion on the highways, and the development of new technologies. If you can afford them, the telephone,[2] a fax machine, a computer with a modem, e-mail, online services and/or the Internet, mail order houses, and the like, all have combined to make a home business feasible, as never before.

It's called *self-employment,* or being *an independent contractor,* or *free-lancing* or *contracting out your services.*[3]

If you're thinking about doing this, working out of your own home, apartment, or condo, you would be joining the more than 23.8 million home-based workers who already do this in the U.S., plus the estimated 25 million additional workers who are *thinking* about doing it.

But you need to begin by being aware of the problems you will face, so that you will know in advance how to deal with them.

---

2. This family includes cellular telephones, 'call-forwarding' -- the technology where people call your one fixed telephone number, and then get automatically forwarded to wherever you have told the phone company you currently are -- and voice/electronic mail.

3. If you decide to launch yourself on this path, be sure to talk to people who have been free-lancers, until you know the name of every pitfall and obstacle in *free-lancing.* Where do you find such people? Well, free-lancers are *everywhere.* Independent screenwriters, copy writers, artists, songwriters, photographers, illustrators, interior designers, video people, film people, consultants, and therapists, are only *some* examples of the type of people who must free-lance, in the very nature of their job. Talk with enough of them, even if they're not free-lancing in the same business you have in mind, until you learn all the pitfalls of free-lancing.

THE THREE MAJOR PROBLEMS
OF HOME BUSINESSES

(1) The first major problem of home businesses, according to experts, is that on average home-based workers *(in the U.S. at least)* only earn 70% of what their full-time office-based equals do. So, you must think carefully whether you could make enough money to survive -- *or even prosper.*

(2) The second major problem of home businesses is that it's often difficult to maintain the balance between business and family time. Sometimes the *family* time gets short-changed, while in other cases the demands of family (particularly with small children) may become so interruptive, that the *business* gets short-changed. So, do investigate thoroughly, ahead of time, *how* you would go about doing this *well.* There are books that can help.

(3) Lastly, a home business puts you into a perpetual job-hunt. Oh, I know, the *theory* about becoming self-employed is that you will thus be able to avoid the job-hunt. And, in the technical sense, you do. But you still have to hunt, and hunt, and hunt for new clients or customers -- who are, in a sense, new *employers* (that is because they *pay* you for the work you are doing). If you are going to be running your own business, you will have to *continually* beat the bushes for new clients or customers -- who will be in fact your short-term -- or long-term -- employers. I mention this, because some of us, when unemployed, are attracted to the idea of starting our own business because this seems like an ideal way to cut short their job-hunt. The irony is, that your own business makes you in a very real sense a *perpetual* job-hunter.

Of course, the dream of most self-employed people is to ultimately become so well known, and so in demand, that clients or customers will be literally beating down your doors -- and you will be able to stop this endless job-hunt. They will come hunting for *you.* But that only happens to a *relative* minority, and your realistic self needs to know that, from the beginning.

The greater likelihood is that you will *always* have to beat the bushes for employers/clients. It may get easier as you get better at it, or it may get harder, if economic conditions take a severe downturn. But it may well be the one aspect of your work that you will *always* cordially dislike.

If you avoid the task of finding new customers *like the plague,* you're probably going to find *"your own business"* is just a glamorous synonym for *'starving.'* I know *many* self-employed people to whom this has happened, and it happened precisely for this reason -- because they couldn't stomach going out to beat the bushes for clients or customers. If that's true for you, you should plan to start out by *hiring, co-opting, or getting someone to volunteer* part-time, to do this for you -- someone who, in fact, 'eats it up.' There are such, out there; you will have to find and link up with one of them.

WHEN YOU DON'T
KNOW WHAT KIND
OF BUSINESS YOU WANT
TO START

Maybe you like the idea of working for yourself. Maybe you love the idea of running your own business. But maybe you haven't the foggiest notion of what kind of business to start. *Minor little detail!*

There are several steps you can take, to nail this down.

First, read. There are oodles of books out there that are *filled* with ideas for home businesses. Browse your local library, or bookstore. If none of the books you look at have any ideas that grab you, businesses that you might consider are: offering home deliveries of local restaurants' dinners, or home delivery of grocery orders from any downtown supermarket. Evening delivery services of laundry, etc. Daytime or evening office cleaning services and/or home cleaning services. Home repairs, especially in the evening or on weekends, of TVs, radios, audio systems, laundries, dishwashers, etc. Lawn care. Care for the elderly in their own homes. Childcare in their own homes. Pick up and delivery of things (even personal stuff, like cleaning) at the office. Automobile care or repair services, with pickup and delivery. Offering short-term business consultancy in various fields. Other successful businesses these days deal with leisure activities.

Secondly, look around your own community, and ask yourself what services or products people seem to need the most. Or what service or product already offered in the community could stand a lot of *improving?* There may be something there that *grabs* you.

The underlying theme to 90% of the businesses that are *out there* these days is *things that save time.* It's what single parents, families where both parents work, and singles who have overcrowded lives, most want.

Third, consider mail order. If you find no needs within your own community, you may want to broaden your search, to ask what is needed in this country -- or the world. After all, mail order businesses can be started *small* at home, and catalogs can be sent *anywhere.* If this interests you, read up on the subject. Also, for heaven's sakes, go talk to other mail order people (for names, just look at the catalogs you're already likely receiving).

Fourth, dream. In evaluating any ideas that you pick up, the first thing you ought to look at are your dreams. What have you always dreamed about doing? Since childhood? Since last week? Now is the time to dust off those dreams.

And please don't pay any attention, for now, to whether those dreams represent *a step up* for you in life, or not. Who cares? Your dreams are yours. You may have been dreaming of earning *more* money. But then again, you may have been dreaming of doing work that you really love, even if it means a lesser salary or income than you have been accustomed to. Don't *judge* your dreams, and don't let anyone else judge them either.

WHEN YOU'VE
INVENTED SOMETHING

If you are inclined toward invention or tinkering, you might want to start by improving on an idea that's already *out there*. Start with something you like, such as bicycles. You might experiment with making -- let us say -- a folding-bicycle. Or, if you like to go to the beach, and your skills run to sewing, you might think about making and selling beach towels with weights sewn in the corners, against windy days.

If you've already invented something, and it's been sitting in your drawer, or the garage, but you've never attempted to duplicate or manufacture it before, now might be a good time to try. Think out very carefully just how you are going to get it manufactured, advertised, and marketed, etc. There are firms out there which claim to specialize in promoting inventions such as yours, for a fee. However, according to the Federal Trade Commission, in a study of 30,000 people who paid such promoters, not a single inventor ever made a profit after giving their invention to such firms.[4] If you want to gamble some of your hard-earned money on such firms, consider whether you might better drop it at the tables in Las Vegas. I think the odds are *better* there.

You're much better off, *of course*, doing your own research as to how one gets an invention marketed. Through the copyright office, and your library, locate other inventors, and ask if they were successful in marketing their own invention. When you find those who were, pick their brains for everything they're worth. Of course one of the first things they're going to tell you is to go get your invention copyrighted or trademarked or patented.

FRANCHISES

If nothing else appeals, you may want to consider a franchise. Franchises exist because some people want to have their own business, but don't want to go through the agony of starting it up. They want to *buy in* on an already established business, and they have the money in their savings with which to do that (or they know where they can get a bank loan). And they don't care if the business in question is not *in the home* (though some franchises can be done from your home, the majority require an outside site).

Fortunately for you, if this interests you, there are a lot of such franchises. In the U.S., for example, there are more than 2,100 franchised businesses, with more than 478,000 outlets, employing more than 6 million people. Your library or bookstore should have books that list many of these, in this country and elsewhere.

In the U.S., the overall failure rate for franchises is less than 4%.[5] You want to keep in mind that some *types* of franchises have a failure rate *far* greater than that. The ten *riskiest* small businesses, according to experts, are local laundries and dry cleaners, used car dealerships, gas stations, local trucking firms, restaurants, infant clothing stores, bakeries, machine shops,

---

4. *San Francisco Chronicle*, 1/26/91.

5. Ray Bard and Sheila Henderson, *Own Your Own Franchise*, Addison Wesley, 1987, p.1.

grocery or meat stores, and car washes -- though I'm sure there will be some new nominees for this list, by the time you read this. *Risky* doesn't mean you can't make them succeed. It only means the odds are greater than they would be with other small businesses.

You want to keep in mind also that some individual franchises are *terrible* -- and that includes well-known names. They charge too much for you to *get on board,* and often they don't do the advertising or other commitments that they promised they would. You can be left a whole lot poorer, and gnashing your teeth.

There isn't a franchising book that doesn't warn you eighteen times to go talk to people who have *already* bought that same franchise, before you ever decide to go with them. And I mean *several* people, not just one. Most experts also warn you to go talk to *other* franchises in the same field, not just the kind you're thinking about signing up with. Maybe there's something better, that your research will uncover.

If you are drawn to the idea of a franchise, because you are in a hurry, and you don't want to do any homework first, *'cause it's just too much trouble,* you will deserve what you get, believe me. That way lies madness.

YOUR OWN BUSINESS
OR FRANCHISE:
WHAT ARE YOUR CHANCES
OF 'MAKING A GO' OF IT?

If you investigate the odds of succeeding at your own business -- whether it be at home or downtown, whether it be of your own devising or is a franchise -- the first thing you will come across are some *intimidating* statistics. Hidden in them is not just bad news, but also some good news.

U.S. Statistics

The following figures are for the U.S., but similar statistics probably can be found in every industrialized country of the world. Currently, in the U.S., 10,200,000 people -- or one out of every twelve people in the workforce -- have started their own business. *But*, at least 65% of all new businesses fail within their first five years of operation -- that's more than one out of every two. A well-known statistic, and the only debate you'll get on it from experts is whether or not the figure is *too low*. 96,100 businesses went bankrupt in 1992.[6] So, if you want to go into business for yourself, there's a great risk that it's going to go belly-up[7] *early on*. That is, as they say, the bad news.

The good news is that *if* you survive this early-on period, things start to look up. The risk decreases. There are two evidences for saying this:

First, only about 25% of new businesses fail *in any given year*; so, taking it on just a year-to-year basis, you have a 75% chance of *not* going belly-up *that* year.[8] Secondly, there are about 28 *old* businesses in the U.S. for every new business that starts up. So, the national bankruptcy/failure rate -- taking *all* businesses into account -- is *much* lower than most people think. In one year recently, out of each 10,000 businesses in the U.S., only 120 failed.[9] That means that 9,880 out of each 10,000 businesses survived.

What these statistics add up to, is that *if* you can make it through the first few years in your home business, you'll probably survive thereafter.

That leaves the BIG question: how *do* you survive those first few difficult years? The answer is: *Research. Homework. Interviewing people.* Before you commit yourself to this new thing, you need to find out something. That *something* can be summarized in the following formula:

---

6. *San Francisco Chronicle*, Thursday, 1/21/93, p. C1.

7. If any of my readers outside the U.S. do not understand the slang phrase "belly-up," other more familiar synonyms would be: bankrupt, out of business, kaput.

8. These figures are from David Birch's *Job Creation In America*. The Free Press, 866 Third Ave., New York, NY 10022. 1987. David is an excellent researcher, and knows more about small businesses than anyone else in the country that I know of; I recommend this book, highly. It describes at length where the new jobs are coming from, and how our smallest companies put the most people to work.

9. 1986, the most recent year for which I have statistics.

A, MINUS B,
EQUALS C

By way of introduction to this subject, in the past twenty-five years I have found it *mindboggling* to discover how many people start a new business, at home or elsewhere, without ever going to talk to anybody else in the same kind of business.

One job-hunter told me she started a homemade candle business, without ever talking to anyone else who had tried a similar endeavor. Her business went belly-up within a year and a half. She concluded: no one should go into such a business. I concluded: she hadn't done her homework, before she started.

To avoid her fate, here are the rules for homework you *must* do, before starting your own home business -- or any kind of new venture. Please *memorize* them:

A – B = C

1. You write out exactly what kind of business you are thinking about starting.

2. You identify towns or cities that are at least twenty-five miles away, and you try to get their phone books, addresses of their Chambers of Commerce, etc.

3. By using the phone book and the Chambers, you try to identify names of three businesses in those towns, that are identical or similar to the business you are thinking of starting. You journey to that town or city, and talk to the founder/owner of same.

4. When you talk to them, you ask them what pitfalls or obstacles they ran into. You ask them how they overcame them. You ask them what skills or knowledges do they think are necessary to running this kind of business successfully. You make a list of the latter. When you've finished talking to all three owners, you put together a list of the skills and knowledges they agreed on, as necessary to running the business. We'll call this list "A."

5. Back home you sit down and inventory your own skills and knowledges, perhaps using Chapters 5 and 6 in this book. We'll call this list "B."

6. Finally, you subtract "B" from "A," and this results in a list we will call "C." That's the list of the skills or knowledges you don't have, but must find -- either by taking courses, or by getting volunteers with those skills, or by hiring someone with those skills.

Why twenty-five miles away? Well, actually, that's a minimum. You want to interview businesses which, *if they were in the same town* with you, would be your rival. And if they were in the same town with you, wouldn't likely tell you how to get started. After all, they're not going to train you just so you can then take business away from them.

But, when a guy, a gal, or a business is twenty-five miles away -- even better, fifty miles away -- you're not as likely to be perceived as a rival, and therefore they're much more likely to tell you what you want to know about their own experience, and how *they* got started, and where the landmines are hidden.

Doubtless at this point you would like an example of this whole process. Okay. Our job-hunter is a woman who has been making harps for some employer, but now is thinking about going into business for herself, not only *making* harps at home, but also *designing* harps, with the aid of a computer. After interviewing several home-based harpmakers and harp designers, and finishing her own self-assessment, her chart of **A – B = C** came out looking like the next page.

If she decides to try her hand at becoming an independent harpmaker and harp designer, she now knows what she needs but lacks: *computer programming, knowledge of the principles of electronics, and accounting.* Column **C.** These she must either go to school to acquire for herself, OR enlist from some friends of hers in those fields, on a volunteer basis, OR go out and hire, part-time.

These are the essential steps for any new enterprise that you are considering: A – B = C. If you want to start up more than one venture, you need to interview people *in each line of work* to find out A – B = C for both jobs.

You may also want to talk to people who have juggled two (or more) careers, at the same time.

HOW CAN YOU DO A – B = C,
IF YOU'VE THOUGHT OF
A BUSINESS OR CAREER
THAT NO ONE'S EVER HEARD OF
BEFORE

No matter how inventive you are, you're probably *not* going to invent a job that *no one* has ever heard of, before. You're only going to invent a job that *most* people have never heard of, before. But the likelihood is *great* that someone, somewhere, in this world of endless creativity, has already put together the kind of job you're dreaming about. Your task: to find her, or him, and interview them thoroughly. And then. . . . well, you know the drill: **A – B = C.**

NEW WAYS TO WORK

Well, we've about covered now some new ways to work. If you're at a turning point in your life, all of these are worth weighing and considering.

Of course, none of the strategies in this section are actually *new* ways to work. They are only *new to you*. Even so, it takes a lot of guts to try something new *for you* in today's economy. It's easier, however, if you keep three rules in mind:

---

1. There is always some risk, in trying something new. Your job is not to avoid risk -- there is no way to do that -- but to make sure ahead of time that the risks are *manageable*.

2. You find this out before you start, by first talking to others who have already done what you are thinking of doing; then you evaluate whether or not you still want to go ahead and try it.

3. Have a Plan B, already laid out, *before you start*, as to what you will do if it doesn't work out; i.e., know where you are going to go, next. Don't wait, *puh-leaze!* Write it out, now. *This is what I'm going to do, if this doesn't work out:* _____

These rules always apply, no matter where you are in your life: just starting out, already employed, unemployed, in mid-life, recovering after a crisis or accident, facing retirement, or whatever. Do take them very seriously.

If you're sharing your life with someone, sit down with that partner or spouse and ask what the implications are *for them* if you try this new thing. Will it require all your joint savings? Will they have to give up things? If so, what? Are they willing to make those sacrifices? And so on.

If you aren't out of work, you will need to debate the wisdom of quitting your job before you start up the new company, or business. And what do the experts say, here? In a word, they say, if you have a job, *don't* quit it. Better by far to move *gradually* into self-employment, doing it as a moonlighting activity first of all, while you are still holding down that regular job somewhere else. That way, you can test out your new enterprise, as you would test a floorboard in an old run-down house, stepping on it cautiously without at first putting your full weight on it, to see whether or not it will support you.

If your investigation revealed that it takes good accounting practices in order to turn a profit, and you don't know a thing about accounting, you go out and hire a (part-time) accountant *immediately* -- or, if you absolutely have no money, you talk an accountant friend of yours into giving you some volunteer time, for a while.

It is up to you to do your research thoroughly, weigh the risks, count the cost, get counsel from those intimately involved with you, and then if you decide you want to do it (whatever *it* is), go ahead and try -- no matter what your well-meaning but pessimistic acquaintances may say.

You only have one life here on this earth, and that life (under God) is *yours* to say how it will be spent, or not spent.

For Further Reading

New books dealing with all kinds of self-employment come out *monthly*. But below are the *kind* of books you will find at your local bookstore or public library:

Philip Holland, *How To Start A Business Without Quitting Your Job: The Moonlight Entrepreneur's Guide*. Ten Speed Press, Post Office Box 7123, Berkeley, CA 94707. 1992.

Sharon Kahn, *101 Best Businesses to Start*. Doubleday, 1540 Broadway, New York, NY 10036. 1988. The categories here are the same as above, plus Healthcare and Fitness, Household Services, Real Estate, Sales and Marketing, and Travel.

Entrepreneur Magazine's *184 Businesses Anyone Can Start and Make a Lot of Money*. 2nd ed., Bantam Books, 1540 Broadway, New York, NY 10036. 1990. Ideas related to Personal Services, Business Services, Food, Retail, Sports and Entertainment, Automotive Businesses, Publishing, and miscellaneous.

Entrepreneur Magazine's *168 More Businesses Anyone Can Start and Make a Lot of Money*. 2nd ed., Bantam Books, 1540 Broadway, New York, NY 10036. 1991. Same categories as above, plus Computer Businesses.

Paul and Sarah Edwards, *Finding Your Perfect Work: The New Career Guide to Making a Living, Creating a Life*. A Jeremy P. Tarcher/Putnam Book, 200 Madison Avenue, New York, NY 10016. 1996. The book features an alphabetical directory of self-employment careers. They advertise this as "The What Color Is Your Parachute for the Next Decade."

Paul and Sarah Edwards, *Working from Home: Everything You Need to Know about Living and Working under the Same Roof*. 3rd ed. J.P. Tarcher, Inc., 200 Madison Avenue, New York, NY 10016. Now revised and expanded. 440 pages. Has a long section on computerizing your home business, and on telecommunicating.

Barbara Brabec, *Homemade Money: Your Homebased Business Success Guide:* 4th ed. Betterway Books, 1507 Dana Avenue, Cincinati, OH 45207. 1992. A very fine book, with an A to Z business section, and a most helpful summary of which states have laws regulating (or prohibiting) certain home-based businesses; it is updated regularly. Barbara also publishes a newsletter, *National Home Business Report*. If you wish more information, you can ask for her catalog, by writing to National Home Business Network, P.O. Box 2137, Naperville, IL 60567.

Lynie Arden, *The Work-at-Home Sourcebook*. 5th ed. 1994. Live Oak Publications, P.O. Box 2193, 1515 23rd St., Boulder, CO 80306.

Homeworking Mothers, a quarterly newsletter for women who want to start their own businesses and work from their homes. Mother's Home Business Network, Box 423, East Meadow, NY 11554.

Cecil C. Hoge, Sr., *Mail Order Moonlighting*. 2nd ed. Ten Speed Press, Box 7123, Berkeley, CA 94707. 1988.

Jeffrey Lant: *The Consultant's Kit: Establishing and Operating Your Successful Consulting Business* (208 pages, $38.50) and *How To Make At Least $100,000 Every Year As A Successful Consultant in Your Own Field: The Complete Guide to Succeeding in the Advice Business* (315 pages, $39.50). Jeffrey Lant Associates, 50 Follen Street, Suite 507, Cambridge, MA 02138. 617-547-6372.

Frank and Sharon Barnett, *Working Together: Entrepreneurial Couples.* Ten Speed Press, P.O. Box 7123, Berkeley, CA 94707. 1989.

Barbara Notarius and Gail Sforza Brewer, *Open Your Own Bed & Breakfast.* 2nd ed. John Wiley & Sons, Inc., Business/Law/General Books Division, 605 Third Ave., New York, NY 10158-0012. 1992.

Jeffrey Maltzman, *Jobs in Paradise: The Definitive Guide to Exotic Jobs Everywhere.* Perennial Library, HarperCollins, 10 East 53rd Street, New York, NY 10022. 1993. Describes jobs at lakes, rivers, coasts and beaches, snow & skiing, tropical islands, mountains, deserts, and so forth. You will probably not want to look so much at the *jobs* described here, as at the *categories,* to help you think out just what *kind* of place you might like to be a telecommuter from. As a place to *start* some informational interviewing, this is a great book -- *if* you're interested in working exactly where you'd also like to spend your leisure time.

Richard C. Levy, *The Inventor's Desktop Companion: A Guide to Successfully Marketing and Protecting Your Ideas.* Visible Ink Press, a division of Gale Research Inc., 835 Penobscot Bldg., Detroit, MI 48226-4094. 1991. From securing a patent for it, to selling it, a very complete compendium.

Fred Grissom & David Pressman, *The Inventor's Notebook.* Nolo Press, 950 Parker St., Berkeley, CA 94710. 1987. A manual to help you keep records about your invention.

Lynie Arden, *101 Franchises You Can Run From Home,* John Wiley & Sons, Professional and Trade Division, 605 Third Ave., New York, NY 10158-0012. 1990.

Franchise Opportunities Handbook, 22nd ed., Sterling Publishing Co., Inc., 387 Park Ave. S., New York, NY 10016. 1991. This is a reprint of the 22nd edition of *Franchise Opportunities Handbook,* issued by the U.S. Government Printing Office. An immensely thorough book, together with a good introductory section about how to investigate a franchise.

Erwin J. Keup, *Franchise Bible: A Comprehensive Guide.* 2 vol. The Oasis Press®/PSI Research, 300 N. Valley Dr., Grants Pass, OR 97526. 1991. Mr. Keup is a lawyer who has specialized in franchise law and franchise consulting for the past 32 years. He covers 'buying an existing business,' as well as franchises. Also, if you have a successful business already, he discusses the pros and cons of turning it into a franchise.

Ray Bard and Sheila Henderson, *Own Your Own Franchise: Everything You Need to Know about the 160 Best Opportunities in America.* A Stonesong Press Book, Addison-Wesley Publishing Co., Inc., Route 128, Reading, MA 01867. 1987.

Robert Laurance Perry, *The 50 Best Low-Investment, High-Profit Franchises.* 1990. Prentice-Hall, Order Dept., 200 Old Tappan Road, Old Tappan, NJ 07675. 1-800-223-2348. Since there is a disturbing trend in franchises these days toward higher and higher start-up fees, up in the $150,000 category or higher, Perry attempts to list ones which people can afford; most of them are less than $20,000, some less than $5,000.

The 220 Best Franchises to Buy. Philip Lief Group's Editors, Bantam Books, 1540 Broadway, New York, NY 10036. 1993. A sourcebook for evaluating the best franchise opportunities.

There are also books that may help you out of the financial thicket, such as James D. Schwartz's *"ENOUGH" A Guide to Reclaiming Your American Dream.* Labrador Press, distributed by RE/MAX International, Inc., 5445 DTC Pkwy., Suite 1200, Englewood, CO 80111. 1992.

Moving

WHEN YOU WANT
A CHANGE OF SCENERY
AND A NEW PLACE
TO LIVE

Our ancestors were nomads. We are the descendants of our ancestors. Surveys reveal that the average person in the U.S. moves eleven times between birth and death. Sometimes that's within the same town; other times it's to a faraway place. Similar patterns of mobility often occur in other countries, as well.

There are three reasons why you might want to move:

(1) Some family member -- say, your ailing or aging mother and father -- may need you, and you decide to move in order to be near them.

(2) You like where you're living, but *you just can't find any work* -- decent-paying work, anyway -- there. It seems as though every job there is filled, numbered, and has a waiting list besides. You've decided you've *got* to move, if you're to find employment. Alternatively, it's too expensive to live where you are, and you want to move somewhere in the country where housing is cheaper, and a family can get by on less.

(3) You can find work where you are, *but* you have reached the point where you decide that *where you live* is more important to you than any other consideration. Maybe you're living in some city, town, or rural area that you detest more, every day you are there. Finally you decide you can't stand it any longer. You've only one life to live, on this earth, and you want to spend the rest of it in a place you really enjoy. This realization can occur when you're twenty, forty, or sixty. If you're retiring, you may particularly want a place where it's always warm, or a place where you can always ski, or whatever. *(Incidentally, nearly four in ten 'baby boomers' who turned fifty in 1996 say they plan to move when they retire, half of these to a different state in the U.S.[1])*

WHEN YOU KNOW EXACTLY
WHERE YOU'RE MOVING

If it's to be with your family, then of course you know the place.

If it's to be with friends you know well, who will support and help you get settled there, then -- again -- you know the place.

If it's your dream city, you've been there on visits before, and now you want to move there permanently, then you know the place.

---

1. *USA Today*, 5/13/96.

In all of these cases, where you *know* where you're going (and you know who's going with you), you need no advice from me. Except about job-hunting, once you get there; in which case, read *Parachute.*

WHEN YOU DON'T KNOW WHERE TO MOVE TO

But there are those other times, when you need or want to move, but have no idea where to move to.

We're back to our first considerations.

What's most on your mind? Jobs, or *a wonderful place?*

Let's look at these two scenarios, taking jobs first:

AND FINDING A JOB IS THE FIRST THING ON YOUR MIND

If jobs are the first thing on your mind, in deciding to move, you have two ways to go.

One is to move where the unemployment rate is low for *all* jobs. In the U.S., your local Federal/State employment office can usually give you the current statistics about all 50 States. You look for the States with the lowest unemployment rate. Currently, the 10 with the lowest rate (where they're desperate for workers) are:

> *Nebraska (the lowest unemployment rate in the nation: only 2.39%),* South Dakota (2.82%), *North Dakota (3.14%),* Iowa (3.28%), *Utah (3.36%),* Minnesota (3.45%), *Wisconsin (3.67%),* Colorado (3.84%), *New Hampshire (3.89%),* and Delaware (4.11%).[2]

• Get a detailed map of each State that interests you, and pick one or more metropolitan areas in those States, so you can call or write to their Chambers of Commerce (pick up your phone and ask *Information* for their phone numbers, in each city).

• Ask those Chambers for all the information they have in writing about businesses which deal with your trade or specialty, and you ask that these lists be sent to you.

• Send them a thank-you note *the day* the stuff arrives, *please.* You may need to contact them again later, perhaps when you're actually in the area, and it will help *you* a lot if *they* can say, *"Oh yes, you're that nice person who sent us a thank-you note when we sent you our materials. First thank-you note we've gotten in three years."* Chances are, they will bend over *backwards* to help you.

If jobs are the first thing on your mind, in deciding to move, there is a second way to go. And that is, to find out what places in the country have a particular need *for your kind of skills.*

This is hard to do in the case of some jobs -- like that of a writer, say, but easier to do if you are a craftsperson or practice a particular trade.

---

2. The Bureau of Labor Statistics.

• In the latter case, go to your local library, and ask the librarian to help you find a trade association directory, or directories.

• Look up the association that deals with your occupation, and jot down the address, phone, fax number, and e-mail address of their national headquarters.

• Fax, write, or phone them and ask if they know where the demand is greatest, in that industry, nationwide. Jot down what they say.

• If they say they don't know, ask who might know. Get said person(s)' address and phone numbers. Contact them.

• If the answer ultimately turns out to be '*several places,*' then you can fall back on the books listed at the end of this section -- such as Richard Boyer's and David Savageau's *Places Rated Almanac* -- to decide which of those is your first choice, which is your second, etc.

• Once you move there, you may feel very stranded and lonely at first.

• If going into a new geographical area is a totally new experience for you, and you have no friends there, just remember there are various ways of meeting people, making friends, and developing contact rather quickly.

• The key is, *find people who share some interest or enthusiasm of yours.*

• There are also athletic clubs, Ys, churches, charitable and community organizations, where you can present yourself and meet people, from the moment you walk in the doors.

• You will soon develop many acquaintances, and some beginning friendships, and the place won't seem so lonely after all.

• Also, visit or write your high school or college before you set out for this new town and find out what graduates live in the area that you are going to be visiting for the first time: they are your friends already, because you went to the same school.

• Once you get there, you will want to talk to key individuals *who can suggest other people you might talk to, as you try to find out what organizations interest you.* You will want to define these key individuals in your distant city ahead of time and let them know you are coming. Your list may include all the people listed above, plus Chamber of Commerce executives, city manager, regional planning offices, appropriate county or state offices in your area of interest, the Mayor, and high-level management in particular companies that look interesting from what you've read or heard about them.

• When you "hit town," you will want to remember the City Directory, the Yellow Pages of your phone book, etc. You *may* want to put a modest-sized advertisement in the paper once you are in your chosen geographical area saying you would like to meet with other people who are following the job-hunting techniques of *What Color Is Your Parachute?* That way you'll form, or join, a kind of 'job-hunters anonymous,' where you can mutually support one another in your hunt.

• One successful job-hunter described how all of this research about *place* can lead as well to information about *jobs:*

"Suppose I arrived cold in some city, the one place in all the world I want to live -- but with no idea of what that city might hold as a match and challenge for my 'personal-talent bank.' I have an economic survey to make, yes; but I also have an equally or more important personal survey to accomplish.

So, I meet pastors, bankers, school principals, physicians, dentists, real estate operators, et al. I would be astonished if opportunities were not brought to my attention, together with numerous offers of personal introduction to key principals. All I would be doing is forging links (referrals) in a chain leading to some eventual jobs. *The referral is the key.*"

IF FINDING
A WONDERFUL PLACE
IS THE FIRST THING
ON YOUR MIND

When you haven't a clue as to where to move, you just want it to be *wonderful*, there are, this time, *three* ways you can go.

• First of all, you can interview all your friends and acquaintances, to ask them what places *they* have loved the most, in the U.S. or in whatever country you live. And *why*. This task can be a lot of fun. And then, out of all the *candidate cities or towns* they propose, choose two or three places that really interest you, for further investigation.

• Alternatively, you can turn to books. In the U.S., there are quite a number of them that rate various cities and towns according to *factors* that may be important to you, such as *weather, crime, educational system, recreational opportunities*, etc. The best of these, by a long shot, is Richard Boyer's and David Savageau's aforementioned *Places Rated Almanac*, listed at the end of this section on *Moving*.

If you live in another country, you may find similar resources for your own country; visit a large bookstore, and ask. One word of caution: do remember, in all these books, that a computer was usually used to sum up, and rate, all the factors. You may find that *the whole* is less than the sum of its *parts* -- i.e., it has the factors you want, but you're less than enchanted with how *it all came together* in the case of this particular place you're thinking about.

• Thirdly, you can do the geographical exercises in *The Quick Job-Hunting Map*, at the beginning of this Resource Guide, which tells you how to do a thorough-going analysis of all the places you have ever lived, in terms of *factors* -- and then how you come up with *names* of places that combine all the factors that were ever important to you in any town or city from your past.

• In the end, you want to try to come up with three names, because if your first choice doesn't pan out for some reason, you will have a backup, and also a backup to your backup.

WHEN YOU WANT TO
'GO RURAL'

It may be you will discover, as you go about this task, that your idea of *paradise* is to 'go rural' -- to move, at last, to 'the country'. Sometimes it's the desire for a simpler life; sometimes, it's the desire for a less expensive cost of living. Whatever the reasons, if this is your vision, take this vision seriously. You only have one life to live, on this earth.

• Just be sure to investigate it *thoroughly*, even as I was just cautioning you, in the case of urban places. "Look before you leap" is always a splendid caution, and it means -- in this particular case -- that if there's a place that sounds good to you, *be sure* to go visit it as a tourist before you up and move there.

• *Go there*, and talk to *everyone*. Get the good side, and the bad. Interview anyone you know, who has moved from urban to rural, and ask them what they like most about the move, *and what they miss the most about their former locale.*

• Then weigh what you learn.

Fortunately, there are a number of resources, books and such, that you can use to explore rural life, if it interests you. They are listed at the end of this section.

EXPLORING THE FARAWAY
PLACE OF YOUR CHOICE

Well, let us suppose that one way or another, you've picked a place.

• It *is* crucial to go visit there, if you possibly can, rather than just letting your choice rest on the fact that the place looks good in a book. You may *hate* this place, on sight. How nice to learn that, *early on*. So, figure out how to get there.

• Do you have a vacation coming to you, that would fall within the time period between now and when you must finally have a job there? Could you visit it on that vacation?

• Could you take a summer job there?

• Go there on leave?

• Once you've turned up some promising job prospects, you will *have* to go there, to that town or city, in almost all cases, for the actual job interview(s). And if this is your first visit to the place, try to go there a week or so ahead of your interviews, so you can look the place over, and decide *Do I really want to move here?* It's a little late to do on-site explorations, but, hey, better late than never!

HOW HARD SHOULD I WORK AT THIS?

We kept score with one man's job-hunt. He was researching a distant place. While still at a distance, by means of diligent research he turned up 107 places that seemed interesting to him. Over a period of some time, he sent a total of 297 letters to them. He also made a total of 126 phone calls to that city. When he was finally able to go there in person, he had narrowed the original 107 that looked interesting, down to just 45. He visited all 45, while there. Having done his homework on himself thoroughly and well, -- and having obviously conducted *this* part of his search in an extremely professional manner, he received 35 job offers. When he had finished his survey, he went back to the one job he most wanted -- and accepted it.

No one can argue that you should be dealing with numbers of this magnitude. But this may at least give you some idea of *how hard you may need to work* at this. Certainly, we're not just talking about five letters and two phone calls. We're talking about rolling up your sleeves, and being *very thorough.*

DOES ALL OF THIS REALLY WORK?

Well, that's a legitimate question. Obviously, thousands if not millions of people have moved to new cities and towns, and found not only work but joyful work there. Obviously, also, many people have moved to new towns or cities and have not been able to find work. Much, much depends upon *the method* they use in their job-search. If you follow diligently the process described in *Parachute*, in the chapters called, "For the Determined Job-Hunter," you will vastly increase your chances of success. Here is how one job-hunter described the whole process, and the way in which it worked for him:

"In 1990, my wife and I took a trip out to the Southwest from our home in Annapolis, Maryland, to see the Grand Canyon and sights like that. We both fell in love with the Southwest, and said, "Wouldn't it be great if I could get a job out here as a highway engineer, and maybe we could work with the Native Americans." Back in Annapolis, I purchased Parachute *and read it with extreme interest. So I started some network planning, and scheduled another upcoming trip to Arizona in February of 1992, planning to visit various engineering offices and check out living conditions.*

"Meanwhile, I visited the U.S.G.S. Headquarters in Reston, Virginia. On the way out, I noticed an ad on the bulletin board for 'Highway Engineer - Bureau of Indian Affairs, Gallup, New Mexico.' Naturally, I applied for the job but received notice that the position had been cancelled. Disappointed, my wife and I decided to each spend a

*day in prayer. On the following day I received a call from that office in Gallup inform-
ing me there was another position for Highway Planner now open; was I still interested? Still interested?!*

"*Using your advice, I called the Bureau in Gallup and got the names of the bosses
of the various divisions or sections that would impinge upon my application. I sent in
the application to the person by name who was the chief decision-maker. In February of
1992 we carried out the trip I had been planning, now including a visit to Gallup.
We visited headquarters there, though they weren't yet ready to formally interview,
since not all applicants had yet been screened. However, it was a useful visit, and on
returning, I wrote Thank You notes to all the people I had met, and hoped for the best.*

"*In March I received another phone call, asking for further information; I used
this to invite myself out for an actual interview, at my expense. My offer was accepted,
I was out there in two days, the interview went well, and I received official notice to report for work in May. We were ecstatic! And we found a house in Gallup, through a
friend in Annapolis who had a friend in Gallup, who knew of a co-worker who was
moving out.*

"*In short, ours is a wonderful story. Who would think a 66 year old man could
leave one job and move into another full-time job, at a salary almost equal to his present one, in a place 2600 miles away, that he and his wife truly love! What a blessing! And what you said has stuck with me all this time: I've remembered to write my
Thank You notes.*"

For Further Reading

Richard Boyer and David Savageau, *Places Rated Almanac: Your Guide to
Finding the Best Places to Live in North America.* Revised ed. 1993. Prentice-Hall,
Order Dept., 200 Old Tappan Road, Old Tappan, NJ 07675. 1-800-223-2348.
A marvelous book. Immensely helpful for anyone weighing where to move

next. All 343 metropolitan areas are ranked and compared for living costs, job outlook, crime, health, transportation, education, the arts, recreation, and climate. Has numerous helpful diagrams, charts, and maps, showing (for example) earthquake risk areas, hurricane and tornado risk areas *(you did see the movie* Twister *didn't you?)*, the snowiest areas, the stormiest areas, the driest areas, and so on. Don't leave home without it.

David Savageau, *Retirement Places Rated.* 3rd ed. 1990. Prentice-Hall, Order Dept., 200 Old Tappan Road, Old Tappan, NJ 07675. 1-800-223-2348. Although purportedly about retirement, it is useful information for anyone. Compares 151 top geographical areas in the U.S.

Norman D. Ford, *50 Healthiest Places to Live and Retire in the U.S.*, Mills & Sanderson, 41 North Rd., Suite 201, Bedford MA 01730-1021.

Lee & Saralee Rosenburg, *50 Fabulous Places to Raise Your Family*, Career Press, 1-800-CAREER-1.

Jill Andresky Fraser, *The Best U.S. Cities for Working Women.* Plume Books, New American Library, 1633 Broadway, New York, NY 10019. 1986.

There is a firm which uses a specialized questionnaire to help a person or family locate three places in the U.S. that fit their expressed personal desires about a place to live. It is run by Andrew Schiller, M.S., a professional geographer, who is thoroughly familiar with *Parachute.* The firm's name is *Relocation Research,* P.O. Box 53391, Knoxville, TN 37950. Write or call, for price: 800-278-9884.

If you are interested in the rural life, there are these resources:

William L. Seavey runs a business called *Greener Pastures Institute,* which publishes a newsletter (sample back issue: $5). He has also written a book which tells you the basic resources for moving to the country or a small town. Its name is *Moving to Small Town America,* 1996, Dearborn Financial Publishers, 800-829-7934. Bill's address is: Greener Pastures Institute, 6301 S. Squaw Valley Rd., Suite 1383, Pahrump, NV 89048-7949, 800-688-6352.

John F. Edwards, *Starting Fresh: How to Plan for a Simpler, Happier, and More Fulfilling New Life in the Country.* Prima Publishing, Sierra Gardens, Suite 130, Roseville, CA 95661. 1988.

Frank Levering and Wanda Urbanska, *Simple Living.* Viking Penguin, 375 Hudson St., New York, NY 10014. 1992.

The Caretaker Gazette, published by Gary C. Dunn, 2380 NE Ellis St., Suite C-16, Pullman, WA 99163-5303. 509-332-0806. $24 for a one-year subscription (six issues), $15 for a six-month subscription (three issues). The only up-to-date source for property caretaking in the world. Landowners searching for caretakers advertise in this *Gazette.* Caretaking is an inexpensive way for you to experience life in a specific geographic area, particularly rural ones. While the majority of the jobs listed are in the U.S., some international positions are also included. A map on the front page of each issue indicates where the employment opportunities are. The June 1994 issue, by way of example, had 50 job listings in 26 states and five countries.

Marilyn and Tom Ross, *Country Bound!™ Trade Your Business Suit Blues For Blue Jean Dreams™.* Communication Creativity, P.O. Box 909, Buena Vista, CO 81211. 1992.

Working Overseas

WHEN YOU WANT TO WORK OVERSEAS

I will assume here that we are talking about job-hunters in the U.S. who want to work in Europe, Africa, Asia, Canada, or South America. However, the same principles apply to those of you who live in other places than the U.S., and want to move here.

First of all, be sure you're not going overseas simply because you're fed up with this country, and think some other place will be the Utopia you've always dreamed about. Of course it may be. But it is much more likely it will not be. Even if (big *if*) you do not find the same things there that irritate you about the U.S., I guarantee you that you will find a whole pack of new things that irritate you.

Regarding the mechanics of going overseas: many people assume you find an overseas job by packing a bag, buying a ticket and passing out resumes once you reach your foreign destination. The reality is that work-permit requirements and high unemployment often make finding jobs in other countries difficult, or impossible. For example, if you were to study employment classifieds in, say, a newspaper from London, England, you would at first sight think you had found some grand opportunities for yourself. *Unfortunately,* these are in most cases job opportunities open only to British nationals or citizens of EEC nations.

What is true in England is true elsewhere. Your U.S. citizenship will actually preclude you from working in a foreign country -- even Canada -- unless your employer can prove that a local national is unavailable to take the job, and can subsequently secure a work permit for *you.*

BEGIN AT HOME

Your wisest approach is to begin your job-hunt for an overseas job while you are still here in the U.S. How do you go about it?

Well, first of all, research the country or countries that interest you, as to living conditions, conditions of employment, et cetera.

Talk to everyone you possibly can who has in fact been overseas, most especially visitors to, or former citizens of, that country or countries that interest you. A nearby large university will probably have such faculty or students *(ask)*. Companies in your city which have overseas branches *(your library should be able to tell you which they are)* should be able to lead you to people also -- possibly to the names and addresses of personnel who are still "over there" to whom you can write for the information you are seeking.

Alternatively, try asking every single person you meet for the next week (at the supermarket checkout, at your work, at home, at church or synagogue, etc.) if they know someone who used to live overseas and now lives here in your city or town. You may be amazed at how many normal looking people are actually world travelers.

By doing research with such people, you will learn a great deal. Find out what they liked and didn't like, about the country which interests you. Find out what they know about the conditions for working over there.

LISTINGS OF JOB OPENINGS

Next, you need to research what kinds of job possibilities exist in that country. Every *successful* overseas search starts with *some* sources of information on "who's hiring now." *Which* sources you access, and how you make use of them, will greatly affect your chances of landing an overseas assignment.

What do I mean? Well, for openers, beware of such sources as employment agencies that promise to find you an overseas job for an advance fee. 98% of their clients *do not* find an overseas job. This fleecing industry has flourished for years, with a few individuals often running scores of companies under an assortment of names. Such companies regularly go out of business or file for bankruptcy *once they've fleeced enough suckers.*[1]

Beware also of directories advertised in newspapers, etc., as *listing overseas employers.* Many, though not all, of these job listings are out of date and tend to report on "who *was* hiring" rather than "who is hiring *now.*"

You can still make effective use of any such directory by taking care that *if* you contact an organization listed therein, you include a cover letter which requests that your resume be kept on file 'for further consideration *if there are no current openings*'. As I have emphasized elsewhere in this book, pure dumb luck -- which means, having your name in 'the right place at the right time' -- often plays a crucial role in finding most jobs. Since you can't get *over there*, at the moment, you will have to rely more heavily on resumes here than I would normally advise, to keep your name in the right place. In the case of overseas employment, the more employers who have your resume, the better.

Rather than the kind of resources mentioned above, I think your best bet for job leads are authoritative directories such as those listed under *For Further Reading* below. Also, in your job-search do not forget that the U.S. Government is a heavy overseas employer. Understandably, in the post-USSR world, with the end of the cold war, there are numerous cutbacks going on

---

1. Write to Stuart Alan Rado, 1500 West 23rd St., Sunset Island #3, Miami Beach, FL 33140, if you wish to know more.

overseas. Nonetheless, this possibility is still well worth exploring. *How* you explore it, is described in the books by Will Cantrell, listed under *Further Reading*.

BACKUP STRATEGIES

If you run into an absolute stone wall in your search for an overseas job, there are two backup strategies for you to consider. The first is to seek an international internship.

The second strategy begins with the fact that many companies operating in this country, both domestic and foreign-owned, *have branches overseas*. Thus, *sometimes* your ticket to getting overseas may be to start working here in the U.S. for such a company, hoping they will eventually send you overseas. It *does* happen. And if it happens, they will likely take care of the visa and work permit red tape, pick up your travel bill, and provide other helpful benefits.

Unfortunately, however, you can't *count* on their ever sending you overseas. Many such firms now prefer to use nationals in the country in question, rather than sending U.S. citizens abroad. In other words, if you take employment with a U.S. firm that has overseas work, hoping that they will send you overseas, understand from the beginning that it's a big fat gamble. *You* have to decide whether you're willing to take that gamble, or not.

If you decide to do either of the above strategies, you'll find the names of such organizations by going to your local library and asking the reference librarian to help you find such directories as these: *Principal International Businesses*, published by Dun's Marketing Service; *International Directory of Corporate Affiliations*, published by Corporate Affiliations Information Services, of the National Register Publishing Company; and *International Organizations, revised annually*, published by Gale Research, Inc.

Lastly, contact every friend you have who already lives overseas -- even if it's not in the country that is your target. Ask for their counsel, advice, help, and prayers. They went before you; hopefully they can now be your guide, and door-opener.

One final word about hunting for an overseas job: above all, be patient. The search for an overseas job takes *more* time than looking for a job in this country. Don't expect to be in an exotic foreign capital within 90 days. Perseverance is the key.

For Further Reading

International Employment Hotline, Box 3030, Oakton, VA 22124. Published monthly by Will Cantrell since 1980, this highly reputable newsletter provides job-search advice and names and addresses of employers currently hiring for international work in government, nonprofit organizations, and private companies. A six-month subscription is $26, one year is $39. *(Incidentally, do not confuse this reputable firm with 'International Employment Hotline' in Amsterdam, Holland, or London; there is no connection between these two firms, whatsoever.)*

Will Cantrell and Francine Modderno, *How To Find an Overseas Job with the U.S. Government.* Worldwise Books, P.O. Box 3030, Oakton, VA 22124.

Comprehensive guide to finding work with the organization that hires the greatest number of Americans abroad. In-depth job descriptions and application procedures are provided for over 17 individual government agencies, along with information on how to complete the government's standard application for employment (SF-171), and how to prepare for and pass the Foreign Service exam. Highly recommended.

Will Cantrell and Francine Modderno, *International Internships and Volunteer Programs.* Worldwise Books, P.O. Box 3030, Oakton, VA 22124. Information on over 150 programs serving as 'stepping-stones' to international careers, for both students and professionals. Positions include salaried and volunteer opportunities, both abroad and also here in the U.S.

ISS Directory of Overseas Schools, by International Schools Services. 500 profiles of overseas schools in 120 countries, with contact names and addresses, teaching staff positions; useful for teachers looking for overseas employment. Available from Worldwise Books, P.O. Box 3030, Oakton, VA 22124.

International Business Travel and Relocation Directory, 6th ed. Gale Research, Inc., 835 Penobscot Bldg., Detroit, MI 48226-4094. It presents all the relevant details for every country in the world.

Sanborn, Robert, Ed.D., *How To Get A Job in Europe: The Insider's Guide.* 2nd ed. Surrey Books, 230 E. Ohio St., Suite 120, Chicago, IL 60611. 1993. Includes tips on how to find a job in the New Europe.

Chambers, Dale, *Passport to Overseas Employment: 100,000 Job Opportunities Abroad.* Prentice-Hall, Order Dept., 200 Old Tappan Road, Old Tappan, NJ 07675. 1-800-223-2348. 1990. Deals with overseas study programs, international careers, temporary employment, airlines and cruises, embassies and consulates, United Nations, and volunteer programs.

Richard Zinks, *Overseas Exotic Jobs.* 8th ed. Zinks International Career Guidance, P.O. Box 790, Richland, MI 49083. 616-629-5770.

Griffith, Susan, *Work Your Way Around the World.* 6th ed. Peterson's Guides, P.O. Box 2123, Princeton, NJ 08543. 1993.

Green, Mary, and Gillmar, Stanley, *How to Be an Importer and Pay for Your World Travel.* 2nd ed. Ten Speed Press, Box 7123, Berkeley, CA 94707. 1993.

Frances Bastress, *The New Relocating Spouse's Guide to Employment: Options & Strategies in the U.S. and Abroad.* 4th ed. 1993. Impact Publications, 9104-N Manassas Drive, Manassas Park, VA 22111.

For teachers wishing to work overseas, the Department of Defense publishes a pamphlet, with application, entitled *Overseas Employment Opportunities for Educators.* Write to U.S. Department of Defense Dependent Schools, Recruitment and Assignments Section, Hoffman Bldg. I, 2461 Eisenhower Ave., Alexandria, VA 22331-1100, for the pamphlet/application.

Your library should also have books such as Angel, Juvenal, *Dictionary of American Firms Operating in Foreign Countries* (World Trade Academy Press).

And to research overseas public companies which sell stock in this country, the Securities Exchange Commission will have their Form 6-K, which they filed in order to be able to sell that stock.

If you want more books about overseas work (or study), write to Worldwise Books, P.O. Box 3030, Oakton, VA 22124, and/or Writer's Digest Books, 1507 Dana Ave., Cincinnati, OH 45207, and ask for their catalogs.

III. Job-Hunting Tools

Researching Companies and Places
Job-Hunting on the Internet
How to Job-Hunt While Still Employed
How to Use Resumes, Agencies & Ads (If You Must)

When You Need To Research Companies or Places

BE NEITHER HAZY NOR LAZY

The surest way to make certain your trip to the library is a total waste of time, is to be *hazy* about what you're trying to find out.

So, please, before you go near a library, write out on a piece of paper, for your own use, "This is the information I am trying to find out *today*:_____." Be specific. Be clear.

For example, do you want to know what the outlook is, in the field that interests you?

Or do you want to know what companies there are, in that field?

Or do you want to find out more about a particular company or organization?

Or do you want to know the names of people within that company or organization?

Or, what?

Think it out ahead of time. Be clear.

Be clear also about why it is important for you to research a company or organization ahead of time. You want to distinguish yourself from all those other job-hunters who walk in on a place and say, "Uh, what exactly do you guys do here?"

Using books -- and contacts -- you want to demonstrate that you cared enough about the place, to learn something about it before you walked in.

WHO DO I TURN TO?

In this section I have listed *some* of the library books which -- as indicated by the experience of career-changers and job-hunters before you -- may prove useful *at one time or another* during the research phase of your career-change or job-hunt.

You may find these resources at your local public library (of course), but don't forget other libraries that may be near you, such as a business library or a local university, college, or community college library.

Some of these books are inexpensive enough for you to purchase, *if you want to* -- from your local bookstore (particularly those dealing with job leads). Browse them, first, to see if they are something you want to be able to refer to, again and again.

Some of these books are not inexpensive. In fact, being reference works, they are *hideously* expensive in many cases, so *thank God* for your local library.

Which book to consult? Well of course, the one that helps you with the particular questions you're trying to find answers to.

The books which follow are categorized by the *primary* arena of their information, though each book or resource may have information that spills over into the other categories:

> 1. **Outlook** (where a particular industry or job-title is going, in the next ten years or so)
>
> 2. **Fields** (Descriptions of Occupations or Industries)
>
> 3. **Companies** (names, brief or extended information about them)
>
> 4. **Individuals** (names, addresses, phone numbers, of people who may serve you as Contacts or Employers)
>
> 5. **Vacancies** or Job Leads (where the jobs are, or at least where some people *claim* the jobs are)
>
> 6. **Job-Hunting** (other books, other approaches, other techniques)

As I indicated, your local library should have many if not most of these resources. Ask your local librarian for help. If there is no librarian available, or at least no *helpful* librarian, there are *(mercifully)* indexes/indices to all these directories:

- Klein's *Guide to American Directories;* and
- *Directories in Print.* Gale Research, Inc., 835 Penobscot Bldg., Detroit, MI 48226-4094, which contains over 15,000 current listings of directories, indexed by title or key word or subject (over 3,500 subject headings).

See also:

Encyclopedia of Business Information Sources. Gale Research, Inc., 835 Penobscot Bldg., Detroit, MI 48226-4094. Identifies electronic, print and live resources dealing with 1,500 business subjects. Their companion volume is entitled *Business Organizations, Agencies and Publications Directory*, listing over 24,000 entries, such as federal government advisory organizations, newsletters, research services, etc.

Directory of Special Libraries and Information Centers. Gale Research, Inc., 835 Penobscot Bldg., Detroit, MI 48226-4094. Lists 22,000 research facilities, on various subjects, maintained by libraries, research libraries, businesses, non-profit organizations, governmental agencies, etc. Detailed subject index, using over 3,500 key words.

And now, to our areas of research:

1. Outlook

Occupational Outlook Handbook. Department of Labor, NTC Publishing Group, 225 W. Touhy Ave., Lincolnwood, IL 60646.

Occupational Outlook Handbook for College Graduates. Superintendent of Documents, U.S. Government.

Petras, Kathryn & Ross, *Jobs '96: By Career, By Industry, By Region.* 1996. Fireside, Rockefeller Center, 1230 Avenue of the Americas, New York, NY 10020. Indicates the outlook, industry by industry. Also lists the leading U.S. companies, associations, directories, and periodicals in each field.

2. Fields

Occupations or Industries

Dictionary of Holland Occupational Codes.

Dictionary of Occupational Titles.

Encyclopedia of Associations, Vol. 1, National Organizations of the U.S.; Vol. 2, Geographic and Executive Indexes; Vol. 3, New Associations and Projects. Gale Research, Inc., 835 Penobscot Bldg., Detroit, MI 48226-4094. Lists 25,000 organizations, associations, clubs and other nonprofit membership groups that are in the business of giving out information. There is a companion series of books: *Regional, State and Local Organizations,* a five-volume set, which lists over 50,000 similar organizations on a regional, state or local level. There is another companion volume, also: *International Organizations.* This lists 4,000 international organizations, concerned with various subjects.

National Trade and Professional Associations of the United States. 29th ed., 1994. Columbia Books, Inc., Publishers, 1212 New York Avenue, N.W., Suite 330, Washington, DC 20005.

Newsletters in Print. Gale Research, Inc., 835 Penobscot Bldg., Detroit, MI 48226-4094. Detailed entry on 10,000 newsletters in various subject fields, or categories. It includes newsletters that are available only online, through a computer and modem.

Standard and Poor's Industry Surveys. Good basic introduction, history, and overview of any industry you may be interested in.

Standard Industrial Classification Manual. 1991. Reprint of material originally published by the U.S. Government Printing Office. Available from: Gordon Press, P.O. Box 459, Bowling Green Station, New York, NY 10003. Gives the Standard Industrial Classification code number for any field or industry -- which is the number used by most business references in their indices.

The Information Please® Business Almanac & Desk Reference, Seth Godin, Editor. Houghton Mifflin Company, 215 Park Ave. So., New York, NY 10003. All kinds of information about industries, with addresses and contacts plus any other business questions you might be curious about (computers, etc.).

U.S. Industrial Outlook. Reprinted from material published by the U.S. Department of Commerce. Available from JIST Works, 720 N. Park Ave., Indianapolis, IN 46202. Covers 350 manufacturing and service industries.

Gives the trends and outlooks for each industry that you may be interested in. Updated annually.

Jobs: What They Are . . . Where They Are . . . What They Pay! by Robert O. Snelling, Sr. and Anne M. Snelling. Fireside, Simon & Schuster Bldg., 1230 Avenue of the Americas, New York, NY 10020. Describes jobs in thirty different fields.

And, for Specific Industries or Fields:

Communications: *Telecommunications Directory.* Gale Research, Inc., 835 Penobscot Bldg., Detroit, MI 48226-4094. Lists over 2,000 national and international firms dealing with communications systems, teleconferencing, videotext, electronic mail, fax services, etc.

Computers: *Information Industry Directory.* Gale Research, Inc., 835 Penobscot Bldg., Detroit, MI 48226-4094. Lists 30,000 computer-based information systems and services, here and abroad. Their companion volume, *Gale Directory of Databases.* Gale Research, Inc., 835 Penobscot Bldg., Detroit, MI 48226-4094, lists trade shows, conventions, users' groups, associations, consultants, etc., worldwide.

Government: In the U.S., the novice government job-hunter assumes that civil service exams introduce a mechanical impartiality to hiring decisions. This is only partially true. If, during your informational interviewing you encounter a federal manager who likes you, and wants to hire you, you can bet your bottom dollar they will do everything they can to guide you through the examination maze -- since any manager worth their salt has long since learned how to creatively use the government's standard operating procedures to their own best advantage. This applies to local and state government positions, as well as federal. For further reading or help:

Krannich, Ronald L., and Krannich, Caryl Rae, *Find a Federal Job Fast!* 2nd ed. 1992. Impact Publications, 4580 Sunshine Court, Woodbridge, VA 22192. They have other federal job-hunting aids, as you will discover when they send you their catalog.

Government Job Finder, by Daniel Lauber. 1996. Planning/Communications, 7215 Oak Ave., River Forest, IL 60305. Lists over 1,600 associations, directories, journals, trade magazines, newsletters, computerized job-listings, online services, job-matching services, salary surveys, etc. -- dealing with local, state or federal government work in the U.S. and abroad -- where contacts may be found, or job-leads advertised. Very thorough.

If you want to work for the Federal government you will have to learn how to fill out a SF-171 form, in many if not most cases. There are guides to help you do this:

Smith, Russ, *The Right SF-171 Writer.* 1994. Impact Publications, 4580 Sunshine Court, Woodbridge, VA 22192.

DataTech's *Quick & Easy 171s.* A software program (for MS-DOS or Windows, only) that produces the SF-171 for Federal job-seekers. Approved by the U.S. Office of Personnel Management. Personal *(single user)* version: $49.95. Order from Impact Publications, 4580 Sunshine Court, Woodbridge, VA 22192.

There is also: *USJOBS Database* (single issue), listing federal jobs nationwide, which you can search by job-title or other parameters. Also has an SF-171 Form Editor, which can turn blank paper into completed SF-171s on your PC. Runs under Windows 3.1. $27.95 from DigiBook Corp., 370 Wall St., Princeton, NJ 08540. Order line: 1-800-734-4371.

United States Government Manual. U.S. Government Printing Office, Stop SSMR, Washington, DC 20402.

Hobbies: *National Recreational Sporting and Hobby Organizations of the U.S.* Columbia Books, Inc., 777 14th St. NW, Washington, DC 20005.

Physical Sciences, Engineering, Biological Sciences: *Directory of Information Resources in the United States.* Washington, DC., Library of Congress.

Research: *Research Center Directory.* Gale Research, Inc., 835 Penobscot Bldg., Detroit, MI 48226-4094. Also: *Research Services Directory.* The two volumes together cover some 13,000 services, facilities, and companies that do research into various subjects, such as feasibility studies, private and public policy, social studies and studies of various cultures, etc.

Statistics: *Statistics Sources.* Gale Research, Inc., 835 Penobscot Bldg., Detroit, MI 48226-4094. Tells you where to find statistics on more than 20,000 specific topics. Key live sources are also featured.

Teaching & Training: *Training and Development Organizations Directory.* Gale Research, Inc., 835 Penobscot Bldg., Detroit, MI 48226-4094. For those of you interested in teaching or training, it lists over 2,500 firms and their areas of interest and expertise.

Public Service Careers: these include such varied occupations as:
- city planner,
- community services officer at a community college,
- gerontology specialist,
- officials dealing with foster parent programs for mentally retarded persons,
- public health officials,
- recreation education,
- social service technician,
- welfare administration,
- workers in the child welfare program,
- workers with the handicapped.

Potential employers for public service occupations or social careers include government (Federal, State, or Local), nonprofit organizations, agencies (independent of state or local government, but often cooperating with them), colleges (particularly community colleges), associations, social welfare agencies, public health departments, correctional institutions, government offices, Job Partnership Training offices, hospitals, rest homes, elementary and secondary schools, parks and recreation agencies, etc.

If you are interested in this general field of social service, you ought to do extensive research, with a heavy emphasis on talking with people actually doing the work you think you would like to do; you will find their names through the national associations in the fields that interest you, also in State departments, and County and City governments (your local reference librarian in your local library can help you locate these associations).

If you know exactly what it is you want to do, but funding is the problem, thorough research on your part will often reveal ways in which funding can be found for positions not yet created; it all depends on your finding a person who knows something about that.

As for what career to choose within this broad category, there are these helps:

Devon Smith, ed., and James LaVeck, asst. ed., *Great Careers: The Fourth of July Guide to Careers, Internships, and Volunteer Opportunities in the Nonprofit Sector.* 2nd ed. Garrett Park Press, Box 190, Garrett Park, MD 20896. 1990. Very useful book with essays and lists of places; includes arts-related careers, and careers dealing with such issues as hunger, animal rights, the environment, homelessness, international jobs, working with people who are disabled, social action, and peace.

Jankowski, Katherine, *The Job Seeker's Guide to Socially Responsible Companies.* 1995. Visible Ink Press™, a division of Gale Research, Inc. 835 Penobscot Bldg., Detroit, MI 48226-4094. An immensely useful book for those who care.

Community Jobs: The Employment Newspaper for the Non-Profit Sector, published by ACCESS: Networking in the Public Interest, 1601 Connecticut Ave., NW, Room 600F, Washington, DC 20009. Lists jobs and internships in nonprofit community organizations. Write directly to them for subscription information.

Peter F. Drucker, *Managing The Non-Profit Organization: Practices and Principles.* HarperCollins Publishers, 10 E. 53rd St., New York, NY 10022. 1990. Very helpful, as is anything from Peter Drucker's pen.

Paul Schmolling, Jr., with William R. Burger and Merrill Youkeles, *Careers in Mental Health: A Guide to Helping Occupations.* Garrett Park Press, Box 190, Garrett Park, MD 20896.

Mary Scott, *Companies With a Conscience: Intimate Portraits of Twelve Firms That Make a Difference.* Birch Lane Press, New York. 1992.

3. Companies

Large Companies

Company/college/association/agency/foundation *Annual Reports.* Get these directly from the personnel department or publicity person at the company, etc., or from the Chamber or your local library.

The Almanac of American Employers 1996-97. Focuses on the 500 largest, fastest growing, most successful corporate employers; available in most public libraries. Covers companies of 2,500+ employees. Plunkett Research, Ltd., P.O. Drawer 8270, Galveston, TX 77553. 409-765-8530.

America's Fastest Growing Employers: The Complete Guide to Finding Jobs with over 275 of America's Hottest Companies, by Carter Smith with Peter C. Hale. Bob Adams, Inc., 260 Center St., Holbrook, MA 02343.

Corporate and Industry Research Reports. Published by R.R. Bowker/Martindale-Hubbell, 121 Chanlon Rd., New Providence, NJ 07974. Can be very helpful.

Corporate Jobs Outlook! A newsletter published every 60 days, available in most public libraries. Covers companies of 500 to 2,500 employees. Plunkett Research, Ltd., P.O. Drawer 8270, Galveston, TX 77553. 409-765-8530.

Corporate Technology Directory. Lists companies by the products they make or the technologies they use. Corporate Technology Information Services, Inc., 12 Alfred St., Suite 200, Woburn, MA 01801-9998.

Directory of American Research and Technology: Organizations Active in Product Development for Business. R.R. Bowker, 121 Chanlon Rd., New Providence, NJ 07974.

Directory of Corporate Affiliations. National Register Publishing Co., Inc.

Dun & Bradstreet's Million Dollar Directory. Very helpful.

Dun & Bradstreet's Million Dollar Directory–Top 50,000 Companies. Very helpful. An abridged version of Dun's *Million Dollar Directory Series*.

Dun & Bradstreet's Reference Book of Corporate Managements.

F & S Indexes (recent articles on firms).

F & S Index of Corporations and Industries. Lists "published articles" by industry and by company name. Updated weekly.

Fitch Corporation Manuals.

Fortune Magazine's 500; they also publish interesting articles during the rest of the year, on major corporations, such as "*America's Most Admired Corporations.*" Visit your local library, and browse back issues.

Hoover's Handbook of American Business, ed. by Gary Hoover, Alta Campbell, and Patrick J. Spain. Publishers: The Reference Press, 6448 Highway 290E., Suite E-104, Austin, TX 78723, 800-486-8666. Profiles of over 500 major U.S. companies. A special section on the companies that have created the most jobs in the last 10 years and those that have eliminated the most jobs.

Hoover's Masterlist of America's Top 2,500 Employers, ed. by Thomas Trotter. The largest and fastest-growing U.S. companies; a software disk for computers that use *Windows* is included.

Hoover's Handbook of World Business, ed. by Patrick J. Spain and James R. Talbot. Profiles of major European, Asian, Latin American, and Canadian companies who employ thousands of Americans both in the U.S. and abroad.

How To Read A Financial Report: Wringing Cash Flow and Other Vital Signs Out of the Numbers, by John A. Tracy, CPA. John Wiley & Sons, Business Law/General Books Division, 605 Third Avenue, New York, NY 10158-0012. Also Chichester, Brisbane, Toronto and Singapore.

Macmillan's Directory of Leading Private Companies.

Moody's Industrial Manual (and other Moody manuals).

Periodicals worth perusing in your public library, in addition to *Fortune,* mentioned above, are *Business Week, Dun's Review, Forbes,* and the *Wall Street Journal*.

Registers of manufacturers for your state or area (e.g., *California Manufacturers Register*).

Standard and Poor's Corporation Records.

Standard and Poor's Industrial Index.

The Adams Jobs Almanac, by the Editors of Bob Adams, Inc. Bob Adams, Inc., 260 Center St., Holbrook, MA 02343. Gives a sampling of the major companies in thirty-one industries, together with the kinds of positions they are usually looking for -- when they're looking. Has a state-by-state index of the major employers, plus an introductory section on career outlooks and job-hunting. This same publisher has a *JobBank Series* which you can find in your local bookstore. Currently there are *JobBank* books for: Atlanta, Boston, the Carolinas, Chicago, Dallas-Fort Worth, Denver, Detroit, Florida, Houston, Los Angeles, Minneapolis/St. Paul, New York, Ohio, Philadelphia, Phoenix, St. Louis, San Francisco, Seattle, Tennessee, and Washington D.C. There is also a National JobBank.

Thomas' Register. Thomas Publishing Co. There are 27 volumes in the Thomas register. All the manufacturers there are of 52,000 products and services, plus catalogs, contacts, and phone numbers.

Walker's Manual of Western Corporations. Walker Western Research Co., 1452 Tilia Ave., San Mateo, CA 94402.

Ward's Business Directory, 6 vols. Gale Research, Inc., 835 Penobscot Bldg., Detroit, MI 48226-4094. Updated yearly. Despite the titles, helpful in identifying smaller companies, as well as large.

Small Companies

Hoover's Handbook of Emerging Companies, ed. by Patrick J. Spain and James R. Talbot. Lists and profiles of 250 smaller, emerging companies with high growth rates. A *sampler* for those seeking employment at smaller companies.

Chamber of Commerce data on an organization or field that interests you (visit the Chamber in the appropriate city or town).

Many public libraries have very efficient database search capabilities, through their computers, and can dig up, copy, and mail to you copies of reports on local companies (for a modest cost). For example, one Pennsylvania job-hunter got the Cleveland (Ohio) Library to send him copies of annual reports on a Cleveland-based company. So, when you get to the point where you're researching organizations, if there's an organization or company that particularly interests you, you might want to try contacting the nearest large public library to that organization's home base, and see what that librarian can turn up for you. (*Please* write and thank her or him, afterward.)

Better Business Bureau report on a particular organization that you may be interested in (call the BBB in the city where the organization is located). These reports sometimes only tell you if there are outstanding, unresolved complaints against a company; if the company has scrambled to settle a complaint in the past, their record will now look pretty good. Still, it's a useful thing to know -- if there are or have been such complaints.

4. Individuals

(As Contacts or Potential Employers)

Consultants and Consulting Organizations Directory. Gale Research, Inc., 835 Penobscot Bldg., Detroit, MI 48226-4094. Lists over 15,000 firms, individuals and organizations engaged in consulting work. Consultants are usually experts in their particular field, and hence may be useful to you in your information search about that job or career-change that you are contemplating.

Dun's Consultants Directory.

Contacts Influential: Commerce and Industry Directory. Businesses in particular market area listed by name, type of business, key personnel, etc. Contacts Influential, Market Research and Development Services, 321 Bush St., Suite 203, San Francisco, CA 94104, if your library doesn't have it.

Standard and Poor's Register of Corporations, Directors and Executives. Key executives in 32,000 leading companies, plus 75,000 directors.

Who's Who in Finance and Industry, and all the other Who's Who books. Useful once you have the name of someone-who-has-the-power-to-hire, and you want to know more about them.

American Society for Training and Development Directory: Who's Who in Training and Development, 1640 King St., Box 1443, Alexandria, VA 22313-2043.

Investor, Banker, Broker Almanac.

American Men and Women of Science.

5. Vacancies or Job Leads

Professional's Job Finder, by Daniel Lauber. 1996. Planning/Communications, 7215 Oak Ave., River Forest, IL 60305. Lists over 2,500 associations, directories, journals, trade magazines, newsletters, computerized job-listings, online services, job-matching services, salary surveys, etc. -- *categorized* very helpfully by fields, industries, and occupations -- where contacts may be found, or job-leads advertised. Includes international job sources. Very thorough.

Non-Profits' and Education Job Finder, by Daniel Lauber. 1996. Planning/Communications, 7215 Oak Ave., River Forest, IL 60305. Lists over 1,350 associations, directories, journals, trade magazines, newsletters, computerized job-listings, online services, job-matching services, foundations, grants, and salary surveys, etc. -- dealing with education and all of the non-profit sector -- where contacts may be found, or job-leads advertised. Very thorough.

JOB HUNTER'S SOURCEBOOK: Where to find employment leads and other job search resources, ed. by LeCompte, Michelle. 1996. Gale Research, Inc., 835 Penobscot Bldg., Detroit, MI 48226-4094. A similar exceptional resource, as it tells you how to find sources of information and job-leads for a whole variety of occupations (155, in all). Somebody did their homework well.

The National Job Hotline Directory: Access more than 3,000 employment hotlines 24 hours a day, by Marcia P. Williams and Sue A. Cubbage. McGraw-Hill, Inc., 1221 Avenue of the Americas, New York, NY 10020.

Yate, Martin, *Knock 'em Dead: The Ultimate Job Seeker's Handbook*. rev. ed. 1994. Bob Adams, Inc., 260 Center St., Holbrook, MA 02343. Omnipresent in U.S. bookstores, currently, this book should be easy to find. Very popular.

The Guide to Internet Job Searching, by Margaret Riley, Frances Roehm, and Steve Oserman. VGM Career Horizons, a division of NTC Publishing Group, 4255 West Touhy Avenue, Lincolnwood (Chicago), IL 60646-1975. 1996. Known on the Web as 'the Riley guide,' I like this book the best of all those which have been coming out about job-hunting and the Internet. The table of contents includes such topics as "Jobs in Business," "Jobs in the Social Sciences," "International Opportunities," etc. An impressive work, representing hundreds of hours of research on 'the Net.'

Stevens, Paul, *Stop Postponing the Rest of Your Life*. 1993. Ten Speed Press, P.O. Box 7123, Berkeley, CA 94707. A classic text from the dean of career counseling in Australia, now revised and updated.

If you did not find the books you were looking for, in this Research section, there are three kinds of places where you can look further.

(1) Your **local bookstores** -- go to more than one, browse, and see what they have. Disadvantage: you have to buy the book, if you want it. Advantage: they've got the latest most up-to-date edition *(usually -- though not always)*. Furthermore, they can order for you almost any book *that is still in print* -- and you'll know *that*, by whether or not it is listed in a reference book most bookstores have, called *Books In Print*. Ask.

(2) Your local **public libraries**, or nearby community college library. If they have a friendly reference librarian, by all means ask to see him or her. They can be worth their weight in gold to you. Tell them your problem or interest, and see what they can dig up. Disadvantage: a library may not have the latest edition of a book (see what edition of *Parachute* they're carrying, for example). Advantage: you can borrow a book for free, and furthermore, the reference librarian often knows of hidden treasures, buried in articles and clippings, which could be the answer to your prayers.

(3) **Mail order**. This is particularly helpful to those who live outside the U.S. There are a number of U.S. mail order places which specialize in career books. Their catalogs are listed on page *277*. Disadvantage: you have to wait to get the book (but if you phone, you can often order them by Federal Express, so sometimes it's *next day* delivery). Advantage: often, you can order it from anywhere in the world, and their listings of career books, tapes, videos and software, are far more extensive than you will find in the average bookstore, or library.

Job-Hunting On The Internet

Table of Contents

Preface

I want to begin by expressing my great debt of gratitude to those who gave me help in understanding and navigating the Internet, during these past two years: my friend Guy Kawasaki, Martin Kimeldorf, Margaret Riley, Mary-Ellen Mort, Nick Donatiello and Deborah Bryant. But most of all I want to express my gratitude for the immeasurable help I have received from my son, Gary Bolles, former editor-in-chief of *Network Computing* Magazine, and former editor-in-chief of *Inter@ctive Week* Magazine. He is one of the leaders in this industry, and has been a fountainhead of knowledge and technical know-how for me.

Needless to say, none of the above are responsible for any of the opinions expressed in this article, or for any misstatement of facts which may be here, for which I alone am responsible.

THE CURRENT SITUATION

If it has escaped your notice that there is a thing called *The Internet* (in general) and the *World Wide Web* (in particular), congratulations! You have *really* managed to get away from it all this past year or two, haven't you!

These two entities seem omnipresent in our society, right now. *Web addresses* appear at the bottom of loads of movie ads, not to mention at the bottom of ads for everything else that moves.

Many newspapers have a column or section which weekly publishes new *Web addresses*, called URLs (*like:* http://www.search.com).[1] Internet addicts, of course, collect new URLs as though they were baseball cards.

---

1. Studying your local newspaper for a week (usually the Business Section) will quickly reveal to you when (and if) they publish new *Web addresses*. Currently, for example, *USA Today* publishes these every Thursday.

Local bookstores have whole sections devoted to *the Web* and the Internet. And, included among these are a goodly number of books devoted to job-hunting on the Internet (See pages *151–152*).

From all of this, you might be forgiven for thinking that everyone is on the Internet except you, poor modemless person that you are. And that you as job-hunter, are hopelessly outdated if you're not using the Internet as part of your job-search.

Well, take heart. You are not as *out of it* as you think. This is the current situation, as I write, despite all impressions and *hype* to the contrary:

At Home

35% of American households have a computer at home;
> **65% do not.**

20% of American households have a modem, and could be online;
> **80% do not.**

11% of American households are actually online, one way or another;
> **89% are not.**

8% of American households are connected to the Web, and the Internet;
> **92% are not.**

0.07% -- or less than one tenth of one percent -- of American households do job-hunting online;
> **99.93% do not.**

> *(These statistics were the latest available as of 6/3/96, and are courtesy of Nick Donatiello, at Odyssey, a noted market research firm.)*

At Work or School

As best the experts can guesstimate, this is the current situation there: Over 60 percent of Internet activity takes place at work, and is, of course, work-related in the majority.[2] 25% of all Americans 16 years of age or older have access to the Internet at work or school;
> **75% do not.**

31% of all Americans 16 years of age or older actually access the Internet, at least on occasion, at home or work or school;
> **69% never do.**

8% of the population actually access the Internet *regularly*;
> **92% do not.**

Of course, if you are already online yourself, the above statistics will seem dead wrong to you, because virtually every friend you have will also be on-line.

It reminds one of the old joke about Sigmund Freud, which was, that he thought the whole world was filled with nothing but neurotics or psychotics,

---

2. Going on the Internet while at work in order to take care of personal business, such as job-hunting, is not a good idea. There is now software which organizations can use that tracks all online activity for every employee, and records every site an employee visits, plus every file he or she downloads.

because those were the only people he ever saw. It is hard to remember that your *sample* of the general population -- the people you attract, and hobnob with -- is greatly skewed by your interests and pursuits. *"Birds of a feather flock together . . ."*

Your impressions aside, the survey evidence is that *currently* most of America (about 92% of the U.S., anyway) are not on the Internet *with any regularity*, if at all -- in spite of the hype and the omnipresence of the Internet in the news.

This, of course, is all going to change dramatically in the months and years ahead. A year ago, only 4% of U.S. households were on the Internet; now 8% are.

This picture will change at a geometric rate, rather than arithmetic, because of the forces that are at work out there: alliances are being formed weekly between communication companies, such as AT&T and other phone companies, computer manufacturers, software giants such as Microsoft, television manufacturers, cable companies, and Internet Service Providers, toward the goal -- sooner, rather than later -- of the Internet being as easy to use as turning on a TV, or picking up a telephone -- using a hardware device costing less than $500, which employs your TV as its screen, and your cable or phone line as its Internet connection.

Anyone who picks this book up four years from now will find this whole section amazingly *quaint* and hopelessly outdated. For, to use the metaphor of Mary-Ellen Mort, founder of the great Web site *JobSmart*, "trying to keep up with the Internet is like trying to keep up with an active mudslide."

But we must talk about things as they are at this moment, even if we know we are essentially taking a snapshot of a gazelle in full flight.

And as things are *at the moment*, 92% of U.S. households are *not* on the Internet, and less than one tenth of one percent of U.S. households do any of their job-hunting on the Internet.

Therefore, we cannot begin by simply talking about job-hunting sites on the Internet. Since the majority of U.S. households are *not* even on the Internet, we must start in a much more elementary way, with a brief overview -- *a beginner's primer* -- of what the Internet is, for those job-hunters or career-changers who are currently *Netless*.[3] If you are already a veteran, of course, you can skip directly to page *142*.

A BEGINNER'S PRIMER: WHAT EXACTLY IS THE INTERNET?

We may think of the last three decades, *computer-wise*, in broad brush strokes such as these:

The '70s may be thought of as largely The Era Of The **Mainframe** Computer. It was a huge thing, that could fill a whole room. Hooked up to it,

---

3. Those who know the Internet backwards and forwards, will probably be driven *nuts* by my oversimplifications in this section.

were *terminals,* smaller machines that were used to run programs on the mainframe. (The mainframe acted as what would later be called *a server --* defined as anything that provides services to another computer.)

With the coming of the '80s we moved into a new era: The Era Of The **Desktop** Computer. Manufacturers were able to put on each person's desk a computer that was self-contained with its own data-storage system -- ultimately, hard disk(s). These were computers requiring connection to nothing else, and, by the late '80s, nearly the equal of some of the old mainframes, in terms of computing power and speed.

With the coming of the '90s we moved into still another era: which may be thought of, loosely, as The **Union** Of Mainframe And Desktop. A *kind-of Mainframe* has returned, not as a replacement for the desktop computer, but as an adjunct to it. What is different from the '70s is that this *kind-of Mainframe* is not constructed as one big computer filling a huge room, but as a number of networks of computer sites around the world deciding to voluntarily link up with each other -- desktop and mainframe alike -- so that *together* they act *as if* they were a *kind-of humongous Mainframe.*

And the name of this *Mainframe-like thing* is <u>The</u> Internet, 'cause it's a series of links *between* (hence: *Inter-*) a whole *network of networks* (hence: *-Net*) of computers around the world.

When, therefore, you connect to the Internet today you are seeking out this thing we might call (by way of *very very* loose metaphor) *The World's Largest Mainframe,* and linking it with your desktop computer - - whereupon you too become *part of the Internet --* which has one part in Michigan, one part in Sweden, one part in Worcester, one part in Australia, one part in Berkeley, and so on and so forth.

But in spite of the scatteredness of its parts, what is ingenious about the thing is that it performs essentially as though it were one.

THE BIRTH OF 'THE BLUES'

I characterized the Internet, above, as a creature of the '90s. Actually, it existed for a couple of decades before that. It just never became really popular with *the masses,* until the '90s. It is easy to explain why.

First proposed in the '60s by RAND Corporation, MIT, and UCLA, the Internet actually began in 1969 as part of the Pentagon's Advanced Research Projects. Their concern was to ensure that information could be sent around the world in peacetime or wartime, even if particular cities -- hence computer sites -- were destroyed *(this is why the Internet breaks down a message into electronic 'packets,' then has those packets take* random *routes to their destination, where they are then reassembled).*

The Pentagon's concerns aside, the Internet quickly got adopted as a kind of high-speed electronic post office, and in the 1980s expanded to include the National Science Foundation's supercomputer sites, as well as university, library, and research centers' sites.

Nonetheless, it remained largely the domain of a kind of 'computer aristocracy': defense people, computer programmers, and academic types. It didn't attract a wider audience for a number of reasons. For one thing, there were several different *models of data*, hence *protocols* or *rules*, that each Internet *host* could adopt. These protocols had such names as *telnet, ftp, gopher, usenet, listserv, e-mail, and the like*, and each node or host computer on the Internet could decide what model or protocol it wished to adopt for its site.

What these protocols had in common was that their data appeared on your computer screen as essentially *text, text, text* -- no color, no pictures, no pizazz, no nothin'. *(You could download pictures to your own computer, but they were binary files which had been* uuencoded, *and basically looked like a mess of gibberish* -- *until once they were downloaded to your desktop computer, you* uudecoded *them, back into their original binary code. Then, and only then, a picture would slowly appear on your desktop. It all was and is a very big royal pain.)*

And that was the state of the Internet when, finally, along came *the World Wide Web*. At last: Lights! Camera! Action! Text in colors: yellows, reds, and blues!

THE WORLD WIDE WEB (W^3)

In 1990, Tim Berners-Lee, at CERN, the European Particle Physics Laboratory in Geneva, Switzerland, conceived the idea of applying an already existent technology called *hypertext* to networked computers. Thus was born (a year later) a new Internet protocol, destined to be called *the World Wide Web*.

Hypertext was used by Tim to magically transport you to a different computer site, different file, etc., *among networked computers* anywhere on the Internet, anywhere in the world -- when you mouse-clicked on a designated word, series of words, graphic, or other *hyperlinks* on your screen.

This enabled users of the Web to leap from one Internet site to another, like a gazelle. In fact, at a time of day when the Web isn't overloaded with traffic, this leaping can be as fast as 1–5 seconds, from site to site. *(On slow days, of course, it can take much longer, and sometimes a site won't even come up on your computer, because too many people are trying to contact it at the same time* -- *and it is overloaded.)*

In a sense, this wasn't new; the protocol called *gopher* already enabled you to leap around this quickly in *gopherspace* on the Internet. But on the Web, married to this ability *to leap* was the ability *to display pictures, graphics, charts, visuals, and sound,* on your computer monitor. Even the old *text, text, text* could be all gussied up, in colors, so that it looked *pretty.*

In terms of the *state of the art* of the Internet, this was like going from radio to color television, in the blink of an eye.

You, the idle consumer, could now get on the Internet, and instead of looking at *text, text, text,* you could see some really interesting graphics and color and visuals on your desktop computer screen. With the World Wide Web, the Internet had acquired a new face, *inter-face,* that is, and new makeup. It had color. It had pictures. It looked *wonderful.*

Moreover, you could create your own '*Web site*' and '*Web page*,' if you wished, and on that page *(or pages)* display whatever you wanted to. It was, and is, democracy in action.

With the invention of *the Web* interface, the Internet suddenly became *really* interesting to average, everyday people. People perked up. The Internet started attracting the masses, by the millions. Even if you didn't have access to a computer at work, a desktop computer at home could give you access to the Internet with just a *modem* (installed or added to your computer), *a telephone line* running from the phone company's wall plug to your modem, and some *Internet Service Provider* -- in some cases your phone company, who, for a fee, would connect you to the Internet.

Then why is it that 92% of U.S. households, currently, aren't yet connected? Well, for a variety of reasons. Cost is one. The learning curve that is required (it is often *steep*) is another. I would say that your feelings about the Internet will largely depend on how many experiences you have that are described in the left-hand column below, vs. how many experiences you have that are described in the right-hand column:

HAPPY EXPERIENCES	**UNHAPPY EXPERIENCES**
The computer equipment necessary for going 'online' is at hand, or easy for you to acquire.	The computer equipment necessary for going 'online' is not at hand, and would be expensive for you to acquire.
The modem is already installed inside your computer, or else connecting it to the computer is 'a piece of cake.'	Connecting the modem to the computer is a process so difficult it can drive you to tears of frustration.
Getting an online provider who has a local access phone number is easy.	Finding a decent online provider where you live, who has a local access phone number, is extremely difficult.
Hooking up via the online provider is easy, because they give you all the information you need in order to be able to do it easily, and they stand by with telephone troubleshooting. Additionally, you have friends who have the same kind of computer you do, are already on the Internet, and are anxious to guide and help you all the way.	Hooking up via the online provider is difficult, because they give you none or little of the information you need in order to be able to do it correctly, and their technicians are unavailable or ignorant of your system. To compound the difficulties, you have no friends who are already on the Internet. Hence, you are basically working blind, here, and are ready to cry at how difficult this all is.
The online provider is inexpensive.	Charges mount by the minute, while you are online to the Web.

You can usually dial right into the Web, without any trouble, through your online provider.	You get the equivalent of constant busy signals from your online provider many times when you try to get on the Internet; their equipment is often overloaded or 'down.'
You have a modem which runs somewhere between 28.8K bps and 128K bps, hence images and Web pages load rather quickly.	You have a modem which runs at 14.4K bps or less, hence images and Web pages load painfully slowly.
Once you are on the Web, you zoom. Your favorite 'search engine' appears on the screen almost immediately, you choose a site and ask your browser to take you there, and you are there almost immediately.	No matter what the speed of your modem, "connections are maddeningly slow, and systems often impenetrable." (*Neil Winton, Reuter.*) E.g., once you are connected to the Web, your favorite 'search engine' does not appear on the screen. Period. *You can't go anyplace.* Or, your browser does appear, you choose a site, and ask your browser to take you there, but you run into a logjam. Or you are rejected with some such message as: "The server may not be accepting connections or may be busy. Try again later." You're going to have to come back later (try midnight) before you can get in.
You can always find the Web page that you are seeking.	You can't find a Web page that you know is out there. You get a message like: "404 Not Found.," or "This server has no DNS." But you *know* it's out there, somewhere.
The Web page you want to see comes up on your screen almost immediately.	It takes too long to download and view the Web pages you want.
When you reach a particular site, you discover it was 'exactly as advertised,' and you find just what you want.	When you reach a particular site, you discover *they lied.* E.g., they claim 15,000 employers are listing their vacancies on that site, but at the time you call you find only 22. Or they claim they have *nationwide job listings,* but you discover *that* totals only 50 -- one for each state. And so forth. And so on.

YOU PUT THE FIRST CLICK HERE,
YOU PUT THE SECOND CLICK THERE

For beginners, here is a brief overview of how you start *surfin' the Web*. Once you are connected to the Internet, your computer monitor will require some kind of *Web* browser, such as Netscape Navigator™, which I use here as my illustration.

Once you have that program, some kind of Web browser, you start it up, and eventually "a page" will be displayed on your computer that looks *more or less* like the one on the next page of this book. *(The look of this Netscape Navigator™ "page" may have changed dramatically by the time this falls into your hands.)*

How did we make *this* "page" come up for display? Well, every piece of information on the Internet, whether it is a Web page, file, Usenet group, or whatever, has **an electronic address,** called its **"Location," "Address,"** or **"URL"** -- *the latter standing for either* Universal Resource Locator, *or* Uniform Resource Locator -- *depending on whom you're talking to.* And the URL for the page I have chosen to go to (C/Net's *Search/Com,* run by a commercial enterprise called C/Net) is:

`http://www.search.com/`

as you can see for yourself in the illustration on the next page.

You bring up this "page" or any Web "page" by typing in its *URL (carefully, without any spaces whatsoever, after deleting anything that was there before)* in the box or on the line called "Go To" *(or, sometimes, "Location" or "Address")*. You then hit the "Return" or "Enter" key on your computer, and -- magically -- your browser will take you to *search/com* -- wherever it is in the world.

The URL takes you directly to the site and file. This is the reason every company or venture is putting their URL at the bottom of their newspaper or magazine ad -- that is, assuming they have a page on the Web.

Once you have brought up a search "page" like this, you will wonder what you are staring at. Well, you are staring at a *search 'engine,'* and its regular form -- waiting to be filled in, but not yet filled in.

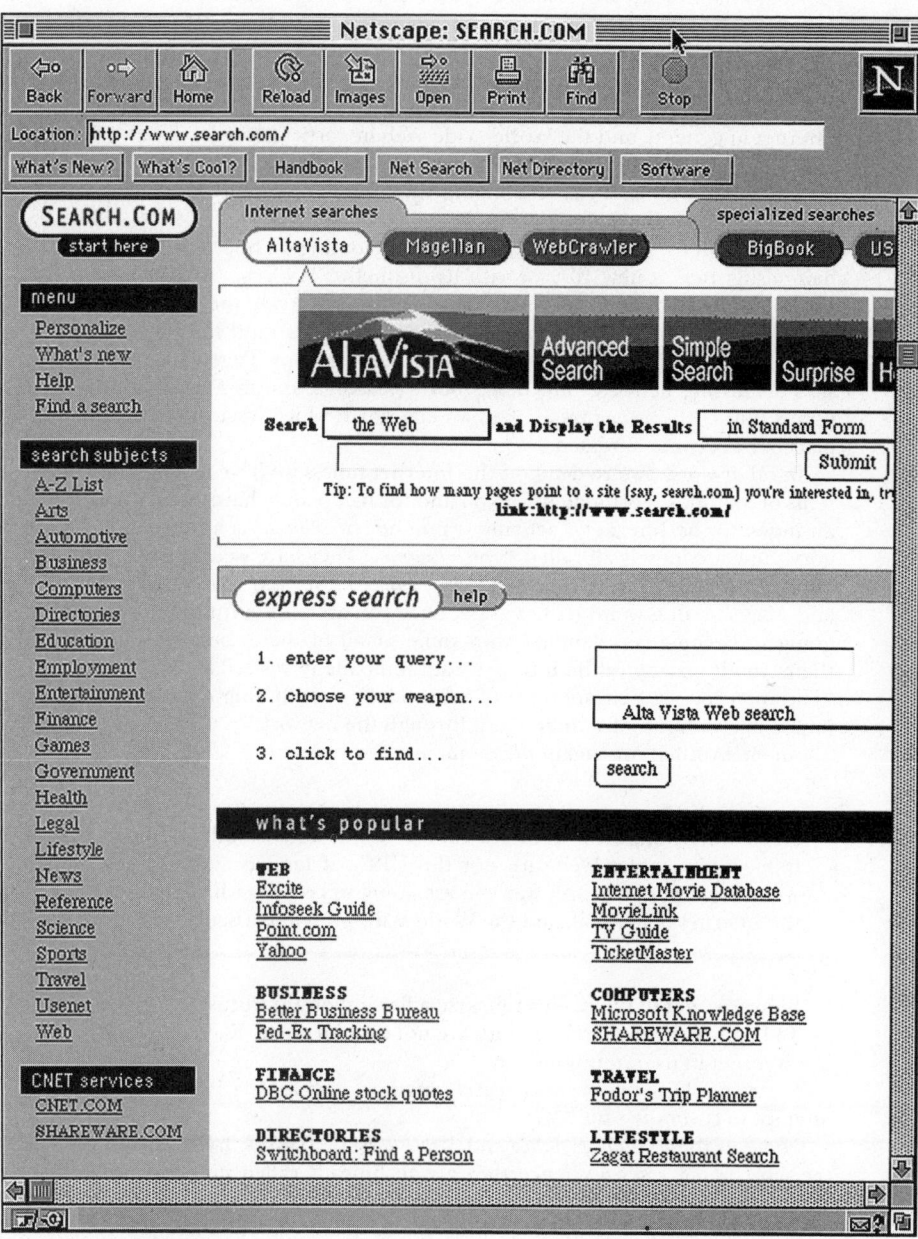

SEARCH ENGINES

Now, what exactly, are 'Search Engines'? Let us begin simply:

URLs are *tres* important. But even if you were to learn the URLs of, say, all the famous employment sites on the Internet, such as America's Job Bank, the Career Center, Career Mosaic. E-Span, the Monster Board, On-Line Career Center, etc., you could not possibly keep up with what's on the Internet in general, and the World Wide Web in particular.

I quoted earlier the words of Mary-Ellen Mort, founder of the wonderful site, *JobSmart,* who said that cataloging the Web is essentially like trying to catalog an active mudslide.

Organizations, groups, and individuals are coming on board the Web at a hair-raising rate: a new *Web site* with its distinctive *Web page* (or pages) gets added every ten minutes, or less. Consequently, as I write, there are at least 30 million Web pages found on 225,000 computers around the world, plus three million articles from 14,000 Usenet news groups. Pages are moving, sites are dying, new sites are being born *endlessly.* And, as Mary-Ellen also points out, URLs *go bad* faster than an egg salad; which means, they get re-placed, or become outdated.

In other words, we're dead on the Internet unless we have a table of con-tents or an index. Fortunately for you and for me, people have come up with an index to the Internet -- actually, a number of *indices.* As an overall cate-gory these are loosely all called *'Search Engines.'* They have weird names, like: *Yahoo, Lycos, Alta Vista, Excite, WebCrawler, InfoSeek, NlightN, HotBot, Open Text,* and *Magellan.* But, weird names aside, once you are on the Internet, you are going to become very familiar with some or all of these, because without them, you'll *never* solve the Internet. Said someone in yesterday's newspaper, "The Internet is a treasure-trove of information, but finding data is next to impossible without software to scout through the network."[4]

Amen, brother. And again I say, Amen.

> Hence, the things it is most critical for you to understand, and be at home with on the Web, are not the URLs of famous sites, but *the search engines.* It's the only way you are going to keep up with what's on the Internet in general, and the World Wide Web in particular.

Before we get to them, let's rehearse a few important truths:

To begin with, all search engines are not created equal. Each one indexes the Internet in its own unique way.

For example, some of these search engines, such as *Alta Vista,* and *Lycos,* attempt to cover the whole Web.

Some of these, such as *Yahoo* and *WebCrawler* or *InfoSeek,* try to cover only the most popular sites -- hence they are technically called *directories,* rather than *search engines.*

---

4. George Avalos, staff writer for the *Contra Costa Times,* 5/31/96.

Some of these attempt to cover a multitude of search engines or directories -- technically called *search services,* such as *MetaCrawler* or *Savvy Search.*

And some of these search engines, directories, or services -- such as the
Point and *C/Net,* -- attempt to evaluate sites, as to usefulness, content, and at-
tractiveness.

And some of these are rumored to be forming alliances -- Yahoo with
Alta Vista, Excite with Magellan, etc. -- which may produce *hybrids* down the
road, that defy prediction, at the moment.

Anyway, *currently,* Netscape Navigator™ has a good detailed description
of each current search engine, directory, or search service, at:

http://home.netscape.com/home/internet-search.html

But we are not through. Further complicating matters, there are search
devices which attempt to explore *other things* on the Internet. For example,
you can search directories of such things as phone numbers, businesses, etc.

And then, there are other types of Internet sites in addition to the Web,
such as *Usenet* (newsgroups) sites, *gopher* sites, *ftp* sites, *e-mail* sites, *Listserv,*
and the like, which have their own search engine *types.* Gopher sites are
searched with two devices called "Archie" and "Veronica."

If you want to know more about these sites and protocols and devices, I
refer you to the "Internet Tools Summary" at:

http://www.december.com/net/tools/toc3.html

Or you may go to the directory called Yahoo. Choose "Computers & The
Internet," then choose, "Internet," then choose from that menu whatever
you are curious about: *gopher, ftp, Usenet, mailing lists (listservs), electronic mail
(e-mail), archie, veronica, or whatever.* Currently that menu is at:

http://www.yahoo.com/Computers_and_Internet/Internet/

If you want to know more about how to fill in a particular search engine's
form, say, the one in our illustration on page *140,* look for an item called
"Help" (it's in the left-hand column in that illustration), double-click on the
word "Help," and they will then guide you through the whole process.

To give you a generalized overview of search devices, I have prepared the
chart, on the next page, *accurate only as of June 1, 1996.* You will want to
use this chart only to get a *sense* of how the different search devices work: the
actual description of them will inevitably be *outdated,* by the time you get to
see this.[5]

---

5. A detailed analysis of these search tools, accurate as of May 1996, is to be found in
Internet World magazine's May 1996 issue. Currently (one cannot predict the future)
you can find it online by going to:

http://pubs.iworld.com/iw-online/

At this Home Page, in small words, you will see: "You can search back issues of
Internet World by <u>cover</u> or by <u>keyword</u>." Mouse-click on the word *keyword,* and when
you see the search form, choose "Internet World" as your database, and type the
words "Search Engine Showdown," without the quotation marks. When that search
gives you its results, mouse-click on the article with that title ("Search Engine
Showdown"), for May, 1996.

Search "Engines"

	Yahoo	MetaCrawler	c/net Search	Alta Vista	Lycos	Excite
URL Address *(no spaces any- where in the address, when you type it in to "Location:")*	http://www. yahoo. com/	http://meta crawler.cs. washington. edu:8080/	http://www. search.com/	http://altavista. digital.com/	http://www. lycos.com/	http://www. excite.com/
Type of Search Device	*Directory*	*Search Service:* An almost simultaneous search with many engines*	*Search Service:* Successive searches with several engines**	*Search Engine*	*Search Engine*	*Search Service,* though it calls itself a search engine
Web Pages Catalogued *(as of 6/3/96)*	Mostly those that are user-submitted	It uses all the pages of all the engines it works with.	The pages catalogued by whatever engine it is using at the time.	30 million Web pages	19 million Web pages	11.5 million Web pages
Can I Browse *By Subject?*	Yes, this is its great strength: it is *beautifully* organized, by librarians.	No	Yes, and lists *all* search engines for a subject, e.g., *employment* has 13 search engines displayed	No`	Yes, using its Service called a2z (A2Z)	Yes, using its Net Directory
What Kinds of Sites Are Included?	The Web	The Web	The Web	The Web Usenet (Newsgroups)	The Web	The Web Usenet (Newsgroups) Reviews Classifieds (from Usenet)

Does it rate the sites in terms of estimated relevancy?	No	No. But it sifts thru the listings, eliminating duplicates.	Depends on which engine it's using.	Yes. In this respect, c/net rated it *the* best search engine	Yes, using its Service called Point: http://www. pointcom.com	It tries to. I find it's often wide of the mark.
Strong Suit of this Particular Device	Superb with subjects and popular sites	Searches many engines at the same time	Vast number of search devices (250) altogether	Has highest number of relevant 'hits' on a search; excels at finding obscure info	Has second highest number of relevant hits	Goes far beyond *the Web* in its searches; and stays current
The Downside to this Device	There's a lot on the Web it knows nothing about; but what it does know, is organized beautifully. I love it.	In spite of the fact you can set a time limit for the search, it can sometimes take *forever*.	Nothing that I've discovered (yet).	It *sometimes* lists many irrelevant sites first (in spite of its claims to the contrary), *and* it is often very slow to add new sites.	For a search engine that covers most of the Web, I have found (*during a keyword search*) that it misses many sites that I know are there.	Many have reported being frustrated by its search results (me included).
Similar Search Services	WebCrawler: http://web crawler.com/ also searches mainstream information and by subject as well	SavvySearch: http://guaral di.cs.colostate. edu:2000/does a genuinely simul- taneous search, *and* with an even larger number of engines	Galaxy: http://galaxy. tradewave.com/ galaxy.html also has an excel- lent subject index, by fields	InfoSeek Guide: http://guide. infoseek.com also has Usenet *and* you can browse by subject. Third best engine at finding relevant sites.		

*Yahoo, Alta Vista, Lycos, Excite, InfoSeek Guide, WebCrawler, Open Text, Galaxy, and Inktomi.
**Yahoo, Alta Vista, Lycos, Excite, InfoSeek Guide, Magellan, shareware com (software), and Lifestyle (Time Warner publications).

And now, on with the question of how you *job-hunt* on the Internet.

JOB-HUNTING COMES, CHAOTICALLY, TO THE INTERNET

As the millions started flocking to the World Wide Web, there were among them -- naturally -- job-hunters and career-changers. Also companies looking for employees. It was inevitable that they should start thinking about how the Internet (in general) and the Web (in particular) could help out.

Five possible uses of the Internet for job-hunters or career-changers occurred to various people. *I will here describe each one of the five, and I will take them* in order -- *from what I consider to be most useful to job-hunters -- on down to what I consider to be least useful:*

#1. For job-hunters and career-changers, the Internet suggests itself as a place to find information or do research on fields, occupations, companies, cities, etc.

#2. For job-hunters and career-changers, the Internet suggests itself as a place to make contacts with people, who can help you find information, or help you get in for an interview, at a particular place.

#3. For job-hunters and career-changers, the Internet suggests itself as a place to get some job-hunting help or career counseling

#4. For job-hunters and career-changers, the Internet suggests itself as a place for you to search for vacancies, listed by employers.

#5. For job-hunters and career-changers, the Internet suggests itself as a place to post your resume

Research. Contacts. Counseling. Vacancies. Resumes. Let us look at each of these five job-hunting uses of the Internet, in turn.

INFORMATION/ RESEARCH

#1. *For job-hunters and career-changers, the Internet suggests itself as a place to find information or do research.*

I have listed this first, because, in essence *all job-hunting is a search for information.*

And the Internet is a superlative place to find information, without the limitations that a normal public library would have. You can access the Internet on holidays, you can access it twenty-four hours a day, and you don't have to even leave the house.

The amount of information you can find on the Internet today is mind-boggling.

I use it daily for issues that have nothing to do with job-hunting. In the past month: I wanted the names of the Seven Dwarfs. *Found that, easily.* I wanted to know the words to an old song. *Found that, easily.* Wanted to know what films a certain actor had appeared in, throughout his career. *Found that, easily.* A member of my family is going to school in Australia. *Easily found* a map of the campus, a map of the town, and an academic calendar for next year, all of which I could print out *in living color.*

It's fun! It's amazing. *And,* when you're using it for job-hunting purposes it can keep you from your job-hunt or career-change for weeks, *all the while giving you the illusion that you are hard at work on it. "Hey, what do you mean I'm not working very hard on my job-hunt? I spent three hours yesterday surfin' the 'Net."*

In other words, when you're job-hunting the Internet furnishes you with a wonderful way to kid yourself.

If you're going to do any job-hunting research on the Internet, I'd say bring carloads of self-discipline. I kid you not, students are flunking out of college because of their addiction to Internet games and *surfing.*

If you're a job-hunter or career-changer using the Internet, and after two weeks you discover that the Internet is all you are doing with your life, disconnect, give your modem to a friend, and go back to job-hunting *the old way.*

In the next five years, we are likely to see 12-Step Programs arise for the Internet-addicted, just as we have for those who can't handle alcohol. Trust me on this.

Effectiveness

The effectiveness of online research in getting a job? Well, that depends of course on what kind of information you're looking for, how essential it is for your job-hunt or career-change that you find this piece of information, etc., etc. In other words, it's impossible to say. We can, however, say this about job-hunting on the Internet & World Wide Web: it can be a great adjunct *to your job-hunt, if rightly used.*

CONTACTS

#2. For job-hunters and career-changers, the Internet suggests itself as a place to make contacts with people, who can help you find information, or help you get in for an interview, at a particular place.

Here is another place where the computer really comes into its own for the job-hunter. I have called this the second most helpful use of the Internet because, in its essence, all job-hunting is a search for people contacts -- that is, for links between you and an employer, or between you and clients.

Through the Internet, you can contact people all over the globe.

If you know who you want to reach, you can do it instantly, without waiting five days for mail to get there -- by using *e-mail*.

If you don't know who you want to reach, you can locate people through *gopher sites, usenet* (a 'newsgroup' devoted to your field of interest, where each of you essentially leaves messages for one another on an electronic bulletin-board, that you have to go visit electronically), and *listservs* (a discussion group like *usenet*, except that it mails each message posted on the bulletin-board to every member's *e-mail box*). There are also '*chat-rooms*' on the Internet and also on commercial services such as *America Online*.

In sum, the number of contacts you can make online, is absolutely mind-boggling.

Any faraway place that interests you, you'll likely find a contact online.

Any question you need an answer to, you'll likely find someone online who knows the answer.

Any organization where you need to know how to meet 'the-person-who-has-the-power-to-hire,' you'll likely find someone online who knows somebody who.

You will want to remember, of course, that anyone you contact on the Internet should be approached -- as in *real* life -- respectfully, politely, courteously, with keen awareness on your part that this is a very busy person, who may or may not be able to respond. If they do give you any help, e-mail thank-you notes should *always* be sent to them, *promptly* (within three days) for the help they gave you.

Effectiveness

My personal estimate of the effectiveness of this use of online, in getting a job: 20% -- that is, out of every one hundred people who make contact with people on the Internet, twenty of them will find a job as a result. Eighty will not.

COUNSELING

#3. *For job-hunters and career-changers, the Internet suggests itself as a place to get some job-hunting help or career counseling.*

Colleges have put some pretty interesting career centers on the Web. I wish I could say the same for all the non-collegiate career centers, but, having roamed a number of such places online, myself, for upwards of two years now -- *and* having talked to other career counselors around the nation and around the world who have also surveyed that scene, I must report that we have found the situation sometimes downright depressing.

What one would *hope* to find on the commercial sites, are:

a) detailed answers to the questions raised by job-hunters, running up to a page or so;

b) written by truly competent career counselors;

c) at no cost to the job-hunter;

d) and without the career counselor or counseling center trying to sell additional services and products (*hidden agendas*).

The reality is often far from this. In fact, my various colleagues around the country, and I, agree that some of the career advice you will find online is absolutely awful. To be sure, the Web is wonderful. But, the fact that inept job-hunting advice is on the Web in living color doesn't magically make that advice useful. *Caveat emptor!*

Having said that, let me add: I think this picture has improved *tremendously* in the last year or so, and I'm much encouraged by what I see. Some really good people are starting to come online. Mary-Ellen Mort's site, *Job-Smart,* is a case in point.

I think the situation will continue to improve.

Effectiveness

My personal estimate of the effectiveness of this use of online, in getting a job: 10% -- that is, out of every one hundred people who seek career counseling on the Internet, ten of them will find a job thereby, due to the coaching that they pick up there. I think ninety will not.

VACANCIES OR 'JOB-POSTINGS'

#4. *For job-hunters and career-changers, the Internet suggests itself as a place for you to search for vacancies, or 'job-postings,' listed on the Internet by* employers.

This is, of course, what makes many job-hunters salivate. Indeed, one *Web site* kept track of its visitors and found that the largest number of those visitors -- 33% -- went to the job-postings, as compared with 26% to the next most popular area there -- salary surveys -- and just 13% to the place where they could put their resume online.

Job-postings! What a lovely sound! *A new place to meet employers.* Thousands of job-opportunities, listed on the Internet! Ah, yes. However, there are two teeny, tiny little problems here.

The first is the fragmentation of the job-postings. The job-hunt in our culture is Neanderthal -- mostly because the *job-market* is so fragmented. Most people sense this. There is no central *marketplace*, no central place for employers and job-hunters to meet each other. So, naturally, when the Internet came along, people hoped it would revolutionize the job-hunt, and offer that one central, unified place, where we might find a list of all available jobs -- at least in our own geographical region, if not in the whole country. That was the hope.

The reality is that reportedly, as I write, we have 11,000 sites on the Internet dealing with jobs or careers. So, if you want to find out what jobs are posted on the Internet, you have to go to hundreds if not thousands of different sites to find that out. Yuk!

The second problem is the infamous *hidden job-market.* You must always keep in mind the fact that 'job-postings' on the Internet are essentially *want ads* -- just like the ones you find in your daily newspaper. Oh, they're free to the employer here (in most cases) -- many times they're posted, in fact, on the employer's own Web site -- and they're called by a more high-falutin' name, like *job-postings*, or *job-banks* -- but *want ads* they remain.

I mention this because employers, generally speaking, prefer every other method of filling vacancies *except* want ads. For many if not most of them, want ads are their *court of last resort*, when all other methods have failed.

If employers can fill their job vacancies without resorting to want ads, they will; and in 80% of all cases, they succeed.

Hence the familiar statistic, for *decades:* "80% of all jobs are never advertised." Never advertised on the Internet, as well as anywhere else. Therefore, even if you were to spend days or weeks visiting every possible site on the Internet where job-postings are to be found, you would still be lacking access to 80 out of every 100 jobs available out there -- due to 'the hidden job-market': *vacancies which employers find ways to fill without ever advertising them.*

And what are those other ways? The diagram on the next page illustrates them. Starting at the bottom, you see how employers typically prefer to fill vacancies: From Within, then by Friends, then Proof, Search Firm, Agency, Resumes, and -- lastly -- Ads (the employers' typical thoughts are within the triangle). Note that job-hunters go in exactly the reverse order from employers, when *they* hunt.

The way a typical
job-hunter
likes to hunt for a job
(starts here)

6 "I will place an ad to find some-one."

Newspaper Ads

Resumes

5 "I will look at some resumes which come in, unsolicited."

Employment Agency for Lower Level Jobs

4 "I want to hire someone for a lower level job, from a stack of potential candidates that some agency has screened for me."

This is called 'a private employ-ment agency,' or - - if it is within the company - - 'the human resources department,' formerly the 'personnel department.' Incidentally, only 15% of all organizations have such an internal department.

Search Firm for Higher Level Jobs

3 "I want to hire someone for a higher level job, from among outstanding people who are presently working for another organization; and I will pay a recruiter to find this outstanding candidate for me."

The agency, thus hired by an employer, is called 'a search firm' or 'headhunter'; only employers can hire such agencies.

A Job-Hunter Who Offers Proof

2 "I want to hire someone who walks in the door and can show me samples of their previous work."

"I want to hire someone whose work a trusted friend of mine has seen and recommends."

That friend may be: mate, best friend, colleague in the same field, or colleague in a different field.

From Within

Employer's Thoughts:

1 "I want to hire someone whose work I have seen." (Promotion from within of a full-time employee, or promotion from within of a part-time employee; hiring a former consultant for a regular position (formerly on a limited contract); hiring a temp for a regular position; hiring a volunteer for a regular position.)

The way a typical employer prefers to fill vacancies (starts here)

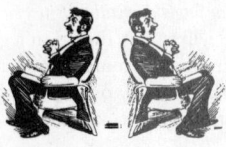

Our Neanderthal Job-Hunting System

If you've already spent *hours* browsing job-postings on one Web site after another, without turning up anything *interesting,* please don't get discouraged: there are tons of jobs *out there,* that the Web knows nothing about![6]

Effectiveness

My personal estimate of the effectiveness of this use of the Internet, in getting a job: one percent, if the job you're looking for is not *computer-related; 40% if it is.*

YOUR RESUME

#5. *For job-hunters and career-changers, the Internet suggests itself as a place to post your resume.*

Many job-hunters think this should be the very best use of the Internet for a job-hunter. Oh, my, oh my! Let's recall some simple truths, here: *a resume is a resume is a resume.* As we have seen, it usually is not a very effective job-hunting tool; and, I'm sorry to report, it doesn't get any better just because it's online. I'll show you what I mean:

Reports from The Field:
The Experience of Seven Actual Job-Hunters
Concerning Their Resume and Job-Postings
On The Internet
This Year

#1. *I have not had any positive reaction to any of my postings of my resume on line. The one exception was a headhunter who asked for my resume. You will get a lot of offers from strange companies or people looking for things that I would describe as pyramid schemes.*

#2. *It was a waste of my time . . . not a single reply!*

#3. *I haven't gotten any responses online. My impression is that if you're not in the computer field, you can pretty much forget finding work online.*

#4. *I found the Internet to be very limited, even for computer employment (which is what I do). Even the 'Entry-Level" newsgroup is full of jobs requiring previous experience. Most of the employer postings seem to be looking for another Albert Einstein with just as many years of experience.*

---

6. *Of course, if one of the postings on the Internet does lead to a job for you -- and it certainly does, for some people -- you can forget everything I just said.* Incidentally, if you find an ad or job-posting online that you like, but they don't give you an e-mail address -- just a postal box number, in their effort to remain anonymous -- you can call that post office and ask for the name of the company or individual renting that box. By law, the post office must provide you with this information.

#5. I didn't actually get my job from the Net, though I made a pass at it. But in the end, I probably reverted to old habits rather than pursuing the job search on the Net the way I said I would. At the same time, the Net definitely played a part in my job hunt, as I pursued many of my contacts via email -- much better than making 'cold' telephone calls, once I'd gotten an email address for a contact in a company (for some reason, a much easier thing than getting direct phone numbers). If I had it to do over again, I would probably do more to take advantage of the Net . . .

#6. I found seeking work online was worthwhile, but I'm in computer programming. After watching the postings for a few weeks, I saw a posting in mid-December which I answered with an e-mailed cover letter and resume. I heard back within a few hours, indicating they would be in touch when they scheduled interviews. While waiting to hear back, I saw another posting for which I considered myself qualified (Note: only two postings that fitted me at all, in four weeks). I answered this one, but never heard back. However, the first one did call me back four weeks later, to set up an appointment, and they offered me the job two weeks after that. I started three weeks after that. But notice how long this process took. While you connect quickly on the Internet, the employment process still moves at a snail's pace 'out there'. You'll need patience. Big time patience.

#7. I feel that online job lists should be viewed with the same healthy skepticism that we offer to want ads. That is, there are many scams, there are comparatively few jobs outside high tech, the government, and academe, and the qualifications sought are either high or highly specialized. Thus, one should not spend any greater time online than he or she would spend looking at the want ads. There is more hype than substance for the so-called average job seeker.

Now, what are we to make of all this? Well, it is obvious that some job-hunters' resumes do get seen by employers on the Internet, and do lead to a job.

Having said that, it's also obvious that in a depressingly large number of cases, *nothing* happens. Zero. Zip. Nada.

So, what's the problem here? Why doesn't your resume get more results, *online?* Well, for a resume to work online, some employer:

has got to be *desperate* to find someone like you,

has got to be at the point in their search for someone like you that they are reduced to reading resumes,

has got to then go online,

has got to accidentally stumble across the site where you posted your resume, and then

has got to take the time and trouble to read it, and then

has got to take the time and trouble to print it out, in all its blah ASCII sameness.

Not only is this a big *pain in the neck* to employers, but there are *at least* 10 million U.S. employers (not to mention other countries') who don't even *think* of the Internet when it's time to hire. Remember the chart about our Neanderthal Job-Hunting System, on page *147*.

Not even *think* of the Internet?? Yes, believe it or not, the CEOs of some very *large* corporations, still haven't got a computer anywhere in sight in their office or in their secretary's office. Just an old faithful *IBM Selectric.* Down through the twentieth century, it has always been true: *job-hunters* flock to a new technology or job-hunting scheme, but a comparatively much smaller proportion of *employers* do.

This isn't just a problem with resumes posted on the Internet. It's been the problem of *all* job-banks, for the last twenty-five years or so. For example, in the case of job-banks I have examined, it has not been uncommon for a job-bank to have, say, 17,000 job-hunters' resumes in its bank, but only 400 employers in that bank *ever*, and only 25–50 employer searches of those 17,000 resumes taking place there *per* week. Some have a much better track record than that, particularly on the Internet, but believe me you will often find it difficult to uncover the specific statistics for the place or places where you post your resume.

So, in many if not most cases, your beautiful resume is just sitting there on the Internet. And sitting there. And sitting there.

But, you're going to put your resume on the Internet, at either a Web or newsgroup site, anyway, aren't you? Sure, you are! It may not get you a job, but your friends will be impressed, when you tell them what you've done! *You?! On the Internet?! Wow!*

There are a number of guides online which tell you exactly *how* to do this, and exactly *where* to do this. They'll tell you the rules about scanning, and the rules about keywords, and so forth. These guides are listed in the URLs section, on page *154.*

Just one caveat: do remember that posting your resume online is the equivalent of nailing your resume to a tree in the town square -- where every employer, solid citizen, salesperson, con artist, pervert, and drunk can see it, and copy down whatever he (or she) wants from it, for follow-up.[7] *Think about it!*

Gary Morris -- who coordinates the Union College Career Development Center *Web site* (http://apollo.union.edu/CDC/CDC.html) -- suggests that if you are posting your portfolio or resume to a public area (such as a Web site) or an online resume database, security should always be a consideration. Gary advises his students to "never include personal or contact information in the body of your resume for safety and security purposes."

I would say that you may want to give your phone number *('cause this is most employers' favorite way of contacting job-hunters),* plus your e-mail address, but **not** your street address, nor business address, nor names of past employers or references *online.* You can always mail this information to an interested employer or recruiter *after* they have contacted you by phone or e-mail.

One final word about resumes *online:* since your resume is going to look *very bland* in plain old ASCII, stripped of all its lovely formatting and the 'nice look' of the original, Martin Kimeldorf suggests that one sentence you

---

7. This includes your present employer, if you have one, since resume postings sometimes get copied from one Internet site to another without your knowledge -- even from *newsgroups* to *the Web,* and vice-versa.

may want to add at the end of your posted resume, is: "An attractive and fully formatted hard copy version of this document is available upon request."

Effectiveness

My personal estimate of the effectiveness of this use of the Internet, in getting a job: less than one half of one percent, if the job you're seeking is not computer-related; 20% effectiveness, if it is.

Well, that is the end of our brief survey of the merits of Job-hunting on the Internet. In sum, I agree with the words of Margaret Riley, everybody's favorite expert on electronic job-hunting: "The Internet is merely an added dimension to the traditional job search, and it is not necessarily an easy dimension to add."

But if you're determined to try it, my advice is: budget only a certain amount of your total job-hunting time to *the Internet part of your job-search* (I'd say 15% of your time, *max*), if you're experienced on the Internet, dive in; if you're new to the Internet, I'd think more seriously about whether or not this is the time to plunge in, when you've got so many other things you should be doing right now (like, inventorying your skills, doing *The Quick Job-Hunting Map*, etc.). But if you decide it is a good time for you to learn to master the Internet, you might want to begin by reading/browsing/keeping at your elbow, one or two of these books, as you then go try some of the URLs listed below.

For Further Help
with The Internet Job Search

The Guide to Internet Job Searching by Margaret F. Riley, Frances Roehm, and Steve Oserman (foreword by Tom Jackson), VGM Career Horizons, a division of NTC Publishing Group, Lincolnwood, Illinois, 1996. *An extraordinary work. If you can buy or read only one book, I suggest that this be it.*

The Riley Guide, as this is called can, incidentally, also be found online as well, at the URL of:

`http://www.jobtrak.com/jobguide/`

Be Your Own Headhunter Online, by Pam Dixon & Sylvia Tiersten. Random House, 1995.

Using the Internet in Your Job Search, by Fred E. Jandt & Mary B. Nemnich. JIST Works, Inc., 1995.

Finding A Job On The Internet, by Alfred and Emily Glossbrenner. McGraw-Hill, 1995.

The On-Line Job Search, by James C. Gonyea (foreword by Tom Jackson). McGraw-Hill, 1995.

Hook Up, Get Hired! The Internet Job Search Revolution, by Joyce Lain Kennedy. John Wiley & Sons, Inc., 1995. *Joyce, a famous syndicated columnist who was very kind to me in the early days of Parachute, has become a pioneer and an acknowledged leader on the subject of electronic job-hunting, by virtue of this book and two earlier ones on the same subject:*

The Electronic Job Search Revolution, by Joyce Lain Kennedy and Thomas J. Morrow. John Wiley & Sons, Inc., 1994.

Electronic Resume Revolution, by Joyce Lain Kennedy and Thomas J. Morrow. John Wiley & Sons, Inc., 1994.

Electronic Resumes for the New Job Market, by Peter D. Weddle. Impact Publications, 1995.

Guerrilla Marketing On-Line, by Jay Conrad Levinson and Charles Rubin, Houghton Mifflin Co., 1995.

WEB ADDRESSES FOR JOB-HUNTERS AND CAREER-CHANGERS

All URLs are to be typed, by you, without any spaces whatsoever, from start to finish, even if they spill over on to more than one line in the text below.

GATEWAY SITES
DEALING WITH CAREERS AND JOB-HUNTING

If you were to start from scratch, find your favorite Internet search engine, and ask it to do a search on the keywords: "careers," "jobs," "employment," "resumes," "job-postings," "career counseling," and the like, you would turn up a sizeable list.

But you don't need to start from scratch. *Fortunately,* a lot of people have already done this search, for you.

Their results are posted at the following *large, gateway* job-sites:

As stated above, the best, by a long shot is **The Riley Guide**; if I could only go to one *gateway* job-site on the Web, this would be it:

    http://www.jobtrak.com/jobguide/

But there are others, as well, which have done a magnificent job of putting together summary lists of what's available. We'll start with:

A Meta-List of Online Job-Services, to be found at the following site (please increase the memory assigned to your Web browser, first, before firing it up, and going to this site, as this is a *huge* file and I have *crashed* several times trying to access it - - *"Out of Memory"*):

    http://rescomp.stanford.edu/jobs/

CareerNet © lists over 11,000 links to jobs, employers, business, education and career service professionals on the Web, plus 6,000 other helpful career resources (which includes Australia and New Zealand, Japan, Germany, and the United Kingdom as well). It is sponsored by Bernard Haldane Associates, and Career Management Resources; It is located at:

    http://www.careers.org/gen/all_gems.htm

Job Search and Employment Opportunities: Best Bets from the Net is at the following gopher URL (Unlike web sites that organize information in *documents*, gopher sites organize and index information by *topics* and include a brief description of each item. Like Web sites, gopher sites maintain links to other sites so that when you conduct a search, you search most gopher sites all at once.):

    gopher://una.hh.lib.umich.edu:70/00/inetdirsstacks/
    employment%3Araytay

Point's Best Sites (Top 5% related to Careers and Jobs) is to be found at:

    http://www.pointcom.com/gifs/reviews/buca.htm

Infoseek Guide has a good list at:

    http://guide-p.infoseek.com/

Once you are on the site, from the left-hand column choose "Business and Finance," then "Careers and Employment." It has at least 1024 sites, and lists "Similar sites" for each item.

Yahoo also has a good list, at:

    http://www.yahoo.com/Business_and_Economy/Employment/

Likewise, **Magellan** has a good "Career and Employment" list at:

    http://www.mckinley.com/

Those are the large *gateway* sites for job-hunting on the Internet. If you want more specific sites, for more specific job-hunting purposes, then the list starts to get much more detailed.

I have listed here a *Sampler*, only, of the types of sites to be found. I have listed these *URLs for Job-Hunters* in five sections, corresponding to the five sections on page *142*. The only difference is, I've listed them in reverse order, *here*, starting with what I think is the *least* useful method of job-hunting on the Internet, and slowly working my way up to what I think are the best uses of the Internet in job-hunting:

1. RESUME SITES
ON THE INTERNET

Some job-hunters *will* want to post their resume on the Internet, in spite of my warnings that this isn't a very effective way to go job-hunting. *I know, you think: just maybe . . .*

So, how can the Internet help you post your resume? Here are some sample sites you can check out:

Good Overall Summary about Resumes is at:
```
http://jobsmart.org/tools/resume/index.htm
```

If you want to know how to write an electronic resume, Joyce Lain Kennedy's insights are to be found at:
```
http://www.mainquad.com/quad/careerfair/resDrop/
style.html
```

The importance of keywords in electronic resumes is to be found at a gopher site, rather than the Web. It's located at the following address, which you can type in to your Web browser (assuming your Internet Service Provider gives you access to *gopherspace*):
```
gopher://merlin.hood.edu:9999/11gopher_root:
%5bcareer_center.job_search%5d
```

If you want to build your resume online, go to:
```
http://www.resumix.com/resume/resume-form.html
```

When it's time to post your resume, a summary of Resume Posting Sites can be found at the following locations:
JobHunt:
```
http://www.rescomp.stanford.edu/jobs.html
```

Yahoo:
```
http://www.yahoo.com/Business_and_Economy/
Employment/Resumes/
```

Galaxy:
```
http://galaxy.einet.net./GJ/employment.html
```

And, also on the Web, sites can be found at the **World Wide Web Employment Office**, which has links to the U.S. and other countries as well. It can be found at:
```
http://www.harbornet.com/biz/office/annex.html
```

Leaving the Web, there are the **Usenet Newsgroups** on the Internet where resumes can also be posted. You can find *lists,* of these at:
```
http://www.yahoo.com/Business_and_Economy/
Employment/Jobs/Usenet/
```

2. JOB-POSTING SITES
ON THE INTERNET

Experts say the major reason job-hunters come on to the Internet, *if they do*, is to look for job-postings. In fact, the ratio is almost 3:1, compared with those who come on the Internet simply to post their resume. In response to such hunger, there are hundreds if not thousands of places that post job vacancies.

What you will not believe, until it happens to you, is that it is possible to hunt through all these listings and *still* not find one job that interests you -- unless of course, you're in the computer field, in which case the Internet is essentially like striking it rich.

Warning to all others: don't get your hopes up, in spite of the number of sites. You may of course get lucky; but don't get depressed or feel there's something wrong with you, if you don't. 80% *at least* of all jobs available are *not* posted on the Internet.

That said, let's see what there is.

There are some pages that have put a number of job-posting *search engines* (*'they' use the term loosely*) all on one page.

The first multiple-site is:

JobBank USA at:
   http://www.jobbankusa.com/
Once you reach this site, mouse-click on "Search Jobs" at the top. It will give you 20 or more employment search engines, for vacancies, all on one page.

Many of the search *directories* or search *engines* themselves, also have multiple *job-posting* sites on one page. Here are some of them:

c/net at:
   http://www.search.com/
Once you reach this site, mouse-click on "Employment" in the left-hand column, under "search engines." It will give you 13 or more employment search engines, for *job-postings*, all on one page.

Point:
   http://www.pointcom.com/
Once you reach this site, choose "View the Top 5% by Category," then "Business," then "Career and Jobs."

a2z, Lycos:
   http://www.lycos.com/ *or: 159*
   http://a2z.lycos.com/
Once you reach either of these sites (they, and *Point* are the same company), choose "Business and Investing," then "Careers and Jobs."

InfoSeek Guide
   http://guide-p.infoseek.com
Once you reach this site, choose "Business & Finance," then "Careers and Employment," then "Company job offers."

Excite:
  http://www.search.com/
Once you reach this site, choose "Net Directory" at the top, then "Business," then "Jobs," then "Job Directories."

100hot
  http://www.100hot.com/
Once you reach this site, choose "Jobs."

ZD Net Jobs Database
  http://www.zdnet.com/zdi/jobs/jobs.html

Multiple listings aside, you will want to familiarize yourself with some of the most famous individual sites, *which get listed again and again in various career indices.* You will already have come across many of these, if you used any of the multiple-site pages listed above, or those listed on page *53.*

Keep in mind that *many* of these sites offer much more than just *job-postings.*

America's Job Bank maintained by the Dept. of Labor, U.S. Employment Service (links 2,000 state Employment Service offices in the U.S.):
  http://www.ajb.dni.us/

BizWomen (intended to be a place where women in business can communicate with one another, post their business card, pick up news about women in business, etc. Still growing):
  http://www.bizwomen.com/

The Black Collegian Job Assistance Selection Service (JASS) is at:
  http://www.black-collegian.com/jobsg.html

Career Magazine offers keyword sifting through jobs-offered postings and offers more information about employers than most online resources:
  http://www.careermag.com/

Career Mosaic is an immensely famous site, located at:
  http://www.careermosaic.com

Career Path (also famous, features some 32,000 ads from eight major newspapers in the U.S.)
  http://www.careerpath.com/

CareerNet © (including business and professional associations) lists over 11,000 links to jobs, employers, business, education, and career service professionals on the Web, plus 6,000 other helpful career resources (which includes Australia and New Zealand, Japan, Germany, and the United Kingdom

as well). It is sponsored by Bernard Haldane Associates, and Career Management Resources, and is located at:
    http://www.careers.org/gen/all_gems.htm

The **CareerNET** Resource and Development Center, sponsored by the Louisiana Department of Labor, is one of my favorite sites; note that it is not to be confused with CareerNet©, which appears above:
    http://www.ldol.state.la.us:80/career1/ldolcp.htm

CareerWeb is at:
    http://www.cweb.com/homepage.html

Catapult (college-related resources) is located at:
    http://www.jobweb.org/catapult/catapult.htm

The College Network (AT&T) Job Station is at:
    http://www.att.com/college/jobs.html

Connect: California Occupational News Network Employing Computerized Telecommunications, is at:
    http://www.cabrillo.cc.ca.us/connect/docs/welcome.html

EINet is at:
    http://galaxy.einet.net/galaxy/Business-and-Commerce/
    General-Products-and-Services/Employment.html

E-Span (Your Online Employment Connection) is at:
    http://www.espan.com/

JobNet, a collection of resources from the Web, Usenet News, gopher, and Listserves is located at:
    http://www.westga.edu/~coop/index.html

JOBTRAK, listing over 2,100 new job postings each day, primarily for college students, graduates, and alumni, is at:
    http://www.jobtrak.com/

JobWeb (run by the National Association of Colleges and Employers):
    http://www.jobweb.org/

The Monster Board, which has over 55,000 postings, a career center, and resume postings as well, is located at:
    http://199.94.216.76:80/

The Online Career Center (sponsored by a non-profit association of leading corporations)
    http://www.occ.com/occ/

The Australian Careers Online Employment Centre is at:
    http://www.careersonline.com.au/jobclub.html

There is a Personality-Type Test Online ("**The Keirsey Temperament Test**") which you fill out online, and then it automatically scores itself. Gives you a Myers-Briggs-type code. *Do take seriously, however, its notice that the labels on the graph at the end of each line should be reversed, for most people, though the final type that is printed out for the test-taker is correct.* The site is to be found at:

    http://sunsite.unc.edu/jembin/mb.pl

An amazingly thorough 74-page *Job Search Guide: Strategies for Professionals* put out by the **USES**, is available online (and can be printed out), at:

    http://www.cabrillo.cc.ca.us/connect/docs/
    jobsearch.html

Career Services at the University of Waterloo has put out a very nice and thorough career guide, as well:

    http://www.adm.uwaterloo.ca/infocecs/CRC/manual-
    home.html

Creative Job Search -- a good site, maintained by Minnesota Department of Economic Security, on skill identification, employment applications, interviews, etc. is to be found at:

    http://mn.jobsearch.org/cjs/cjs_site/cjs-home.htm

Informational Interviewing is at:

    http://danenet.wicip.org/jets/jet-9407-p.html

Pencom Career Center, offers an interactive salary guide, nationwide job listings, and articles on careers:

    http://www.pencomsi.com/careerhome.html

JobSmart, noted above, also has a superb collection of salary surveys.

The Career Action Center in Palo Alto is at:

    http://www.gatenet.com/cac/

Worklife (Paul Stevens' centre in Australia) is at:

    http://www.ozemail.com.au/~worklife/

Oh, and incidentally, this chapter is on the web at:

    http://www.washingtonpost.com/parachute

4. SITES FOR DEVELOPING CONTACTS
ON THE INTERNET

The Internet is *everybody's* favorite place to make contacts, and since contacts are the name of the game (at least in *creative* job-hunting), here are some ways of developing contacts that you'll want to know about:

One of your best bets for finding contacts who share your interest, is to discover a Usenet Newsgroup or ListServ Mailing List, in essence an e-mail discussion group centered around the field of interest that you are trying to find a contact for. **Synapse Internet** has a good search page, at:

```
http://www.synapse.net/~radio/finding.htm
```

The Contact Center Network lists over 6,000 organizations, publications and directories of nonprofits, and community organizational interests, and is located at:

```
http://www.contact.org/
```

Archie and *Veronica* Searches of *gopher* sites on the Internet, to find people who share your interests, can be conducted from:

```
http://www.arn.net/
```

Finding contacts by interest field can also be helped by NeoSoft™ **Publicly Accessible Mailing Lists**, a wonderful list that can be accessed by subject, or name, or title, which is to be found at:

```
http://www.neosoft.com/internet/paml/
```

Once you know the name of a contact, you of course want to be able to find them. Well, the **Four11** Search Engine has 100 million telephone listings in the U.S. Just type in the name of the person and the State they live in, and this program may turn up the address, zip code, and phone number for them. Of course, it may also turn up *dozens* of similar names if you are searching in large metropolitan areas, and sometimes the addresses may be outdated or wrong. Still, it's a start, and it's located at:

```
http://www.Four11.com/cgi-bin/Four11Main?
fonesearch&FormId=
```

Another mammoth directory, **WhoWhere**, searches not only for phone numbers, but also for e-mail addresses, companies on the Net, and the Yellow Pages. It is located at:

```
http://www.whowhere.com/
```

5. FOR RESEARCH ON THE INTERNET

You'll want, first of all, of course, to know how to find **standard reference works** on the Web, like: *dictionaries, encyclopedias,* and the like.

Okay, **Yahoo** has a good collection of them at:

```
http:www.yahoo.com/Reference/
```

And **CareerNET Resource and Development Center** has a good list of reference works, including ERIC, CARL, Usenet Search, an Online Dictionary of Computing, Internet Public Library, a congressional bill-tracking database, directories to nonprofit organizations, etc.: You will find this at:

```
http://www.ldol.state.la.us:80/career1/hp_refer.htm
```

Now, on to specific tasks related to careers. First of all, there is the researching of:

Occupational Fields

The place to begin, of course, is with the **Occupational Outlook Handbook**, which can be found at:
    http://stats.bls.gov/oco/oco1000.htm

You may wish to supplement this with the **Occupational Outlook Quarterly**, to be found at:
    http://stats.bls.gov/empooq0.htm

Or with **Bureau of Labor Statistics** figures and articles concerning the future of particular occupations, at:
    http://stats.bls.gov/blshome.html

Fields are roughly parallel to *Subjects*, and there is a **Clearinghouse for Subject Guides** located at:
    http://www.lib.umich.edu/chhome.html

Fields are roughly parallel with *Associations*, or *Professional Associations*, and these are listed on **Yahoo**, at:
    http://www.yahoo.com/Economy/Organizations/
    Professional/

Fields are roughly parallel to *Professional Societies*, and there are **Job Databases by Professional Societies** and other Institutions listed at:
    http://www.rpi.edu/dept/cdc/society/

Fields are also roughly parallel to *Majors*, in college of course, and there is a description of approximately 460 majors, and which 4-year or 2-year colleges offer those majors in the U.S. at **JobTrak**:
    http://www.jobtrak.com/docs/collegelist.html

Fields are roughly parallel also to *categories* in phone books, and these are to be found in the **AT&T Toll-Free Internet Directory** at:
    http://www.tollfree.att.net/dir800/

Salaries

Another part of your occupational research will, inevitably, involve salaries. The best list of salary surveys on the Net, that I know of, is located at **JobSmart**:
    http://jobsmart.org/tools/salary/index.htm

Companies, Organizations, Or Businesses

Once you've researched an occupational field, or occupation, you will of course want information on particular companies, organizations, or businesses. To help you in this task, some Internet search engines and directories have compiled lists for you:

Yahoo has some help at:
http://www.yahoo.com/
Once you're at this site, choose "Business," then "Companies," then "Indices." Companies are listed by fields.

InfoSeek Guide also has a good list:
http://guide-p.infoseek.com
Once you're at this site, choose "Business & Finance," then "Resources & directories," then "Business directories."

Accufind has help as well:
http://nln.com/
Once you're at this site, choose "Biz," then look under the heading, "Public Company Information." Choose which directories you then want to use.

100hot websites has lists:
http://www.100hot.com
Once you're at this site, choose "Business" *and/or* "Jobs."

excite:
http://www.excite.com/
Once you're at this site, choose "NetDirectory," then "Business," then "Companies."

Once you know the name of an organization or company, you'll of course want to be able to research it. **Starting Point** has a wonderful collection of Commercial Directories listed at:
http://www.stpt.com/busine.html

Mansfield University's Library also has a wonderful collection of a whole bunch of *Business and Economics References* -- Business Yellow Pages, Canadian Statistics, Hoover's, Edgar (SEC database), etc. -- listed at:
http://www.mnsfld.edu/~library/mu-biz.html

LookupUSA, sponsored by American Business Information, Inc. lists 88 million households and 11 million businesses. They can give you a full company profile with key executives, number of employees, sales volume, lines of business, fax numbers, and more are available, by phone call, for $3. They are to be found at:
http://www.abii.com/

IBM InfoMarket Service has information on more than 10 million companies, though if detailed, these reports will be for a price:
http://www.infomarket.ibm.com/

Dun & Bradstreet, Inc. alsò has information on more than 10 million companies, though -- again -- if detailed, these reports will be for a price:
http://www.dbisna.com/dbis/product/secure.htm

As far as *locating* a business is concerned, once you know its name, there are *huge* telephone directories on the Web, which are searchable. **NYNEX** has one such directory at:
http://s13.bigyellow.com/

Special Populations Or Special Problems

Lastly, of course, you'll want resources dealing with special populations or special problems. I have listed a potpourri, here, of the kind of thing found on the Internet.

Resources for Minorities on the Internet can be found on the Internet. Give your favorite search engine this assignment, and see what it turns up. It will find such things as **Virtual Job Fair**'s site:
http://www.vjf.com/pub/docs/jobsearch.html

Resources for Women can be found on the Internet. Give your favorite search engine this assignment, and see what it turns up. It will find such things as **Pleiades Network**'s site:
http://www.pleiades-net.com/lists/orgs.html
Also at **FeMiNa**:
http://www.femina.com/
Also at **Women Online:**
http://www.women-online.com/women/
Also at **iGuide**:
http://www.iguide.com/insites/13/3/1/index.htm

Resources for Gay and Lesbians can be found on the Internet. Give your favorite search engine this assignment, and see what it turns up. It will find, for example, sites such as: **Bach Personnel**, a personnel agency in San Francisco which is targeted at, but not limited to, the Gay and Lesbian Community. Its site is at:
http://www.best.com/~bach/hstory.html

Resources for the Elderly, particularly dealing with Social Security, can be found on the Internet. Give your favorite search engine this assignment, and see what it turns up. It will find such things as the **Social Security Administration**:
http://www.ssa.gov/pubs/10069.html

Resources for People with Disabilities, particularly related to the ADA, can be found on the Internet. Give your favorite search engine this assignment, and see what it turns up. It will find such things as **The Job Accommodation Network**:

http://janweb.icdi.wvu.edu/kinder/

Resources for Those Seeking Work with Nonprofits can be found on the Internet. Give your favorite search engine this assignment, and see what it turns up. In my estimation, the best list, called a **Nonprofit Resources Catalog**, maintained by Phillip A. Walker, is to be found at:

http://www.clark.net/pub/pwalker/General_
Nonprofit_Resources/
There is also **The Contact Directory to Nonprofits**, with several directories:

http://www.contact.org/sample/dir.htm

Magellan also has an excellent list at:

http://www.mckinley.com/
Once you are at this site, choose "Business," then "Nonprofits."
4Work also has job listings from various business and not-for-profit organizations, internships, youth positions, and volunteer work. When I searched this site, I found the listings *limited*. However, looking down the road, it does include a nifty search tool: by registering your name, e-mail address, keyword, and geographic specifications, you are automatically updated via e-mail whenever a new posting occurs, that matches your specifications of what you are looking for:

http://www.4work.com/
Also, a site called **Good Works** has a list of non-profits doing good in the community, at **Essential Information**, founded by Ralph Nader:

http://www.essential.org/goodworks/

Resources for Those Seeking Self-Employment can be found on the Internet. Give your favorite search engine this assignment, and see what it turns up. It will find such things as **Working Solo**, which has a Site for Independent Entrepreneurs, that lists 1,200 business resources for those seeking self-employment. The site is located at:

http://www.workingsolo.com/
And let us not forget the obvious friend of self-employed businesspersons, the U.S. **Small Business Administration** or SBA, which has its site at:

http://www.sbaonline.sba.gov/
Should you want information on patents, copyrights, NAFTA, the SBA Online, etc. , The Information Center's **Business Resource Center** is located at:

http://www.greatinfo.com/business_cntr/bus_res.html
Two search engine sites maintain similar lists. First of all, **excite** at:

http:///www.excite.com
Once you are at the site, choose "NetDirectory," then "Business," then "Patents and Intellectual Property."
Then, **Yahoo:**

http://www.yahoo.com/
Once you are at the site, choose "Business," then "Intellectual Property."

Resources for Those Interested in Volunteering or in Internships can be found on the Internet. Give your favorite search engine this assignment, and see what it turns up. It will find such things as the **4Work** site I mentioned earlier, at:

http://www.4work.com/

Resources for Those Seeking Temp Work can be found on the Internet. Give your favorite search engine this assignment, and see what it turns up. For example, at **Temp Access**, there is a listing of 14,000 Temporary Agencies in the U.S.:

http://www.tempaccess.com/home2.html

Incidentally, people are always asking me, *what is your vision for the Web: what do you think it* should *do for job-hunters?* Well, since we're talking about temporary agencies here, I am reminded of the fact that New York City has a truly exemplary use of what the Web could be. It's called **The Red Guide**, and it's found at:

http://www.panix.com/~grvsmth/redguide/

In addition to a useful "Tips for Temps" section, it is most importantly a site where people who have worked for temporary agencies in NYC can write in afterwards, about their experience with those agencies. (Choose "Review Database".)

If the Web were to have such sites nationwide, divided by geographical region, and not only for temporary agencies, but all other job-counseling centers, counselors, and services, where job-hunters could report their experiences, positive and negative, then the Web would begin to do something that only it can do, *job-hunt-wise.*

If it were to follow this up by having one unified site in all the world for resumes, one unified site in all the world for job-postings, with powerful search capabilities,

And if it were to follow this up by designing a set of protocols, procedures, and standards -- such as Tim Berners-Lee has designed, and is designing, for the World Wide Web -- as to how job-hunters and employers alike list what they are looking for and what they have to offer, thus enabling job-hunter and employer to at least speak a common language to each other,

Then I think we would see the Internet begin to fulfill its potential to add something terrific to the job-hunt process, rather than its present tendency to merely ape or *tidy up* the Neanderthal job-hunting system that already existed, out there, long before the Internet ever came along.

How Do I Job-Hunt While I'm Still Employed?

The U.S. government did a study of job-hunting about ten years ago, and discovered that in a typical month 4.2% of all *employed* workers -- that's one out of every twenty -- went looking for another job that month, while still employed at their old job.

If that same percentage holds true today, then this means that 5,250,000 people are currently job-hunting while still employed.

How do employed job-hunters go about their search, while still at their present job? Over the past twenty-five years, I have asked employed job-hunters this very question, and the distillation of their advice to you -- based on their own successful experience -- is this:

• **Press evenings into service.** Do the original homework on yourself that you will need, figuring out what your skills are and what it is you want to do, as well as where you want to do it. Later on in your job-search, use evenings also to write thank-you notes, send out letters, and the like.

• **Press lunch hours into service,** for the actual calling upon potential employers, if they are in the city where you presently work. People take lunch hours at all different times: 11:15 a.m., 11:45, 12 noon, 12:30, 1 p.m. While you are on your lunch hour, somebody you want to see hasn't gone to lunch yet, or has just come back. Sometimes you can move your lunch hour -- if the place where you are presently working is flexible about that -- to the 11 a.m.–12 noon time slot. If you "brown-bag it," you will have time to eat lunch and also make and keep one appointment, particularly if your intent is to make the interview no longer than twenty minutes -- a good idea, in any case, for the exploratory or information interview.

• **Press late afternoons into service.** Many people you will want to see are on an executive or management level, and they often do not get away from their offices promptly at 5. It is appropriate to estimate how long it will take you to get across town to them, and ask them if they could see you that long after your quitting time, on a particular day.

• **Press holidays into service.** Holidays fall into two classes: those which everyone observes, like Christmas and New Year's Day; and those which *some* people observe, like Washington's Birthday, etc. In the case of the latter kind of holiday, if you have it off, you will sometimes be able to visit the people you want to see at their offfices that day, because they do not have it off.

• **Press Saturdays into service.** Sometimes the people you want to see are working on Saturday, and are willing to set up appointments for Saturday.

• **Press your sick leave into service.** In some organizations, workers accumulate sick leave, and have the right to take it as time off. If that is the case with you, use such days off judiciously, to visit potential employers who interest you.

• **Press your vacations into service.** If you are dead serious about the importance of your job-hunt or career-change, it is not too great a sacrifice to devote one year's vacation time to your job-hunt. This is especially important if you are trying to secure employment in a distant city. Schedule your vacation in that city, and make arrangements and appointments, by letter and phone, ahead of time. Indeed, if you have sufficient savings, the following stratagem may be one you would like to consider as well. If you have a whole list of people and places you need to visit, and you cannot wait until your vacation time, you have the right to ask your present employer if you can have a leave of absence *without pay.* So long as the time requested is no longer than a week or so, and so long as it is scheduled at the convenience of the employer (i.e., not in the week that they need you the most, there), this request will often be honored. You can give, as the reason, the simple truth: Personal Business.

Job-hunting while you are employed will not necessarily come quickly to a conclusion. So, be prepared for this job-hunt to take some time. Just determine to keep at it, with every spare hour you can find. It can be done, and it can be done successfully.

Should you feel guilty about job-hunting while you are still employed? Not in today's world. Remember these simple truths:

Your employer has certain rights, including the right to lay you off at any time, for cause, for downsizing, for merger, for anything. And, your employer has the right to prepare for this act of firing ahead of time, laying the groundwork, transferring part of your work to other colleagues, etc.

You, the employee, have the same rights, including the right to quit at any time. And you have the right to prepare for this act of quitting ahead of time, laying the groundwork through interviewing and job-searching.

Resumes, Agencies, & Ads

(If You Must)

My favorite comment this year about resumes came from a student graduating from the University of Texas at Austin. *"I can't begin to tell you how grateful I am that you wrote this book. I will be graduating this May and will be gainfully employed by an employer of my choice thereafter. I have the job I want, in the field I love (aviation) while my friends are still sending out resumes! To this day, I have never written nor used such a useless piece of paper! I think I'll put all of my friends out of their misery by telling them to quit wasting time on resumes, and buy them all a copy of your book!"*

Why are his fellow students having so much trouble finding jobs? Well, you remember the track record of resumes, don't you? Only one job-offer tendered and accepted, for every 1470 resumes that are floating around out there in the world of work.

So why don't resumes work better than they do? Why don't employers put more faith in them?

Well, let's start with the word "lying."

As far back as 1992, it was being discovered that 'an unacceptably high' number of 15- to 30-year-olds believed it was okay to lie and cheat at work or school. One-third of them said they were willing to lie on a resume.

This trend is not restricted to the young. People in high places -- executives, superintendents of schools, and the like -- have falsely claimed doctorates, and otherwise lied on their resumes. And been caught.

Thus, experts estimate that one-third to one-half of all job-hunters lie on their resumes.

They lie by: inflating their title or responsibilities, omitting their firings or failures, inflating their results, inflating their credentials, hiding jobs where they did terribly, and a lot of other subterfuges.

If you were an employer, how much faith would you put in a piece of paper where you know there are lies on one-third to one-half of them?

> Resume: An ingenious device that turns a human being into an object (an eight and a half by eleven inches piece of paper). This transformation device is then often used to try and convince people we have never met to invest thousands of dollars in us, by hiring us for a job we have not yet specifically identified.
>
> *Michael Bryant*

Still, you're probably determined to use one, so let's look at some things you'll need to keep in mind about resumes, agencies, and ads:

A Summary of What We Know About Resumes

RÉSUMÉ **rez-e-mā** n {F. *résumé* fr. pp. of *résumer* to resume, summarize] SUMMARY *specif:* a short account of one's career and qualifications prepared typically by an applicant for a position.

Webster's

Resumes have a lousy track record. A study of employers done a number of years ago discovered that there was one job offer tendered and accepted, for every 1470 resumes that employers received, from job-hunters. Would you take a plane flight if you knew that only one out of every 1470 planes ever made it to its destination?

The few for whom resumes work talk a lot about it; the vast majority for whom resumes don't work, usually keep quiet about it. Hence, the widespread impression that 'this is a method which works for almost everyone.'

If you believe resumes generally work, and you send out loads of resumes, and you don't even get a nibble, you're going to think that something is wrong with *you*. Hence, plummeting self-esteem, thence depression, emotional paralysis, and worse symptoms *often* follow. This has happened to tens of thousands of job-hunters. It has even happened to me. Don't let it happen to you. You have to get back to point #1, above: resumes have a lousy track record. If you don't get even a nibble, that doesn't mean that anything's wrong with you. Something's desperately wrong with resumes . . . as a job-hunting technique.

Those employers who like resumes like them because they enable employers to screen you out *fast* without ever 'wasting their time' on an interview. *Most* employers, or their subordinates, can *screen you out* in approximately thirty seconds, if your resume is sitting in a stack of, say, fifty, on their desk. And if it's in a stack of several hundred, the employer picks up speed and -- we know by actual count -- can screen you out in as little as eight seconds. So, in eight to thirty seconds, *you're gone*. And, with it, any chance for a job there.

In spite of the evidence, almost everyone -- including career counselors and job-hunting books -- will advise you to send out your resume *(or 'curriculum vitae,' c.v. for short)* to a lot of employers, and in answer to a lot of ads for job vacancies. Many people love the *idea* of a resume, no matter how ineffective it is. Never was love more blind. Only 1 in 1470 gets through, remember.

Many employers *hate* resumes. Period. Many others use them, but distrust them, because so many job-hunters lie about their qualifications -- *and are found out.*

Many organizations send no response in answer to resumes. You'll have to guess whether they ever saw your resume, or 'deep-sixed' it, unopened and unread.

Job-hunters will always love resumes, in spite of all the above, be-cause job-hunters *hate* rejection. With resumes, your name gets out there, and though it usually doesn't lead to a job, at least you're not standing there in front of a would-be employer, staring into his or her face while you hear the bad news. With resumes, it's rejection all right. But it doesn't feel so . . . *personal.* Resumes are a nice way to kid ourselves, so that we *feel* we are doing some-thing about our job-hunt, even if -- so far as effectively finding a job is concerned -- we are actually doing next to nothing.

Government/State Employment Agencies

The second job-hunting strategy that we instinctively turn to, in our Neanderthal job-hunting system, is agencies.

Agencies seem like a wonderful idea, when you are unemployed. My goodness, there's actually someone out there who can link employers looking for jobs with very-qualified me. We all like to think that somewhere out there is just such a switchboard, where all the employers and all the job-hunters, in an area, can come to find each other.

Unhappily, no place in this country has even a clue as to where all the jobs are. The best that any place can offer you is a kind of sampling, a sort of smorgasbord, if you will, of some of the jobs that are available, out there.

So, if you want a sampling, you will naturally want to visit an agency. Agencies are of several types: federal/state; private; and those retained by employers. Let's look at them in turn, beginning with The Federal/State Employment Service.

The local State employment office in your town or city is actually part of a nationwide Federal network, called "The United States Employment Service," or USES for short. USES has seen its staff and budget, nationwide, greatly reduced in recent years.

About one-tenth of these offices offer job-search workshops, from time to time -- depending on the demand, and whether or not a counselor is available who knows how to teach such a workshop. Beyond that, they have listings of some of the jobs available in your geographical area -- usually ones that employers have already tried to fill in every other way they can.

According to one study, USES placed only 13.7% of those who sought a job there. This means of course that they failed to find a job for 86.3% of the job-hunters who went there to find a job.

They are not, therefore, helpful to most job-hunters. But if you research the firms very thoroughly, and find one that deals with your field or specialty, it's always worth sending them your resume -- just in case. Don't count on anything happening, though. You're essentially praying for lightning to strike.[1]

Is there any place out there, set up by employers where employer and job-hunter can meet face-to-face? Well, there are job-fairs in various places around the country, held at various times of the year. Ask your local Chamber of Commerce if they know of any. These are often remarkably unproductive, but some job-hunters have struck pay-dirt by going to them.

On some college campuses, recruiters from various companies show up to interview seniors (and sometimes others) for jobs they have vacant. But it's a very dicey process, and you should by no means count on it. Most often it leads absolutely nowhere.

---

1. There are places that will sell you lists. For example:

Directory of Executive Recruiters, published by Consultant News, Templeton Rd., Fitzwilliam, NH 03447. Published yearly. Lists several hundred firms and the industries served.

Directory of Personnel Consultants by Specialization (Industry Grouping). Published by the National Association of Personnel Consultants, Round House Square, 3133 Mt. Vernon Ave., Alexandria, VA 22305. 1-703-684-0180.

If you want to know more about executive search, there is: John Lucht, *Rites of Passage at $100,000+,* rev. ed. Henry Holt and Co., 115 W. 18th, New York, NY 10011. 800-247-3912. Review by one of our readers: "This book describes in depth the methods of headhunters, what to expect and how to deal with them on an on-going basis. Highly recommended for anyone in middle-management or above. . . ."

Ads In Newspapers

The third job-hunting strategy that we instinctively turn to, in our Neanderthal job-hunting system -- after resumes and agencies -- is want ads.

Want ads are found in your local newspaper -- in the classified section, and/or in the business section, sports section, education section, or Sunday edition. Also, for management or financial job-hunters, ads are to be found in the *Wall Street Journal* (especially Tuesday's and Wednesday's editions).

Some phrases are designed to lure you in, while concealing what the job is really about. Beware! Examples:

"Energetic self-starter wanted" (= You'll be working on commission)
"Good organizational skills" (= You'll be handling the filing)
"Make an investment in your future" (= This is a franchise or pyramid scheme)
"Much client contact" (= You handle the phone, or make 'cold calls' on clients)
"Planning and coordinating" (= You book the boss's travel arrangements)
"Opportunity of a lifetime" (= Nowhere else will you find such a low salary and so much work)
"Management training position" or "Varied, interesting travel" (= You'll be a salesperson with a wide territory)

Within 48–96 hours after an ad appears (the third day is usually the peak), an employer will typically receive from 20 to 1000 or more resumes, and will proceed to systematically *screen out* 95 to 98 out of every 100.

Many classified ads include the employers' phone number, because they want to see if they can *screen you out* over the telephone, without ever having to take the time to see you in person. This is always to your disadvantage. Therefore, most experts say, don't say anything over the phone, except that you want to set up an appointment. One way to avoid being drawn into conversation, designed to screen you out over the phone, is simply to say: "I'm sorry I can't talk now; I'm at work."

A study conducted in two "typical" cities -- one large, one small -- revealed, and I quote, that "85% of the employers in San Francisco, and 75% in Salt Lake City, did not hire any employees through want ads" during a typical year. Yes, that said *any* employees, *during the whole year.*[2] In other words, if you use ads, they only give you access to (at most) 25% of the employers in that city, during the entire year.

As if all of this weren't bad enough, your job-hunting career with ads is further compromised by the fact that some of the ads you see are fakes.

Some employers run fake ads to test the loyalty of their employees (the ad lists only a box number to write to).[3]

Some employment agencies run fake ads, usually listing jobs that have already been filled, in order to draw you in (the old 'bait and switch' process).

Some swindlers run fake ads, pretending they are employers, so that they can get your money (the clue is: the ad gives you a 900 number to call) or get your Social Security number and the number of your driver's license (don't ever give these out over the phone, in response to an ad). With these two numbers alone, from you, they can often take you to the cleaners with some of the con games they've invented.

---

2. Olympus Research Corporation, "A Study to Test the Feasibility of Determining Whether Classified Ads in Daily Newspapers Are an Accurate Reflection of Local Labor Markets and of Significance to Employers and Job Seekers." 1973. Now out of print.

3. I am citing an actual case here, as my example.

Want Ads Not In Newspapers

• For Nonprofit Organizations Doing Public or Community Service: ACCESS, Networking in the Public Interest, 1001 Connecticut Ave., N.W., Suite 838, Washington, D.C. 20036. 202-785-4233. Fax: 202-785-4212. Amy Kincaid, Executive Director. Listings of job opportunities in the nonprofit sector, ranging from entry level to Executive positions, are disseminated through three publications: (1) *Community Jobs: The National Employment Newspaper For The Non-profit Sector;* (2) *Community Jobs/ NJ, NY,* a bi-monthly publication; (3) *Community Jobs/D.C.,* a bi-monthly publication. ACCESS also provides career development services specifically geared toward the nonprofit job-seeker. Write, call, or fax, for details, if you are interested.

• For teachers: *The NESC Jobs Newsletters* are published by the National Education Service Center, P.O. Box 1279, Dept. PB, Riverton, WY 82501. 1-307-856-0170. Between March and August, this weekly series of newsletters lists about 58,000 job openings annually. Each week's edition contains only new listings, none repeated. The newsletters are published year 'round, with fewer listings in the months August to March. You select one or more of fourteen different job categories, and receive listings of jobs in those categories only.

• For The Blind: Job Opportunities for the Blind, 1800 Johnson St., Baltimore, MD 21230. 1-410-659-9314, or 1-800-638-7518. Exists to inform blind applicants about positions that are open with public and private employers throughout the country. Maintains a computerized listing. Also, they have cassette instructions on everything for the blind job-seeker. Operated by the National Federation of the Blind in partnership with the U.S. Department of Labor.

• For Jobs Outdoors: Environmental Opportunities, Box 788, Walpole, NH 03608, publishes a monthly listing of environmental jobs and internships, with the same name (Environmental Opportunities). Each issue contains sixty to one hundred full-time positions in a variety of disciplines. 1-603-756-4553.

• For Jobs in Horticulture: Ferrell's JOBS IN HORTICULTURE, P. O. Box 156, Mechanicsburg, PA 17055-0156. A semi-monthly guide to opportunities. $22.95 for six issues (3 months worth).

- For Jobs Overseas: *International Employment Hotline,* a monthly newsletter which lists international employment opportunities. *International Employment Hot line,* Cantrell Corp., Box 3030, Oakton, VA 22124.

- For Government Jobs: *Federal Career Opportunities,* published biweekly by Federal Research Service, Inc., 243 Church St. NW, Vienna, VA 22183. 1-703-281-0200. Each issue is 64 pages, and lists 3,200+ currently available federal jobs, in both the U.S. and overseas.

- For Jobs in Criminal Justice: The *NELS Monthly Bulletin,* National Employment Listing Service, Criminal Justice Center, Sam Houston State Univ., Huntsville, TX 77341. 1-409-294-1592. A nonprofit service providing information on current job opportunities in the criminal justice and social services fields.

- For Jobs in The Christian Church: Intercristo is a national Christian organization that lists over 18,000 jobs, covering hun-dreds of vocational categories within over 1,000 Christian service organizations in the U.S. or overseas. Their service is called Christian Placement Network. *(Jeff Trautman, Executive Director.)* In 1992, 12,500 people used the Christian Placement Network; one out of every twenty-five job-hunters who used this service found a job thereby. (That, of course, means twenty-four out of twenty-five didn't.) Our readers feel that many of these listings are in very conservative church settings, but if that (and the odds) don't bother you, you can contact them at 19303 Fremont Ave. N., Seattle, WA 98133, (phone number: 1-800-426-1342, or 1-206-546-7330), and ask to be listed with them for three months (cost: $41.50). *More general* information about Christians in the world of work (again, from a conservative point of view) is to be found in the *Strategic Careers Project Forum,* published bi-monthly by Inter-Varsity Christian Fellowship of the U.S.A., Box 7895, Madison, WI 53707-7895.

David Swanson, *The Resume Solution; How To Write (and Use) A Resume That Gets Results.* 1991. JIST Works, Inc., 720 North Park Ave., Indianapolis, IN 46202-3431. This is a relatively new book on resumes, with tips not to be found in other books. It is very popular. (Dave has been on my staff at my workshops since 1978.)

Tom Jackson, with Ellen Jackson, *The* New *Perfect Resume.* 1996, revised. Anchor Press/Doubleday, Garden City, NY 11530. This is Tom's best-selling book, and with good reason. This edition is completely updated with 100+ resume samples and with internal career advice.

Timothy D. Haft, *Trashproof Resumes: Your Guide to Cracking the Job Market.* 1995. *The Princeton Review,* Random House, Inc., 201 E. 50th St., New York, NY 10022. Geared primarily to college students and recent college graduates. Well done.

There are a number of books out there devoted to *cover letters,* either to go with a resume or by themselves instead of a resume. These include:

Krannich, Ronald L. and Caryl Rae, *Dynamite Cover Letters.* 1992, Impact Publications, 9104-N Manassas Drive, Manassas Park, VA 22111.

William S. Frank, *200 Letters for Job Hunters.* rev. ed. 1993. Ten Speed Press, Box 7123, Berkeley, CA 94707.

If the above sampling is not enough for you, see your local bookstore.

IV. Job-Hunting
for
Special Populations

Job-Hunting and High School Students,
including Summer Jobs
Job-Hunting and College Students
Job-Hunting and Women
Job-Hunting and Executives
Job-Hunting and Retirement
Job-Hunting and Ex-Military
Job-Hunting and Clergy
Job-Hunting and The So-Called 'Handicapped'
Job-Hunting and Minorities
Job-Hunting and Gays and Lesbians
Job-Hunting and Immigrants to the U.S.
Job-Hunting and 'People in Recovery'
Job-Hunting and Ex-Offenders

Job-Hunting
for
Special
Populations

The main body of *Parachute* tells you 98% of what you need to know, in order to successfully conduct your job-hunt. However, for those of you who are in one of the groups listed below, I do have some further comments and counsel.

High School
Students

And Job-Hunting

If you are a high school graduate (or student) looking for work, you already know that you face especial difficulties during your job-hunt. You *can* overcome these difficulties. But you do need to be aware of what they are.

To begin with the bad news, in the U.S. only 18% of executives would hire a high school graduate for an entry-level job, according to a recent survey.[1] One employer (Nynex), for example, had to test 60,000 applicants to fill 3,000 job vacancies. When another employer (BellSouth) tested technician applicants, only 8 out of every 100 passed.

What's the problem? Bad work habits, say 78% of all employers.[2] That means U.S. high school graduates as a whole, often have a most unfortunate reputation for failing to show up regularly, balking at doing tasks they consider 'beneath them,' failing to accomplish assigned tasks, arguing that as long as they just keep busy they are doing their job, and failing to go 'the extra mile.'

What's the problem? It's also reading, writing, and 'rithmetic. In 1945, the written vocabulary of a 6- to 14-year-old American was 25,000 words. Today it is only 10,000. The average young adult in the U.S. is reading at only a 2.6 level of English proficiency, while current jobs require a proficiency, on average, of 3.0 (*going up to 3.6 by the year 2000, experts say*).

Furthermore, in the area of skills, 90% of all employers feel that high school graduates "do not know how to solve complex problems."

So, if you are still in high school, **get these skills** -- reading, writing, math, keyboarding (computers), and knowing how to solve problems -- while you are still there. Also, learn what good work habits are, if you have to go and interview every manager of fast-food places within ten miles -- asking them the question: what is the mark of a really good employee here? what is the mark of a really bad employee here? Make a list of what they say are good work habits, and follow that list slavishly at whatever job you then take thereafter.

If you are already *out* of high school, consider seriously going to night school at your local high school or community college, and picking up the skills listed in the previous paragraph, if you don't already have them.

If you are having difficulty finding work, then you must read, mark, learn and inwardly digest the chapters in *Parachute* called "For the Determined Job-Hunter," and *do* the Quick Job-Hunting Map here in this *Workbook*.

The rules you must follow in your job-hunt are easy to master, since they are the same for you as they are for everyone: *Know your skills. Know what kind of work you want to do. Talk to people who are doing it. Find out how they like*

---

1. Reported in *USA Today*, 3/27/96.

2. According to a 1991 Harris Poll, reported in *USA Today*, 5/1/92.

the work, how they found their job. Do some research, in your chosen geographical area, on organizations which interest you, to find what they do and what kinds of problems they or their industry are wrestling with. Then identify and seek out the person who actually has the power to hire you there, for the job you want; use your contacts to get in to see him or her. Show this person with the power to hire you how you can help them with their problems; and how you would stand out as 'one employee in a hundred.' In all of this, cut no corners, take no shortcuts.

Remember this *above all:* all employers divide into two groups: those who will be bothered by the fact you are of high school age, and those who won't be -- and will hire you, so long as you can do the job. Your task is to find the second group of employers, and just thank the first very politely for their time.

For Further Reading

The Guide To Basic Skills Jobs: 2nd ed., *Vols. 1 and II.* 1993. RPM Press, Inc., P.O. Box 31483. Tucson, AZ 85751. 602-886-1990. A catalog of viable jobs for individuals with only basic work skills and/or limited education and/or limited general aptitudes -- such as persons with physical impairments, limited English proficiency, migrant workers, welfare recipients, persons with mental illness, etc. The database is *broken out* from the *D.O.T.*, but a concise, easy-to-use classification system is added. This volume identifies over 5,000 major occupations which require no more than an eighth-grade level of education, and no more than one year of specific vocational preparation. Based upon research originally done by occupational analysts at North Carolina State University, and U.S.E.S. *Immensely useful book* if you counsel any of the above populations.

Hayes, Charles D., *Proving You're Qualified: Strategies for Competent People without College Degrees.* 1995. Autodidactic Press, P.O. Box 872749, Wasilla, AL 99687. The title says it all; very useful book.

Barkley, Nella, *How to Help Your Child Land The Right Job (without being a pain in the neck).* 1993. Workman Publishing Company, Inc., 708 Broadway, New York, NY 10003. Nella worked with John Crystal for a number of years before he died in 1988, and now heads his Center.

For summer jobs in the U.S. or elsewhere, there are directories for high school or college students. They are updated annually, and the year of their revision often appears in their title:

Beusterien, Pat, ed., *Summer Employment Directory of the United States.* Peterson's Guides, P.O. Box 2123, Princeton, NJ 08543.

Hatchwell, Emily, ed., *Directory of Summer Jobs in Britain.* Peterson's Guides, P.O. Box 2123, Princeton, NJ 08543.

Woodworth, David, ed., *Directory of Overseas Summer Jobs.* Issued in annual revisions. Peterson's Guides, P.O. Box 2123, Princeton, NJ 08543.

College Students

And Job-Hunting

College is no longer just for 18-year-olds. Some 42% of college students today are over the age of 24, according to the National Center for Education Studies. *(Source: ReCareering Newsletter, March-April 1995)*

If you are a college graduate looking for work, you already know that you face especial difficulties during your job-hunt. You *can* overcome these difficulties. But you do need to be aware of what they are.

The major problem is the false belief that there is a job out there that goes with the degree. *After all, don't corporate recruiters just come on campus during your senior year, and clamor for you to come work for them?* Well, no, they don't. In the U.S., for example, only one in three graduates has a job waiting for them at graduation time. At some colleges or universities, that figure was only one in ten.[3]

In most cases, therefore, you are going to have to take charge of your own job-hunt. The race for the best jobs belongs not to the strong, but to those who take initiative, are persistent, and know how to conduct their job-hunt themselves.

Summer jobs or internships may stand you in good stead, as you go through college. Remember that one out of seven students, in some sections of the country, get their job at the place where they interned.[4] So, internships might be an important part of your planning during the four years. There is a company called Back Door Experiences, which has a comprehensive guidebook for those seeking a short-term work experience (internship, seasonal job, program abroad, etc.). Cost is $30. For a free information packet you can write the author, Michael Landes, at 1414 Arbutus Ave., Chico, CA 95926-2660. 916-343-3867, 800-552-PATH.

If you are still having difficulty finding work, then you must read, mark, learn and inwardly digest the chapters in *Parachute* called "For the Determined Job-Hunter," and *do* the Quick Job-Hunting Map here in this *Workbook.*

The rules you must follow in your job-hunt are easy to master, since they are the same for you as they are for everyone: *Know your skills. Know what kind of work you want to do. Talk to people who are doing it. Find out how they like the work, how they found their job. Do some research, in your chosen geographical area, on organizations which interest you, to find what they do and what kinds of problems they or their industry are wrestling with. Then identify and seek out the person who actually has the power to hire you there, for the job you want; use your contacts to get in to see him or her. Show this person with the power to hire you how you can help them with their problems; and how you would stand out as 'one employee in a hundred.'* In all of this, cut no corners, take no shortcuts.

Remember this *above all:* all employers divide into two groups: those who

---

3. *USA Today,* 5/1/92

4. *San Francisco Chronicle,* 5/27/92

will be bothered by the fact you are a recent college graduate, and those who won't be -- and will hire you, so long as you can do the job. Your task is to find the second group of employers, and just thank the first very politely for their time.

For Further Reading

Figler, Howard, *Liberal Education and Careers Today.* 1989. Garrett Park Press, Box 190, Garrett Park, MD 20896. Good stuff, as is everything from Howard's pen.

Books on summer jobs are listed at the end of the previous section.

Women

And Job-Hunting

If you are a woman looking for work, you already know that you face especial difficulties during your job-hunt. You *can* overcome these difficulties. But you do need to be aware of what they are.

The advice for women who go job-hunting is the same as it is for men:

If you are having difficulty finding work, then you must read, mark, learn and inwardly digest the chapters in *Parachute* called "For the Determined Job-Hunter," and *do* the Quick Job-Hunting Map here in this *Workbook.*

The rules you must follow in your job-hunt are easy to master, since they are the same for you as they are for everyone: *Know your skills. Know what kind of work you want to do. Talk to people who are doing it. Find out how they like the work, how they found their job. Do some research, in your chosen geographical area, on organizations which interest you, to find what they do and what kinds of problems they or their industry are wrestling with. Then identify and seek out the person who actually has the power to hire you there, for the job you want; use your contacts to get in to see him or her. Show this person with the power to hire you how you can help them with their problems; and how you would stand out as 'one employee in a hundred.'* In all of this, cut no corners, take no shortcuts.

Remember this *above all:* all employers divide into two groups: those who will be bothered by the fact you are a woman, and those who won't be -- and will hire you, so long as you can do the job. Your task is to find the second group of employers, and just thank the first very politely for their time.

Once hired, women do face four unique problems.

(1) **Salary** is a major one. Women are notoriously underpaid, even when of equal experience and training to men in the same company or firm. There are several strategies for dealing with this inequity.

• Some women go into a field belonging predominantly to men, where salary inequities are generally rarer.

• Some women go into a new field, where the salary is more likely to be equitable.

• Some search for unusual job-titles, as -- again -- they are then more likely to be paid an equitable wage.

• Some women prefer to negotiate for a higher salary before they even accept the job offer. And indeed you *can* increase the salary offered you, *if* you know something about salary negotiation, before you go in for the job interview. Be *sure* and study pages 208ff, in *Parachute.*

(2) Related to salary is the problem of **child-care.** For the working poor, child-care costs often represent at least one fifth of their income, which of course reduces the *net* amount of their already-low paycheck by at least that much.

(3) The third problem is **getting promoted.** You have to figure out who the decision-makers are, concerning any promotion you may be qualified for. You have to educate them, whether with a yearly report to your immediate supervisor, copy to the decision-makers, detailing your accomplishments for the year -- or whatever may occur to you. It also helps to volunteer to work on committees or in other departments, so you get experience in many areas there at your place of business. It helps to ask for feedback from co-workers and your supervisor, as to how you could do the work better. It helps if you *ask* for more responsibility, particularly those kinds where there is a definite contribution to the profit or loss side of your place of business. About all else, ask for what you want, gently, kindly, persistently. Robin Wolaner, vice president of Time Publishing Ventures, was quoted in the press recently as saying that early in her career "I kept expecting people to give me things because I deserved it. Then I realized you had to raise your hand." Mark this well!

(4) The fourth problem for women after they get the job, is that of **the invisible 'glass ceiling.'** This now well-known phrase refers to the difficulty women have, in getting promoted beyond a certain point. At lower levels, women are not running into as much trouble getting promoted as they used to. But when they get to higher levels, the going gets much tougher, as their head hits *the glass ceiling!* This explains why so many women are gravitating eventually to small organizations, or forming their own companies. The National Association of Women Business Owners estimates that there are over 7.7 million businesses in the U.S. owned by women.

(5) The fifth and final problem facing women especially is that of **sexual harassment** or abuse in the workplace.

• While harassment in this crazy topsy-turvy world can sometimes be inflicted by women managers on the men or women they work with, or by males on males, the vast majority of harassment is done by males to females: and the harassment ranges from subtle to yucky to gross to demonic. This is particularly likely in 'the blue-collar world,' or any job where men are the dominant job-holders.

• The crux of the problem lies in *some* men's ignorance, some men's meanness, some men's *power* needs, and some men's assumption that women basically think like they do. As for the latter, no, no, men and women do not think alike, as John Gray has been spending some years convincing the world. *Men are from Mars, Women are from Venus.*

• Evidence: 75% of men in the workplace find sexual advances from the opposite sex *flattering*, while 75% of women in the workplace find them *offensive.*[5]

• Further evidence: many good-hearted men regard an offer to help a woman colleague or client, particularly outside of working hours, as innocent; whereas many good-hearted women are deeply suspicious of such offers, often due to prior experience with such offers from bad-hearted men, who intended it as a prelude to seduction.

Now, if you are a woman and someone in your workplace is overtly harassing you, sexually or otherwise, making your life truly miserable, you have three courses of action open to you:

• The first is to pray he or she will go away. Sometimes they will. It helps if you give a nice unambiguous "No" to any sexual propositions -- veiled or overt -- and a nice firm, "I'm going to pretend this conversation never took place" in response to any crude language. Silence is not golden. If you have kept silent, please when next you go home, practice in front of a mirror if you must, "I will not keep silent. I will tell this person, No, no, no. I will not keep silent." If you can't bring yourself to break your silence, then I urge you to do whatever you need to do, with therapy, group work, or whatever, to build up your self-confidence. If you have already said No, and it hasn't changed a thing, then plan on leaving. Incidentally, when women are asked why they did not protest harassment on the job, their universal reply is: "Because I couldn't afford to risk losing the job." Sometimes that's because they love the work, and the pay is fabulous. More often than not, however, this clinging to their present job-turned-bad arises from their lack of confidence in their ability to go find another job of equal merit. In other words, their problem is lack of knowledge about the job-hunt. Go fix *that* lack of knowledge, and you will be better able to decide what to do about the harassment. Study this book. You *must* realize that you do have the ability to find another job of equal merit, and without harassment.

• The second course of action is to file a lawsuit. It is an idea which is becoming increasingly attractive, especially if you have witnesses to the offending behavior, and a lawyer who is experienced with these kinds of cases. The only thing you must recognize is that such a lawsuit sometimes takes *forever,* and I mean *forever.* As I write, the Equal Employment Opportunity Commission in the U.S. has a backlog of 97,000 cases.[6] Count the cost, also: I have counseled three women whose lawsuit, some years ago, dramatically affected their present employability. Future employers may see you as 'a troublemaker.' You can mitigate this, perhaps, before you file, by trying to

---

5. According to a survey done in the U.S., in 1992.
6. If you decide to file a suit, you must consult a lawyer *experienced in such matters.* You may also wish to read articles such as "Getting Justice Is No Easy Task," in the May 13, 1996 issue of *Business Week.* Look it up in the archives at your local library, or online (the *Business Week* site on America Online).

find out if any of your co-workers have endured such harassment, and getting them to enter into the lawsuit with you -- so that it is more of a group action. Needless to say, if you're planning on retiring, or going into business for yourself, or if you plan on going to work for some new employer -- female or male -- who will regard you as a heroine on account of this lawsuit, then this last point is moot.

• The third course of action open to you, as I mentioned earlier, is to leave. Don't tell yourself, *"Hey, it's a good job and I like everything else about it, so I'll just put up with the sexual innuendos, leers, or abuse."* No, no:

> A 'good job' with sexual harassment present
> is by definition a bad job.

My advice to you, for what it's worth, is that if you are being harassed, and you decide not to file a suit, *don't* trade your self-esteem just for a paycheck. Make plans -- even long-range plans -- to leave, if your tormentor doesn't leave first! Prepare the groundwork *now* by increasing your command of the job-hunt. Devour this book. Do all the exercises. Really sharpen your job-hunting skills. And when you're confident about your ability to go find another job, go find it.

For Further Reading

The WomanSource Catalog & Review: Tools for Connecting the Community of Women, edited by Ilene Rosoff. Celestial Arts, P.O. Box 7123, Berkeley, CA 94707. 1995. Countless resources for women; an immensely helpful book.

Petrocelli, William, and Repa, Barbara Kate, *Sexual Harassment on the Job: What it is and how to stop it.* Nolo Press, 950 Parker St., Berkeley, CA 94710-9867. 1995. Very enlightening and helpful.

McCann, Nancy Dodd, and McGinn, Thomas A., *Harassed: 100 Women Define Inappropriate Behavior in the Workplace.* Business One Irwin, Homewood, IL 60430. 1992. Discusses one situation after another, and then tells what percentage of the women in their survey felt this situation represented harassment. Men will find this very enlightening.

Nivens, Beatryce, *Careers for Women without College Degrees.* McGraw-Hill Book Company, 11 West 19th St., New York, NY 10011. 1988. Has some useful information about the skills required for some typical occupations that a woman might be considering. She has also written: *How To Change Careers.* 1990. The Putnam Publishing Group, 390 Murray Hill Pkwy., Dept. B, East Rutherford, NJ 07073.

Caroline Bird, *Lives of Our Own: Secrets of Salty Old Women.* Houghton Mifflin, 1995.

Executives

And Job-Hunting

Well, you may have quit or you may have been let go. If the latter, be aware that if you are a U.S. executive or manager in your middle years or beyond, working in an organization of 20 or more employees, and you feel you were let go because of your age -- even if it was in the midst of a downsizing -- you may have a discrimination case under a U.S. law called the Age Discrimination in Employment Act (ADEA).

Merely saying, "I *feel* I was let go because of my age" isn't sufficient. You need evidence. So, keep a record of *any* statements made to you by your superiors that substantiate your claim and your *feelings* ('we need younger blood in here,' or 'we could get two college graduates for what we are paying you,' etc.). Poor performance ratings, suddenly, after years of good ones -- with no reason -- may also substantiate your claim. If you have such evidence, and you decide you do want to pursue legal remedies, a stamped self-addressed envelope sent to the National Employment Lawyers Association, 600 Harrison St., #535, San Francisco, CA 94107 will get you names of attorneys who practice employment law. Hie thee to one of them, evidence in hand, and see what they think.

If this route is of no interest to you, as well it may not be for any number of good reasons, and you just want to get on with your next job-hunt, be aware that because of your age and other factors you will face some subtle difficulties during your upcoming job-hunt. You *can* overcome these difficulties. But you do need to be aware of what they are. And, how to overcome them.

The first is, there are a lot of other executives who are job-hunting at the same time you are. The current mania for downsizing, mergers and so forth, has hit white-collar workers *hard*. There are a lot of middle- to upper-level managers out there, who suddenly find themselves looking for work after twenty years at a place. That's why the average job-search period for executives, recently, was 6.8 months.[7]

Secondly, the length of your job-search will likely be related to your age, and the amount of salary that you are seeking. One large outplacement firm kept records and discovered that if an executive was 25–34 years of age, the average length of their job-hunt was about 20 weeks, but if over 55 years in age, it took almost 30 weeks. They further discovered that for those seeking an annual salary of $40,000 to $75,000, the average length of their job-hunt was about 25 weeks, while for those seeking more than $100,000, the average length of their job-hunt was almost 30 weeks.[8] That's what you *may* be up against.

---

7. According to Drake Beam Morin Inc., for the year 1990.

8. Reported in the *National Business Employment Weekly,* in the 8/27/89 edition. Statistics were for the year 1989.

However, these statistics reflect the manner in which executives go job-hunting. Many are completely baffled by this process, and have *no idea* how to go job-hunting -- except to rely almost exclusively on the sending out of resumes. That route always has a bad track record, and may account for why the average job-hunt of executives takes so long. A better job-hunting method would equal a shorter time out of work, in many, many cases.

If you are having difficulty finding work, then you must reconsider *how* you are conducting your job-hunt. Do read, mark, learn and inwardly digest the chapter in *Parachute* called "The Determined Job-Hunter," and *do* the Quick Job-Hunting Map here in this *Workbook*.

The rules you must follow in your job-hunt are easy to master, since they are the same for you as they are for everyone: *Know your skills. Know what kind of work you want to do. Talk to people who are doing it. Find out how they like the work, how they found their job. Do some research, in your chosen geographical area, on organizations which interest you, to find what they do and what kinds of problems they or their industry are wrestling with. Then identify and seek out the person who actually has the power to hire you there, for the job you want; use your contacts to get in to see him or her. Show this person with the power to hire you how you can help them with their problems; and how you would stand out as 'one employee in a hundred.'* In all of this, cut no corners, take no shortcuts.

Remember this *above all:* all employers divide into two groups: those who will be bothered by your age or by the fact that you were laid off in a downsizing or merger, and those who won't be -- and will hire you, so long as you can do the job. Your task is to find the second group of employers, and just thank the first very politely for their time.

When you are being interviewed, be aware that in the U.S. the ADEA forbids the employer to ask your age.

For Further Reading

Burton, Mary Lindley, and Wedemeyer, Richard A., *In Transition: From the Harvard Business School Club of New York's Career Management Seminar.* HarperBusiness, 10 E. 53rd St., New York, NY 10022. 1991.

Retirement

And Job-Hunting

'Retirement' has become a nebulous concept. It used to mean *not working* -- sitting on the front porch, or on the beach, or taking a cruise -- but in general enjoying a life of leisure. However, a recent *Gallup Poll/USA Today* survey turned up the fact that 70% of baby boomers said they expect to work after they 'retire,' whether that is at age 65 or earlier.[9] So now, 'retirement' often means simply a time for a *career change*, if one doesn't continue at what one has always been doing.

Incidentally, the number of people in the U.S. who retire annually is nearly 2 million, and the median age (of retirement) currently is age 62. In fact, one-third of all retirees do so by age 55.[10]

Of course, not *everyone* works after they 'retire.' For many, retirement *is* retirement. They drop out of the workforce, and half of them, according to a relatively recent study,[11] are satisfied with that situation, while one-quarter are very unhappy over the fact that they aren't working. (In point of fact, one out of three retired men does return to the workforce, usually within two years.)[12] *The remaining one-quarter not accounted for above, are people who are simply unable to work, presumably because of their health.*

In the U.S., if you are a retiree receiving Social Security, and have decided to go looking for work, your desire to work will be complicated by the Social Security requirements, which amount to a kind of *disincentive* to work. In 1996, the law is this: once you are 62 years of age, and through the time you are 64, you lose $1 of Social Security benefits for every $2 earned above $8,280; once you are 65 and through the time you are 69, you lose $1 of benefits for every $3 earned above $12,500.

In 1997, this latter limit rises to $13,500; in 1998, to $14,500; in 1999, to $15,500; in the year 2000, to $17,000; in 2001, to $25,000; and in the year 2002, to $30,000.

The limit for the 62–64 year age range remains *indexed* to the cost of living for each year, so the changes there should be comparatively slight.

In any and all of these years, if you are past your 70th birthday, you can earn without limit, and you will lose none of your benefits no matter how much you earn.

---

9. *USA Today*, 4/29/96.

10. *Monthly Labor Review*, July 1992, "Trends in retirement age by sex, 1950-2005."

11. Reported in *The New York Times*, 4/22/90.

12. Reported in *American Demographics*, 12/90. Statistics for women in retirement were not covered in the article.

> These Social Security rules and limits do get changed by Congress
> and time, so be sure not to take my word for any of this, but check
> with your local Social Security office to find out if this has changed
> between the time I write this and the time you read this; and remem-
> ber, you're still subject to the regular employment taxes, on what you
> earn, just like everyone else.

If you want to work primarily (or solely) to supplement your retirement
income, the foregoing may be a disincentive. On the other hand, if you want
to work for the pure joy of working, the economic disincentive will probably
not faze you. *And,* you can always volunteer your time without cost to the
place where you are dying to serve.

If you do decide to job-hunt, you may face particular difficulties because
of your age, as you know. You can overcome those difficulties, of course, but
to do so you must read, mark, learn and inwardly digest the chapter in
Parachute called "The Determined Job-Hunter," and *do* the Quick Job-
Hunting Map here in this *Workbook.*

The rules you must follow in your job-hunt are easy to master, since they
are the same for you as they are for everyone: *Know your skills. Know what
kind of work you want to do. Talk to people who are doing it. Find out how they like
the work, how they found their job. Do some research, in your chosen geographical
area, on organizations which interest you, to find what they do and what kinds of
problems they or their industry are wrestling with. Then identify and seek out the person who actually has the power to hire you there, for the job you want; use your contacts to get in to see him or her. Show this person with the power to hire you how you
can help them with their problems; and how you would stand out as 'one employee in
a hundred.'* In all of this, cut no corners, take no shortcuts.

Remember this above all: all employers divide into two groups: those who
will be bothered by your age, and those who won't be -- and will hire you, so
long as you can do the job. Your task is to find the second group of employers, and just thank the first very politely for their time.

For Further Reading

If you want some guidance about possible places to retire to, in the U.S.,
there are these resources:

Richard Boyer and David Savageau, *Places Rated Almanac: Your Guide to
Finding the Best Places to Live in North America.* rev. ed. 1993. Prentice-Hall, 15
Columbus Circle, New York, NY 10023. A marvelous book. Immensely helpful for anyone weighing where to move next. All 343 metropolitan areas are
ranked and compared for living costs, job outlook, crime, health, transportation, education, the arts, recreation, and climate. Has numerous helpful diagrams, charts, and maps, showing (for example) earthquake risk areas,
tornado and hurricane risk areas, the snowiest areas, the stormiest areas, the
driest areas, and so on. Highly recommended. A knockout of a book.

Savageau, David, *Retirement Places Rated.* 3rd ed. 1990. Prentice Hall Press,
15 Columbus Circle, New York, NY 10023. 151 top retirement areas ranked

and compared for costs of living, housing, climate, personal safety, services, work opportunities, and leisure living. Highly recommended. Tremendously useful. He updates it periodically.

If you want to know what retired people do, by way of work, after retirement, the classic on this subject is:

Bird, Caroline, *Second Careers: New Ways to Work After 50.* 1992. Little, Brown and Company, Time Warner Bldg., 1271 Avenue of the Americas, New York, NY 10020. The subject of this book is not what 'seniors' *ought* to do after age 50, but what in fact they *do* do . . . and why. This book is her 'report to the nation' of her analysis of some 36,000 questionnaires sent in by readers of *Modern Maturity* Magazine. Highly recommended.

Ex-Military

And Job-Hunting

If you are an ex-military person who has decided to look for work outside the military, in the general workplace, you already know that you will have some problems convincing the world you know *anything* except how to wage war. You *can* convince them, but it will take work.

Your major problem is that you speak a different language from those out there in the world. You have been living in a sub-culture within our general culture, and this sub-culture is in many respects like the general job-market, *except* that it has its own unique vocabulary. It is *crucial* that you sit down and inventory the skills you have been using during your time in the military. Take especial care to take your skills and fields of knowledge out of the military *jargon*, and translate them into language that is understood in the general marketplace.

There are three aids to help you do this:

The first is 'The Quick Job-Hunting Map' at the beginning of this workbook.

Secondly, each service's personnel manuals has a section where military jobs and tasks are cross-coded to the civilian *Dictionary of Occupational Titles.*

Thirdly, there is a two-volume Military Occupation Training Data series, available from Defense Manpower Data Center, 1600 Wilson Blvd., Suite 400, Arlington VA 22209, which does the same thing.

If you are or were an officer, you should know that the Retired Officers Association (TROA), 201 N. Washington Street, Alexandria, VA 22314-2529, 703-838-8117, has an Officer Placement Service which maintains a comprehensive job-search library, a computerized placement service, and resume critiques for their members. It is, unfortunately, open only to officers, and only to those who become members of TROA.

Officer or not, your salvation depends on the same creative job-hunting -- and career-changing -- methods as anyone else.

If you are having difficulty finding work, then you must read, mark, learn and inwardly digest the chapter in *Parachute* called "The Determined Job-Hunter," and *do* the Quick Job-Hunting Map here in this *Workbook*.

The rules you must follow in your job-hunt are easy to master, since they are the same for you as they are for everyone: *Know your skills. Know what kind of work you want to do. Talk to people who are doing it. Find out how they like the work, how they found their job. Do some research, in your chosen geographical area, on organizations which interest you, to find what they do and what kinds of problems they or their industry are wrestling with. Then identify and seek out the person who actually has the power to hire you there, for the job you want; use your contacts to get in to see him or her. Show this person with the power to hire you how you can help them with their problems; and how you would stand out as 'one employee in a hundred.'* In all of this, cut no corners, take no shortcuts.

Remember this *above all:* all employers divide into two groups: those who will be bothered by the fact you were in the military, and those who won't be -- and will hire you, so long as you can do the job. Your task is to find the second group of employers, and just thank the first very politely for their time.

For Further Reading

Schlachter, Gail Ann, and Weber, R. David, *Financial Aid for Veterans, Military Personnel, and Their Dependents 1990–1991.* 1990. Reference Service Press, 1100 Industrial Road, Suite 9, San Carlos, CA 94070. Outlines over 1,000 programs open to veterans and their dependents. See if there is an updated version, by the time you read this.

Clergy
And Job-Hunting

If you are an ordained person who has decided to look for work outside the church, in the general workplace, you already know that you will have some problems convincing the world you know *anything* except theology. As a matter of fact, you *can* convince them, but it will take work.

Your major problem is that you speak a different language from those out there in the world. Like the military (above), you have been living in a sub-culture within our general culture, which describes your skills and work-experience in its own unique vocabulary. It is *crucial* that you sit down and inventory the skills you have been using during your time in the church, and that you take especial care to *translate* your skills and fields of knowledge out of the clerical *jargon* and into language that is understood in the general marketplace.

You must read, mark, learn and inwardly digest the chapters in *Parachute* called "For the Determined Job-Hunter," and *do* the Quick Job-Hunting Map here in this *Workbook*.

The rules you must follow in your job-hunt are easy to master, since they are the same for you as they are for everyone: *Know your skills. Know what kind of work you want to do. Talk to people who are doing it. Find out how they like the work, how they found their job. Do some research, in your chosen geographical area, on organizations which interest you, to find what they do and what kinds of problems they or their industry are wrestling with. Then identify and seek out the person who actually has the power to hire you there, for the job you want; use your contacts to get in to see him or her. Show this person with the power to hire you how you can help them with their problems; and how you would stand out as 'one employee in a hundred.'* In all of this, cut no corners, take no shortcuts.

Remember this *above all:* all employers divide into two groups: those who will be bothered by the fact you were in the clergy, and those who won't be -- and will hire you, so long as you can do the job. Your task is to find the second group of employers, and just thank the first very politely for their time.

For Further Reading

In case you want further reading, or counseling, the books and counselors who look at job-hunting and career-changing particularly from a religious point of view are to be found on page *230 ff.*

The So-Called
Handicapped

And Job-Hunting

If you are a person with a handicap or disability, and are looking for work, you already know that you face especial difficulties during your job-hunt. You *can* overcome these difficulties. But you do need to be aware of what they are.

The first is that of *language*. There is much debate in our culture about how to describe those of us who have disabilities or handicaps. This debate is founded on the belief that *language* enshrines prejudice, and that if we can change the language we can change the prejudice. I understand the logic of this, but am dumbfounded at how obstinate prejudice is, in the face of *all* attempts to alter it. I have reluctantly come to the conclusion that changing *language* does not change the human *heart*. Hence, I think *politically correct* language is misguided, as it has turned the whole matter of disability into a joke: *physically-challenged*, etc.

I think you can call yourself whatever you wish. I liked a wonderful senior deaf and blind woman who was interviewed in the national press this past year. She said, "I'm not *disabled* -- like a car. I'm *handicapped* -- as in golf."

There are, of course, employers who are prejudiced, irrespective of what language you use to describe yourself. If you have a physical, mental, emotional, or other disability, and are looking for work, *of course* you are going to run into them. It helps if you remember this above all: all employers divide into *two* groups: those who will be bothered by your disability, and those who won't be -- and will hire you, so long as you can do the job.

Your task is to find the second group of employers, and just thank the first very politely for their time, plus secure any referrals they may be able to suggest.

If you are having difficulty finding work, then you must read, mark, learn and inwardly digest the chapter in *Parachute* called "The Determined Job-Hunter," and *do* the Quick Job-Hunting Map here in this *Workbook*.

The rules you must follow in your job-hunt are easy to master, since they are the same for you as they are for everyone: *Know your skills. Know what kind of work you want to do. Talk to people who are doing it. Find out how they like the work, how they found their job. Do some research, in your chosen geographical area, on organizations which interest you, to find what they do and what kinds of problems they or their industry are wrestling with. Then identify and seek out the person who actually has the power to hire you there, for the job you want; use your contacts to get in to see him or her. Show this person with the power to hire you how you can help them with their problems; and how you would stand out as 'one employee in a hundred.'* In all of this, cut no corners, take no shortcuts.

For Further Reading

I would like to list here all the resources available to you in your job-hunt, but this has proved to be a list that is too long for this *Workbook*. The list is available as a separate booklet, together with some extended advice on my part as to how you conduct interviews, and so forth; you can order it from the publisher if you want further help. It may also be in your local bookstore. It is:

Bolles, Richard N., *Job-Hunting Tips For The So-Called Handicapped or People Who Have Disabilities. A Supplement to What Color Is Your Parachute?* 1991. Order from Ten Speed Press, Box 7123, Berkeley, CA 94707. 61 pp. $4.95.[13]

Titles published since my booklet, include:

Jeffrey Allen's *Successful Job Search Strategies for the Disabled: Understanding the ADA.* 1994. John Wiley & Sons, Inc., 605 Third Ave., New York, NY 10158.

Gail Ann Schlachter & R. David Weber, *Financial Aid for the Disabled and Their Families, 1996-1998.* 1996. Reference Service Press, Suite 9, 1100 Industrial Rd., San Carlos CA 94070-4131.

Minorities

And Job-Hunting

If you are a member of some minority group looking for work, you already know that you may face especial difficulties during your job-hunt. You *can* overcome these difficulties. But you do need to be aware of what they are.

The principal one is the mental view that others have, by which they see the whole world in terms of 'tribes.' I call this mental view *tribalism*, and I regard it as the root of most of the troubles throughout the world: cf. Ireland, Bosnia, Iraq, the Middle East, Liberia, Somalia, Russia, and -- *of course* -- the U.S. So long as whites remain dominant among employers, here, *tribalism* and its bastard offspring, *prejudice*, is something you have to take into account.

If you are having difficulty finding work in the face of such prejudice, then you *must* read, mark, learn and inwardly digest the chapters in *Parachute* called "For the Determined Job-Hunter," and *do* the Quick Job-Hunting Map here in this *Workbook*.

The rules you must follow in your job-hunt are easy to master, since they are the same for you as they are for everyone: *Know your skills. Know what*

---

13. If you wish to save this money, you can consult your local library to see if it has a copy of the booklet, *or* a copy of the 1990 or 1991 editions of *Parachute*, since this stuff first appeared as an Appendix in the back of those editions.

kind of work you want to do. Talk to people who are doing it. Find out how they like the work, how they found their job. Do some research, in your chosen geographical area, on organizations which interest you, to find what they do and what kinds of problems they or their industry are wrestling with. Then identify and seek out the person who actually has the power to hire you there, for the job you want; use your contacts to get in to see him or her. Show this person with the power to hire you how you can help them with their problems; and how you would stand out as 'one employee in a hundred.' In all of this, cut no corners, take no shortcuts.

Remember this *above all:* all employers divide into two groups: those who will be bothered by the fact you belong to a minority, and those who won't be -- and will hire you, so long as you can do the job. Your task is to find the second group of employers, and just thank the first very politely for their time.

For Further Reading

Johnson, Willis L., ed., *Directory of Special Programs for Minority Group Members: Career Information Services, Employment Skills Banks, Financial Aid Sources,* 5th ed. 1990. Garrett Park Press, Box 190, Garrett Park, MD 20896.

Minority Organizations: A National Directory. 4th ed. 1992. Garrett Park Press, Box 190, Garrett Park, MD 20896. An annotated directory of 9,700 Black, Hispanic, Native American, and Asian American organizations.

The Black Resource Guide. 10th ed., 1992. Black Resource Guide, Inc., 501 Oneida Pl., NW, Washington, DC 20011. A comprehensive list of over 3,000 black resources or organizations in the U.S.

Gays & Lesbians

And Job-Hunting

If you are a gay or lesbian looking for work, and want to be 'up front' about this, you already know that you will face especial difficulties during your job-hunt. You *can* overcome these difficulties.

Over the past decade or two, 'the Gay movement' in the U.S. and elsewhere in the world has made tremendous strides in gaining acceptance for their members within the broader society. Nonetheless, this is still 'but a drop in the bucket.' Vast antagonism to homosexuals still remains, making your orientation a definite handicap when you approach employers, looking for a job.

Of course you can go looking for companies known to be the best places for you to work. There is, for example, a book by Ed Mickens, called *The 100 Best Companies for Gay Men and Lesbians,* Pocket Books, Simon & Schuster, 1994.

Further, if you are in the San Francisco area or want to be, there is a Personnel Agency whose mission is "to increase employment opportunities targeted, but not limited to, the Gay and Lesbian Community." They are at 2358 Market St., near Castro, in San Francisco, CA 94114. Their phone is 415-626-4663, and they also have a site on the Internet: http://www.best. com/~bach/

But if you want to conduct a broad search, and simply choose a company that is your preferred place to work, without knowing anything about their prejudice or lack of prejudice, your reception is less certain.

If you are having difficulty finding work in the face of such prejudice, then you *must* read, mark, learn and inwardly digest the chapters in *Parachute* called "For the Determined Job-Hunter," and *do* the Quick Job-Hunting Map here in this *Workbook.*

The rules you must follow in your job-hunt are easy to master, since they are the same for you as they are for everyone: *Know your skills. Know what kind of work you want to do. Talk to people who are doing it. Find out how they like the work, how they found their job. Do some research, in your chosen geographical area, on organizations which interest you, to find what they do and what kinds of problems they or their industry are wrestling with. Then identify and seek out the person who actually has the power to hire you there, for the job you want; use your contacts to get in to see him or her. Show this person with the power to hire you how you can help them with their problems; and how you would stand out as 'one employee in a hundred.'* In all of this, cut no corners, take no shortcuts.

Remember this *above all:* all employers divide into two groups: those who will be bothered by the fact that you are a gay or lesbian, and those who absolutely won't, and will hire you if you are able to do the job. Your task is to find the second group of employers, and just thank the first very politely for their time.

For Further Reading

The Alyson Almanac: The Fact Book of the Lesbian and Gay Community, Boston, Alyson Publications, Inc., 40 Plympton St., Boston, MA 02118. 1993. Has a section on laws and attitudes, state by state and in over 100 countries.

The Gay and Lesbian Address Book, by the editors of *Out* Magazine, Perigree, published by Berkley Publishing Group, 200 Madison Ave., New York, NY 10016. 1995. Lists all kinds of organizations and individuals.

The Big Gay Book: A Man's Survival Guide for the '90s, edited by John Preston. Plume, a division of Penguin Books USA Inc., 375 Hudson St., New York, NY 10014. 1991. Lists all kinds of organizations.

The Corporate Closet: The Professional Lives of Gay Men in America, by James D. Woods with Jay H. Lucas. The Free Press, a division of Macmillan, Inc., 866 Third Ave., New York, NY 10022. 1994. Discusses all the different issues about how to conduct oneself in the workplace: the asexual professional, dodging the issue, playing it straight, etc.

Immigrants

And Job-Hunting

If you are newly arrived in the U.S., and are looking for work, you already know that you face especial difficulties during your job-hunt. You *can* overcome these difficulties. But you do need to be aware of what they are. And, how to overcome them.

Most of what you need to know, on both counts, can be learned in two ways. First of all, by talking to other immigrants, who have been here longer than you have, and have already 'learned the ropes.' And secondly, by reading *Parachute* thoroughly.

You will discover the chief job-hunting handicaps you need to overcome are your level of education, and your fluency (or lack of fluency) in English. See the earlier section on "High School Students and Job-Hunting."

If you are having difficulty finding work, then you must read, mark, learn and inwardly digest the chapters in *Parachute* called "For the Determined Job-Hunter," and *do* the Quick Job-Hunting Map here in this *Workbook*.

The rules you must follow in your job-hunt are easy to master, since they are the same for you as they are for everyone: *Know your skills. Know what kind of work you want to do. Talk to people who are doing it. Find out how they like the work, how they found their job. Do some research, in your chosen geographical area, on organizations which interest you, to find what they do and what kinds of problems they or their industry are wrestling with. Then identify and seek out the person who actually has the power to hire you there, for the job you want; use your contacts to get in to see him or her. Show this person with the power to hire you how you can help them with their problems; and how you would stand out as 'one employee in a hundred.'* In all of this, cut no corners, take no shortcuts.

Remember this *above all:* all employers divide into two groups: those who will be bothered by the fact you are newly arrived in this country, and those who won't be -- and will hire you, so long as you can do the job. Your task is to find the second group of employers, and just thank the first very politely for their time.

For Further Reading

Friedenberg, Joan E., Ph.D., and Bradley, Curtis H., Ph.D., *Finding a Job in the United States.* 1988, 1986. NTC Publishing Group, 4255 W. Touhy Ave., Lincolnwood, IL 60646-1975. A guide for immigrants, refugees, limited-English-proficient job-seekers, foreign-born professionals -- anyone who is seeking work in the United States. It contains job information based on the successful experience of job-seekers, plus advice from the U.S. Department of Labor. Includes information about American job customs and laws related to immigration, as well as a systematic plan for job-hunting.

Also, Stephen Rosen, Chairman of the Science and Technology Advisory Board, 575 Madison Ave., 22nd Floor, New York, NY 10022-2585, 212-940-6415, specializes in working with newly arrived immigrants with a science, engineering, or professional background -- his specialty is Russian immigrants, in particular. For people in the New York City area, he runs a 12-session program called Scientific Career Transitions, for which there is no charge.

People In Recovery
And Job-Hunting

If you are a person with a previous history of substance abuse, and you are now 'in recovery' and are looking for work, you already know what I'm going to say: you may face especial difficulties during the hiring interviews. You *can* overcome these difficulties. But in order to do so, you must read, mark, learn and inwardly digest the chapters in *Parachute* called "For the Determined Job-Hunter," and *do* the Quick Job-Hunting Map here in this *Workbook*.

The rules you must follow in your job-hunt are easy to master, since they are the same for you as they are for everyone: *Know your skills. Know what kind of work you want to do. Talk to people who are doing it. Find out how they like the work, how they found their job. Do some research, in your chosen geographical area, on organizations which interest you, to find what they do and what kinds of problems they or their industry are wrestling with. Then identify and seek out the person who actually has the power to hire you there, for the job you want; use your contacts to get in to see him or her. Show this person with the power to hire you how you can help them with their problems; and how you would stand out as 'one employee in a hundred.'* In all of this, cut no corners, take no shortcuts.

Remember this *above all:* all employers divide into two groups: those who will be bothered by the fact you are in recovery, and those who won't be -- and will hire you, so long as you can do the job. Your task is to find the second group of employers, and just thank the first very politely for their time.

For Further Reading

Tanenbaum, Nat, and Eric A., *The Career Seekers: A Program for Career Recovery.* 1988. This book is for people who are actively practicing any 12-step program, or are in counseling for co-dependency; but its principles apply to all who see themselves as 'recovering people.' A useful supplement to *Parachute*. Order from Nat Tanenbaum, 21 Timberlane Circle, Pisgah Forest, NC 28768, 704-884-2995.

Whitfield, M.D., Charles L., *A Gift to Myself.* 1990. Health Communications, Inc., 3201 SW 15th St., Deerfield Beach, FL 33442. Deals with root emotional issues often blocking job-hunters in recovery.

Ex-Offenders

And Job-Hunting

Currently, more than 5.1 million people in the U.S. are behind bars or on parole or probation.

If you are an ex-offender, and are looking for work, *of course* you are going to face especial difficulties during the hiring interviews, because of your history. You *can* deal with this problem, though you may need help.

If you decide you want to work on getting a college degree while you are in prison, get your hands on a book by John Bear called *College Degrees by Mail: 100 Good Schools that Offer Bachelor's, Master's, Doctorates and Law Degrees by Home Study*. 1997. Ten Speed Press, Box 7123, Berkeley, CA 94707. It has an Appendix entitled, "Advice for People in Prison."

Once you're out, and job-hunting, the Federal/State Employment Offices can often be of particular assistance to ex-offenders. All offices can provide for bonding of ex-offenders, if needed to obtain employment. They also have information on tax breaks for employers who hire ex-offenders. The larger offices even have Ex-Offender Specialists.

There is also *The Fortune Society*, 39 W. 19th St. (between 5th & 6th Avenues), New York, NY 10011. 212-206-7070. JoAnne Page, Executive Director. This Society works primarily with people who can come to their office, but they can also direct ex-offenders to the *Prisoners' Assistance Directory*, developed by the ACLU; the *Directory of Programs Serving Families of Adult Offenders*, published by the U.S. Department of Justice; *Post-Release Assistance Programs for Prisoners*, published by McFarland & Co., Inc.; and the *Guide to Community Services*, a publication of the Community Resource Network -- all of which will list resources for the area of the country in which you wish to find employment. The Society publishes the *Fortune News*, which is sent to you if you send them a contribution.

If all else fails, contact your local Chamber of Commerce or United Way, to see if they can tell you which community service organizations work with ex-offenders in your town or city.

If, in spite of all these resources, you are still having trouble finding work, then you *must* read, mark, learn and inwardly digest the chapters in *Parachute* called "For the Determined Job-Hunter," and *do* the Quick Job-Hunting Map here in this *Workbook*.

The rules you must follow in your job-hunt are easy to master, since they are the same for you as they are for everyone: *Know your skills. Know what kind of work you want to do. Talk to people who are doing it. Find out how they like the work, how they found their job. Do some research, in your chosen geographical area, on organizations which interest you, to find what they do and what kinds of problems they or their industry are wrestling with. Then identify and seek out the person who actually has the power to hire you there, for the job you want; use your contacts to get in to see him or her. Show this person with the power to hire you how you can help them with their problems; and how you would stand out as 'one employee in a hundred.'* In all of this, cut no corners, take no shortcuts.

Remember this *above all:* all employers divide into two groups: those who will be bothered by your incarceration, and those who won't be -- and will hire you, so long as you can do the job. Your task is to find the second group of employers, and just thank the first very politely for their time.

For Further Reading

The Correctional Educator, Annual Employment Issue, published by the Correctional Education Company, $15 for this special issue. Errol Craig Sull, President, 370 Franklin St., Buffalo, NY 14202. 716-849-0247. Fax: 716-845-5393. $79 for five issues annually. Sample copy sent on request. Also: *The Ex-Inmate's Complete Guide to Successful Employment,* by Errol Craig Sull. $29.95 plus $5.00 Shipping & Handling.

American Correctional Association, 8025 Laurel Lakes Ct., Laurel, MD 20707-5075. 301-206-5059 or 800-825-2665. Publishes: "As Free As An Eagle."

Interstate Publishers, P.O. Box 50, Danville, IL 61834-0050. 217-446-0500 or 800-843-4774. Publishes a parole planning manual called "From the Inside Out."

Open Inc., P.O. Box 566025, Dallas TX 75356-6025. 214-271-1971. Offender Preparation and Education Network. Publishes "99 Days & a Get-up," and "Man, I Need a Job!"

Manatee Publishing, 4835 North O'Conner St., #134435, Irving, TX 75062. Publishes: "Getting Out and Staying Out."

Want More Resources?

If you want more books than are included in the preceding sections, there are three places where you can look:

(1) Your **local bookstores** -- go to more than one, browse, and see what they have. Disadvantage: you have to buy the book, if you want it. Advantage: they've got the latest most up-to-date edition *(usually -- though not always)*. Furthermore, they can order for you almost any book *that is still in print* -- and you'll know *that*, by whether or not it is listed in a reference book most bookstores have, called *Books In Print.* Ask.

(2) Your local **public libraries**, or nearby community college library. If they have a friendly reference librarian, by all means ask to see him or her. They can be worth their weight in gold to you. Tell them your problem or interest, and see what they can dig up. Disadvantage: a library may not have the latest edition of a book (see what edition of *Parachute* they're carrying, for example). Advantage: you can borrow a book for free, and furthermore, the reference librarian often knows of hidden treasures elsewhere in the library, buried in articles and clippings, which could be the answer to your prayers.

(3) **Mail order**. This is particularly helpful to those who live outside the U.S. There are a number of U.S. mail order places which specialize in career-related or job-hunting books for special populations. Their catalogs are listed in the section for Career Counselors, beginning on page *277ff*. Disadvantage: you have to wait to get the book, though if you phone, you can often order them by Federal Express, so sometimes it's *next day* delivery. Advantage: often you can order it from anywhere in the world, and their listings of career books, tapes, videos and software, are far more extensive than you will find in the average bookstore, or library.

V. How to Find Your Mission in Life

God
and One's Choice of Vocation

Introduction

As I started writing this section, I toyed at first with the idea of following what might be described as an "all-paths approach" to religion. But, after much thought, I decided not to try that. This, because I have read many other writers who tried, and I felt the approach failed miserably. An "all-paths" approach to religion ends up being a "no-paths" approach, even as a woman or man who tries to please everyone ends up pleasing no one. It is the old story of the "universal" vs. the "particular."

Those of us who do career counseling could predict, ahead of time, that trying to stay universal is not likely to be helpful, in writing about religion. We know well from our own field that truly helpful career counseling depends upon defining the **particularity** or uniqueness of each person we try to help. No employer wants to know only what you have in common with everyone else. He or she wants to know what makes you unique and individual. As I have argued throughout this book, the identification and inventory of your uniqueness or *particularity* is crucial if you are ever to find meaningful work.

This particularity invades and carries over to *everything* a person does; it is not suddenly "jettisonable" when he or she turns to religion. Therefore, when I or anyone else writes about religion I believe we **must** write out of our own particularity -- which *starts*, in my case, with the fact that I write, and think, and breathe as a Christian -- as you might expect from the fact that I have been an ordained Episcopalian minister for the last forty-three years. Understandably, then, this article speaks from a Christian perspective. I want you to be aware of that, at the outset.

Balanced against this is the fact that I have always been acutely sensitive to the fact that this is a pluralistic society in which we live, and that I owe a great deal to my readers who may have religious convictions quite different from my own. It has turned out that the people who work or have worked here in my office with me, over the years, have been predominantly of other faiths, mainly Jewish. Furthermore, **Parachute's** more than 5 million readers have not only included Christians of every variety and persuasion, Mormons, Christian Scientists, Jews, members of the Baha'i faith, Hindus, Buddhists, adherents of Islam, but also believers in 'new age' religions, secularists, humanists, agnostics, atheists, and many others. I have therefore tried to be very courteous toward the feelings of all my readers, *while at the same time* counting on them to translate my Christian thought forms into their own thought forms. This ability to thus translate is the indispensable *sine qua non* of anyone who wants to communicate helpfully with others, these days.

In the Judeo-Christian tradition from which I come, one of the indignant Biblical questions is, "Has God forgotten to be gracious?" The answer was a clear No. I think it is important *for all of us* also to seek the same goal. I have therefore labored to make this section gracious as well as helpful.

R. N. B.

How to Find Your Mission in Life

God and One's
Choice of Vocation

How I Came To Write This

Some time ago, a woman asked me how you go about finding out what your Mission in life is. She assumed I would know what she was talking about, because of a diagram which appears a number of times in one of my other books, The Three Boxes of Life:

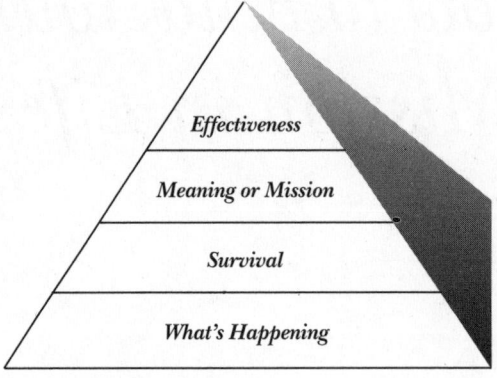

The Issues of the Job-Hunt

As this diagram asserts, the question of one's Mission in life arises naturally as a part of many people's job-hunt.

She told me that what she was looking for was not some careful, dispassionate, philosophical answer, where every statement is hedged about with cautions and caveats -- "It may be . . .' or " It seems to me . . ." Nor did she want to know why I thought what I did, or how I learned it, or what Scriptures support it. "I want you to just speak with passion and conviction," she said, "out of what you most truly feel and believe. For it is some vision that I want. I am hungry for a vision of what I can be. So, just speak to me of what you most truly feel and believe about our mission in life. I will know how to translate your vision into my own thought forms for my own life, when I reflect afterwards upon what you have said. But I want you to talk about this now with passion and conviction -- please."

And so, I did. And I will now tell you what I said to her.

The Motive for Finding
A Sense of Mission in Life

We begin with the fact that, according to fifty years of opinion polls conducted by the Gallup Organization, 94% of us believe in God, 90% of us pray, 88% of us believe God loves us, and 33% of us report we have had a life-changing religious experience (*The People's Religion: American Faith in the 90s.* Macmillan & Co. 1989).

It is hardly surprising therefore, that so many of us are searching these days for some sense of mission. Career counselors are often afraid to give help or guidance here, for fear they will be perceived as trying to talk people into religious belief. It is a groundless fear. Clearly, the overwhelming majority of U.S. job-hunters and career-changers already have their religious beliefs well in place.

But, we want some guidance and help in this area, because we want to *marry* our religious **beliefs** with our **work**, rather than leaving the two -- our religion and our work -- compartmentalized, as two areas of our life which never talk to each other. We *want* them to talk to each other and uplift each other.

This marriage takes the particular form of a search for a Sense of Mission because of our conviction that God has made each of us unique, even as our fingerprints attest. We feel that we are not just another grain of sand lying on the beach called humanity, unnumbered and lost in the 5 billion mass, but that God caused us to be born and put here for some unique reason: so that we might contribute to Life here on earth something no one else can contribute in quite the same way. At its very minimum, then, when we search for a sense of Mission we are searching for reassurance that the world is at least a little bit richer for our being here; and a little bit poorer after our going.

Every keen observer of human nature will know what I mean when I say that those who have found some sense of Mission have a very special joy, "which no one can take from them." It is wonderful to feel that beyond eating, sleeping, working, having pleasure and *it may be* marrying, having children, and growing older, you were set here on Earth for some special purpose, *and* that you can gain some idea of what that purpose is.

So, how does one go about this search?

I would emphasize, at the outset, two cautions. First of all, though I will explain the steps that seem to me to be involved in finding one's Mission -- based on the learnings I have accumulated over some sixty years, I want to caution you that these steps are not the only Way -- by any means. Many people have discovered their Mission by taking other paths. And you may, too. But hopefully what I have to say may shed some light upon whatever path you take.

My second caution is simply this: you would be wise not to try to approach this problem of "your Mission in life" as primarily an **intellectual** puzzle -- for the mind, and the mind alone, to solve. To paraphrase Kahlil Gibran, *Faith* is an oasis in the heart that is not reached merely by the journey of the mind. It is your will and your heart that must be involved in the search as well as your mind. To put it quite simply, it takes the total person to learn one's total Mission.

It also takes the total disciplines of the ages -- not only modern knowledge but also ancient thought, including the wisdom of religion, faith, and the spiritual matters. For, to put it quite bluntly, the question of Mission inevitably leads us to God.

The Main Obstacle in Finding Your Mission in Life: Job-Hunting Compartmentalized from Our Religion or Faith

Mission challenges us to see our job-hunt in relationship to our faith in God, because *Mission* is a religious concept, from beginning to end. It is defined by Webster's as "a continuing task or responsibility that one is destined or fitted to do or specially called upon to undertake," and historically has had two major synonyms: *Calling* and *Vocation*. These, of course, are the same word in two different languages, English and Latin. Regardless of which word is used, it is obvious upon reflection, that a Vocation or Calling implies *Someone who calls*, and that a destiny implies *Someone who determined the destination for us*. Thus, unless one opts for a military or governmental view of the matter, the concept of Mission with relationship to our whole life lands us inevitably in the lap of God, before we have even begun.

There is always the temptation to try to speak of this subject of *Mission* in a secular fashion, without reference to God, as though it might be simply "a purpose you choose for your own life, by identifying your enthusiasms, and then using the clues you find from that exercise to get some purpose you can choose for your life." The language of this temptation is ironic because the substitute word used for "Mission" -- *Enthusiasm* -- is derived from the Greek, '*en theos*,' and literally means "God in us."

It is no accident that so many of the leaders in the job-hunting field over the years -- the late John Crystal, Arthur Miller, Ralph Mattson, Tom and Ellie Jackson, Bernard Haldane, Arthur and Marie Kirn, and myself -- have been people of faith. If you would figure out your Mission in life, you must also be willing to think about God in connection with your job-hunt.

The Secret of Finding Your Mission in Life: Taking It in Stages

The puzzle of figuring out what your Mission in life is, will likely take some time. It is not a *problem* to be solved in a day and a night. It is a *learning process* which has steps to it, much like the process by which we all learned to eat. As a baby we did not tackle adult food right off. As we all recall, there were three stages: first there had to be the mother's milk or bottle, then strained baby foods, and finally -- after teeth and time -- the stuff that grownups chew. Three stages -- and the two earlier stages were not to be disparaged. It was all Eating, just different forms of Eating -- appropriate to our development at the time. But each stage had to be mastered, in turn, before the next could be approached.

The Three Stages of Mission: What We Need to Learn

By coincidence, there are usually three stages also to learning what your Mission in life is, and the two earlier stages are likewise not to be disparaged. It is all "Mission" -- just different forms of Mission, appropriate to your development at the time. But each stage has to be mastered, in turn, before the next can be approached. And so, you may say either of two things: You may say that you have *Three Missions in Life.* Or you may say that you have *One Mission in Life, with three parts to it.* But there is a sense in which you must discover what those three parts are, each in turn, before you can fully answer the question, "What is my Mission in life?" Of course, there is another sense in which you never master any of these stages, but are always growing in understanding and mastery of them, throughout your whole life here on Earth.

As it has been impressed on me by observing many people over the years (admittedly through *Christian spectacles*), it appears that the three parts to your Mission here on Earth can be defined generally as follows:

(1) *Your first Mission here on Earth* is one which you share with the rest of the human race, but it is no less your individual Mission for the fact that it is shared: and it is, **to seek to stand hour by hour in the conscious presence of God, the One from whom your Mission is derived.** *The Missioner before the Mission,* is the rule. In religious language, your Mission here is: *to know God, and enjoy Him forever, and to see His hand in all His works.*

(2) Secondly, once you have begun doing that in an earnest way, *your second Mission here on Earth* is also one which you share with the rest of the human race, but it is no less your individual mission for the fact that it is shared: and that is, **to do what you can, moment by moment, day by day, step by step, to make this world a better place, following the leading and guidance of God's Spirit within you and around you.**

(3) Thirdly, once you have begun doing that in a serious way, *your third Mission here on Earth* is one which is uniquely yours, and that is:

a) **to exercise that Talent which you particularly came to Earth to use -- your greatest gift, which you most delight to use,**

b) **in the place(s) or setting(s) which God has caused to appeal to you the most,**

c) **and for those purposes which God most needs to have done in the world.**

When fleshed out, and spelled out, I think you will find that there you have the definition of your Mission in life. Or, to put it another way, these are the three Missions which you have in life.

The Two Rhythms of the Dance of Mission: Unlearning, Learning, Unlearning, Learning

The distinctive characteristic of these three stages is that in each we are forced to *let go* of some fundamental assumptions which the world has *falsely* taught us, about the nature of our Mission. In other words, throughout this quest and at each stage we find ourselves engaged not merely in a process of *Learning*. We are also engaged in a process of *Un*learning. Thus, we can restate the above three Learnings, in terms of what we also need to *un*learn at each stage:

• We need in the first Stage to *un*learn the idea that our Mission is primarily to keep busy *doing* something (here on Earth), and learn instead that our Mission is first of all to keep busy being something (here on Earth). In Christian language (and others as well), we might say that we were sent here to learn how *to be* sons of God, and daughters of God, before anything else. "*Our Father, who art in heaven . . .*"

• In the second stage, "Being" issues into "Doing." At this stage, we need to *un*learn the idea that everything about our Mission must be *unique* to us, and learn instead that some parts of our Mission here on Earth are *shared* by all human beings: e.g., we were all sent here to bring more gratitude, more kindness, more forgiveness, and more love, into the world. We share this Mission because the task is too large to be accomplished by just one individual.

• We need in the third stage to *un*learn the idea that that part of our Mission which is truly unique, and most truly ours, is something Our Creator just *orders* us to do, without any agreement from our spirit, mind, and heart. (On the other hand, neither is it something that each of us chooses and then merely asks God to bless.) We need to learn that God so honors our free will, that He has ordained our unique Mission be something which we have some part in choosing.

• In this third stage we need also to *un*learn the idea that our unique Mission must consist of some achievement which all the world will see, -- and learn instead that as the stone does not always know what ripples it has caused in the pond whose surface it impacts, so neither we nor those who watch our life will always know *what we have achieved* by our life and by our Mission. *It may be* that by the grace of God we helped bring about a profound change for the better in the lives of other souls around us, but it also may be that this takes place beyond our sight, or after we have gone on. And we may never know what we have accomplished, until we see Him face-to-face after this life is past.

• Most finally, we need to *un*learn the idea that what we have accomplished is our doing, and ours alone. It is God's Spirit breathing in us and through us which helps us to do whatever we do, and so the singular first person pronoun is never appropriate, but only the plural. Not "*I* accomplished this" but "*We* accomplished this, God and I, working together . . ."

That should give you a general overview. But I would like to add some random comments on my part about each of these three Missions of ours here on Earth.

Some Random Comments About Your First Mission in Life

Your first Mission here on Earth is one which you share with the rest of the human race, but it is no less your individual Mission for the fact that it is shared: and that is, **to seek to stand hour by hour in the conscious presence of God, the One from whom your Mission is derived**. The Missioner before the Mission, is the rule. In religious language, your Mission is: to know God, and enjoy Him for ever, and to see His hand in all His works.

Comment 1: How We Might Think of God

Each of us has to go about this primary Mission according to the tenets of his or her own particular religion. But I will speak what I know out of the context of my own particular faith, and you may perhaps translate and apply it to yours. I will speak as a Christian, who believes (passionately) that Christ is the Way and the Truth and the Life. But I also believe, with St. Peter, "that God shows no partiality, but in every nation any one who fears him and does what is right is acceptable to him." (Acts 10:34-35)

Now, Jesus claimed many unique things about Himself and His Mission; but He also spoke of Himself as the great prototype for us all. He called himself "the Son of Man," and He said, "I assure you that the man who believes in me will do the same things that I have done, yes, and he will do even greater things than these . . ." (John 14:12)

Emboldened by His identification of us with His life and His Mission, we might want to remember how He spoke about His Life here on Earth. He put it in this context: "**I came from the Father and have come into the world; again, I am leaving the world and going to the Father.**" (John 16:28)

If there is a sense in which this is, in even the faintest way, true also of our lives (and I shall say in a moment in what sense I think it is true), then instead of calling our great Creator "God" or "Father" right off, we might begin our approach to the subject of religion by referring to the One Who gave us our Mission and sent us to this planet not as "God" or "Father" but -- *just to help our thinking* -- as: "**The One From Whom We Came and The One To Whom We Shall Return**," when this life is done.

If our life here on Earth be at all like Christ's, then this is a true way to think about the One who gave us our Mission. We are not some kind of eternal, pre-existent *being*. We are **creatures**, who once did not exist, and then came into Being, and continue to have our Being, only at the will of our great Creator. But as creatures we are both body and soul; and although we know our body was created in our mother's womb, our soul's origin is a great mystery. Where it came from, at what moment the Lord created it, is something we cannot know. It is not unreasonable to suppose, however, that the great God created our *soul* before it entered our body, and in that sense we did indeed stand before God before we were born; and He is indeed **"The One From Whom We Came and The One To Whom We Shall Return."**

Therefore, before we go searching for "what work was I sent here to do?" we need to establish or in a truer sense *reestablish* -- contact with this **"One From Whom We Came and The One To Whom We Shall Return."** Without this reaching out of the creature to the great Creator, without this reaching out of *the creature with a Mission* to *the One Who Gave Us That Mission*, the question *what is my Mission in life?* is void and null. The *what* is rooted in the *Who;* absent the Personal, one cannot meaningfully discuss The Thing. It is like the adult who cries, "I want to get married," without giving any consideration to *who* it is they want to marry.

Comment 2: How We Might Think of Religion or Faith

In light of this larger view of our creatureliness, we can see that *religion* or *faith* is not a question of whether or not we choose to (*as it is so commonly put*) "have a relationship with God." Looking at our life in a larger context than just our life here on Earth, it becomes apparent that some sort of relationship with God is a given for us, about which we have absolutely no choice. God and we **were and are** related, during the time of our soul's existence before our birth and in the time of our soul's continued existence after our death. The only choice we have is what to do about **The Time In Between**, i.e., what we want the nature of our relationship with God to be during our time here on Earth and how that will affect the *nature* of the relationship, then, after death.

One of the corollaries of all this is that by the very act of being born into a human body, it is an inevitable that we undergo a kind of *amnesia* -- an amnesia which typically embraces not only our nine months in the womb, our baby years, and almost one-third of each day (sleeping), but more importantly any memory of our origin or our destiny. We wander on Earth as an amnesia victim. To seek after Faith, therefore, is to seek to climb back out of that amnesia. Religion or faith is **the hard reclaiming of knowledge we once knew as a certainty**.

Comment 3: The First Obstacle to Executing This Mission

This first Mission of ours here on Earth is not the easiest of Missions, simply because it is the first. Indeed, in many ways, it is the most difficult. All can see that our life here on Earth is a very physical life. We eat, we drink, we sleep, we long to be held, and to hold. We inherit a physical body, with very physical appetites, we walk on the physical earth, and we acquire physical possessions. It is the most alluring of temptations, *in our amnesia*, to come up with just a *Physical* interpretation of this life: to think that the Universe is merely interested in the survival of species. Given this interpretation, the story of our individual life could be simply told: we are born, grow up, pro-create, and die.

But we are ever recalled to do what we came here to do: that without re-jecting the joy of the Physicalness of this life, such as the love of the blue sky and the green grass, we are to reach out beyond all this to **recall** and recover a *Spiritual* interpretation of our life. *Beyond* the physical and *within* the physi-calness of this life, to detect a Spirit and a Person from beyond this Earth who is with us and in us -- the very real and loving and awesome Presence of the great Creator from whom we came -- and the One to whom we once again shall go.

Comment 4: The Second Obstacle to Executing This Mission

It is one of the conditions of our earthly amnesia and our creatureliness that, sadly enough, some very *human* and very *rebellious* part of us *likes* the idea of living in a world where we can be our own god -- and therefore loves the purely Physical interpretation of life, and finds it *anguish* to relinquish it. Traditional Christian vocabulary calls this "**sin**" and has a lot to say about the difficulty it poses for this first part of our Mission. All who live a thoughtful life know that it is true: our greatest enemy in carrying out this first Mission of ours is indeed *our own* heart and our own rebellion.

Comment 5: Further Thoughts About What Makes Us Special and Unique

As I said earlier, many of us come to this issue of our Mission in life, be-cause we want to feel that we are unique. And what we mean by that, is that we hope to discover some "specialness" intrinsic to us, which is our birth-right, and which no one can take from us. What we, however, discover from a thorough exploration of this topic, is that we are indeed special -- but only because God thinks us so. Our specialness and uniqueness reside in Him, and His love, rather than in anything intrinsic to our own *being*. The proper appreciation of this distinction causes our feet to carry us in the end not to the City called Pride, but to the Temple called Gratitude.

> What is religion? Religion is the service of God
> out of grateful love for what God has done for us.
> The Christian religion, more particularly, is the
> service of God out of grateful love for what God
> has done for us in Christ.
>
> Phillips Brooks, author of
> *O Little Town of Bethlehem*

Comment 6: The Unconscious Doing of
The Work We Came To Do

You may have *already* wrestled with this first part of your Mission here on Earth. You may not have called it that. You may have called it simply "learning to believe in God." But if you ask what your Mission is in life, this one was and is the precondition of all else that you came here to do. Absent this Mission, and it is folly to talk about the rest. So, if you have been seeking faith, or seeking to strengthen your faith, you have -- willy nilly -- already been about *the doing of the Mission you were given*. Born into **This Time In Between**, you have found His hand again, and reclasped it. You are therefore ready to go on with His Spirit to tackle together what you came here to do -- the other parts of your Mission.

Some Random Comments About
Your Second Mission in Life

Your second Mission here on Earth is also one which you share with the rest of the human race, but it is no less your individual mission for the fact that it is shared: and that is, **to do what you can moment by moment, day by day, step by step, to make this world a better place -- following the leading and guidance of God's Spirit within you and around you**.

Comment 1: The Uncomfortableness of
One Step at a Time

Imagine yourself out walking in your neighborhood one night, and suddenly you find yourself surrounded by such a dense fog, that you have lost your bearings and cannot find your way. Suddenly, a friend appears out of the fog, and asks you to put your hand in theirs, and they will lead you home. And you, not being able to tell where you are going, trustingly follow them, even though you can only see one step at a time. Eventually you arrive safely home, filled with gratitude. But as you reflect upon the experience the next day, you realize how unsettling it was to have to keep walking when you could see only one step at a time, even though you had guidance in which you knew you could trust.

Now I have asked you to imagine all of this, because this is the essence of the second Mission to which *you* are called -- and *I* am called -- in this life. It is all very different than we had imagined. When the question, "*What is your Mission in life?*" is first broached, and we have put our hand in God's, as it were, we imagine that we will be taken up to *some mountaintop*, from which we can see far into the distance. And that we will hear a voice in our ear, saying, "Look, look, see that distant city? That is the goal of your Mission; that is where everything is leading, every step of your way."

But instead of the mountaintop, we find ourself in *the valley* -- wandering often in a fog. And the voice in our ear says something quite different from what we thought we would hear. It says, "**Your Mission is to take one step at a time, even when you don't yet see where it all is leading, or what the Grand Plan is, or what your overall Mission in life is. Trust Me; I will lead you.**"

Comment 2: The Nature of This Step-by-Step Mission

As I said, in every situation you find yourself, you have been sent here to do whatever you can -- moment by moment -- that will bring more gratitude, more kindness, more forgiveness, more honesty, and more love into this world.

There are dozens of such moments every day. Moments when you stand -- as it were -- at a spiritual crossroads, with two ways lying before you. Such moments are typically called "**moments of decision.**" It does not matter what the frame or content of each particular decision is. It all devolves, in the end, into just two roads before you, *every time*. **The one** will lead to *less* gratitude, *less* kindness, *less* forgiveness, *less* honesty, or *less* love in the world. **The other** will lead to *more* gratitude, *more* kindness, *more* forgiveness, *more* honesty, or *more* love in the world. Your Mission, each moment, is to seek to choose the latter spiritual road, rather than the former, *every time*.

Comment 3: Some Examples of This Step-by-Step Mission

I will give a few examples, so that the nature of this part of your Mission may be unmistakably clear.

You are out on the freeway, in your car. Someone has gotten into the wrong lane, to the right of *your* lane, and needs to move over into the lane you are in. You *see* their need to cut in, ahead of you. **Decision time.** In your mind's eye you see two spiritual roads lying before you: the one leading to less kindness in the world (you speed up, to shut this driver out, and don't let them move over), the other leading to more kindness in the world (you let the driver cut in). **Since you know this is part of your Mission, part of the reason why you came to Earth, your calling is clear. You know which road to take, which decision to make.**

You are hard at work at your desk, when suddenly an interruption comes. The phone rings, or someone is at the door. They need something from you, a question of some of your time and attention. **Decision time.** In your mind's eye you see two spiritual roads lying before you: the one leading to less love in the world (you tell them you're just too busy to be bothered), the other leading to more love in the world (you put aside your work, decide that God may have sent this person to you, and say, "Yes, what can I do to help you?"). **Since you know this is part of your Mission, part of the reason why you came to Earth, your calling is clear. You know which road to take, which decision to make.**

Your mate does something that hurts your feelings. **Decision time.** In your mind's eye you see two spiritual roads lying before you: the one leading to less forgiveness in the world (you institute an icy silence between the two of you, and think of how you can punish them or otherwise get even), the

other leading to more forgiveness in the world (you go over and take them in your arms, speak the truth about your hurt feelings, and assure them of your love). **Since you know this is part of your Mission, part of the reason why you came to Earth, your calling is clear. You know which road to take, which decision to make.**

You have not behaved at your most noble, recently. And now you are face-to-face with someone who asks you a question about what happened. **Decision time.** In your mind's eye you see two spiritual roads lying before you: the one leading to less honesty in the world (you lie about what happened, or what you were feeling, because you fear losing their respect or their love), the other leading to more honesty in the world (you tell the truth, together with how you feel about it, in retrospect). **Since you know this is part of your Mission, part of the reason why you came to Earth, your calling is clear. You know which road to take, which decision to make.**

Comment 4: The Spectacle Which Makes the Angels Laugh

It is necessary to explain this part of our Mission in some detail, because so many times you will see people wringing their hands, and saying, "*I want to know what my Mission in life is,*" all the while they are cutting people off on the highway, refusing to give time to people, punishing their mate for having hurt their feelings, and lying about what they did. And it will seem to you that the angels must laugh to see this spectacle. *For these people wringing their hands,* their Mission was right there, on the freeway, in the interruption, in the hurt, and at the confrontation.

Comment 5: The Valley vs. The Mountaintop

At some point in your life your Mission may involve some grand *mountaintop experience,* where you say to yourself, "This, this, is why I came into the world. I know it. I know it." *But until then,* your Mission is here in *the valley,* and the fog, and the little callings moment by moment, day by day. More to the point, it is likely you cannot ever get to your mountaintop Mission unless you have first exercised your stewardship faithfully in the valley.

It is an ancient principle, to which Jesus alluded often, that if you don't use the information the Universe has already given you, you cannot expect it will give you any more. If you aren't being faithful in small things, how can you expect to be given charge over larger things? (Luke 16:10,11,12; 19:11–24) If you aren't trying to bring more gratitude, kindness, forgiveness, honesty, and love into the world each day, you can hardly expect that you will be entrusted with the Mission to help bring peace into the world or anything else large and important. If we do not live out our day-by-day Mission in the valley, we cannot expect we are yet ready for a larger *mountaintop* Mission.

Comment 6: The Importance of Not Thinking of This Mission As 'Just A Training Camp'

The valley is not just a kind of "training camp." There is in your imagination even now an invisible *spiritual* mountaintop to which you may go, if you wish to see where all this is leading. And what will you see there, in the imagination of your heart, but the goal toward which all this is pointed: **that Earth might be more like heaven. That human's life might be more like God's.** That is the large achievement toward which all our day by day Missions *in the valley* are moving. This is a *large* order, but it is accomplished by faithful attention to the doing of our great Creator's **will** in little things as well as in large. It is much like the building of the pyramids in Egypt, which was accomplished by the dragging of a lot of individual pieces of stone by a lot of individual men.

The valley, the fog, the going step-by-step, is no mere training camp. The goal is real, however large. "**Thy Kingdom come, Thy will be done, on Earth, as it is in heaven.**"

Some Random Comments About Your Third Mission in Life

Your third Mission here on Earth is one which is uniquely yours, and that is:

a) **to exercise that Talent which you particularly came to Earth to use -- your greatest gift which you most delight to use**

b) **in those place(s) or setting(s) which God has caused to appeal to you the most,**

c) **and for those purposes which God most needs to have done in the world.**

Comment 1: Our Mission Is Already Written, "in Our Members"

It is customary in trying to identify this part of our Mission, to advise that we should ask God, in prayer, to speak to us -- and **tell us** plainly what our Mission is. We look for a voice in the air, a thought in our head, a dream in the night, a sign in the events of the day, to reveal this thing which is otherwise *(it is said)* completely hidden. Sometimes, from just such answered prayer, people do indeed discover what their Mission is, beyond all doubt and uncertainty.

But having to wait for the voice of God to reveal what our Mission is, is not the truest picture of our situation. St. Paul, in Romans, speaks of a law "written in our members," -- and this phrase has a telling application to the question of **how** God reveals to each of us our unique Mission in life. Read again the definition of our third Mission (above) and you will see: the clear implication of the definition is that God has **already** revealed His will to us concerning our vocation and Mission, by causing it to be "**written in our members**." We are to begin deciphering our unique Mission by studying our talents and skills, and more particularly which ones (or One) we most rejoice to use.

God actually has written His will *twice* in our members: *first in the talents* which He lodged there, and secondly *in His guidance of our heart*, as to which talent gives us the greatest pleasure from its exercise (**it is usually the one which, when we use it, causes us to lose all sense of time**).

Even as the anthropologist can examine ancient inscriptions, and divine from them the daily life of a long lost people, so we by examining **our talents** and **our heart** can *more often than we dream* divine the Will of the Living God. For true it is, our Mission is not something He **will** reveal; it is something He **has already** revealed. It is not to be found written in the sky; it is to be found written in our members.

Comment 2: Career Counseling: We Need You

Arguably, our first two Missions in life could be learned from religion alone -- without any reference whatsoever to career counseling, the subject of this book. Why then should career counseling claim that this question about our Mission in life is its proper concern, *in any way?*

It is when we come to this third Mission, which hinges so crucially on the question of our Talents, skills, and gifts, that we see the answer. If you've read the body of this book, before turning to this Epilogue, you know without my even saying it, how much the identification of Talents, gifts, or skills is the province of career counseling. Its expertise, indeed its *raison d'etre*, lies precisely in the identification, classification, and (forgive me) "prioritization" of Talents, skills, and gifts. To put the matter quite simply, career counseling knows how to do this better than any other discipline -- **including** traditional religion. This is not a defect of religion, but the fulfillment of something Jesus promised: "When the Spirit of truth comes, He will guide you into all truth." (John 16:12) Career counseling is part (we may hope) of that promised late-coming truth. It can therefore be of inestimable help to the pilgrim who is trying to figure out what their greatest, and most enjoyable, talent is, as a step toward identifying their unique Mission in life.

If career counseling needs religion as its helpmate in the first two stages of identifying our Mission in life, religion repays the compliment by clearly needing career counseling as **its** helpmate here in the third stage.

And this place where you are in your life right now -- facing the job-hunt and all its anxiety -- is the perfect time to seek the union within your own mind and heart of both career counseling (as in the pages of this book) and your faith in God.

Comment 3: How Our Mission Got Chosen: A Scenario for the Romantic

It is a mystery which we cannot fathom, in this life at least, as to why one of us has this talent, and the other one has that; why God chose to give one gift -- and Mission -- to one person, and a different gift -- and Mission -- to another. Since we do not know, and in some degree cannot know, we are certainly left free to speculate, and imagine.

We may imagine that before we came to Earth, our souls, *our Breath, our Light,* stood before the great Creator and volunteered for this Mission. And God and we, together, chose what that Mission would be and what particular gifts would be needed, which He then agreed to give us, after our birth. Thus, our Mission was not a command given peremptorily by an unloving Creator to a reluctant slave without a vote, but was a task jointly designed by us both, in which as fast as the great Creator said, "**I wish**" our hearts responded, "**Oh, yes.**" As mentioned in an earlier Comment, it may be helpful to think of the condition of our becoming human as that we became amnesiac about any consciousness our soul had before birth -- and therefore amnesiac about the nature or manner in which our Mission was designed.

Our searching for our Mission now is therefore a searching to recover the memory of something we ourselves had a part in designing.

I am admittedly a hopeless romantic, so of course I like this picture. If you also are a hopeless romantic, you may like it too. There's also the chance that it just may be true. We will not know until we see Him face-to-face.

Comment 4: Mission As Intersection

There are all different kinds of voices calling you to all different kinds of work, and the problem is to find out which is the voice of God rather than that of society, say, or the superego, or self-interest. By and large a good rule for finding out is this: the kind of work God usually calls you to is the kind of work (a) that you need most to do and (b) the world most needs to have done. If you really get a kick out of your work, you've presumably met requirement (a), but if your work is writing TV deodorant commercials, the chances are you've missed requirement (b). On the other hand, if your work is being a doctor in a leper colony, you have probably met (b), but if most of the time you're bored and depressed by it, the chances are you haven't only bypassed (a) but probably aren't helping your patients much either. Neither the hair shirt nor the soft birth will do. **The place God calls you to is the place where your deep gladness and the world's deep hunger meet.**

Fred Buechner
Wishful Thinking -- A Theological ABC

Excerpted from *Wishful Thinking – A Theological ABC* by Frederick Buechner. Copyright ©1973 by Frederick Buechner. Reprinted with permission of HarperCollins, Inc.

Comment 5: Examples of Mission As Intersection

Your unique and individual mission will most likely turn out to be a mission of Love, acted out in one or all of three arenas: either in the Kingdom of the Mind, whose goal is to bring more Truth into the world; or in the Kingdom of the Heart, whose goal is to bring more beauty into the world; or in the Kingdom of the Will, whose goal is to bring more Perfection into the world, through Service.

Here are some examples:

"My mission is, out of the rich reservoir of love which God seems to have given me, to nurture and show love to others -- most particularly to those who are suffering from incurable diseases."

"My mission is to draw maps for people to show them how to get to God."

"My mission is to create the purest foods I can, to help people's bodies not get in the way of their spiritual growth."

"My mission is to make the finest harps I can so that people can hear the voice of God in the wind."

"My mission is to make people laugh, so that the travail of this earthly life doesn't seem quite so hard to them."

"My mission is to help people know the truth, in love, about what is happening out in the world, so that there will be more honesty in the world."

"My mission is to weep with those who weep, so that in my arms they may feel themselves in the arms of that Eternal Love which sent me and which created them."

"My mission is to create beautiful gardens, so that in the lilies of the field people may behold the Beauty of God and be reminded of the Beauty of Holiness."

Comment 6: Life As Long As Your Mission Requires

Knowing that you came to Earth for a reason, and knowing what that Mission is, throws an entirely different light upon your life from now on. You are, generally speaking, delivered from any further fear about how long you have to live. You may settle it in your heart that you are here until God chooses to think that you have accomplished your Mission, or until God has a greater Mission for you in another Realm. You need to be a good steward of what He has given you, while you are here; but you do not need to be an anxious steward or stewardess.

You need to attend to your health, *but you do not need to constantly worry about it*. You need to meditate on your death, *but you do not need to be constantly preoccupied with it*. To paraphrase the glorious words of G. K. Chesterton: **"We now have a strong desire for living combined with a strange carelessness about dying. We desire life like water and yet are ready to drink death like wine."** We know that we are here to do what we came to do, and we need not worry about anything else.

Final Comment: A Job-Hunt Done Well

If you approach your job-hunt as an opportunity to work on this issue as well as the issue of how you will keep body and soul together, then hopefully your job-hunt will end with your being able to say: "Life has deep meaning to me, now. I have discovered more than my ideal job; I have found my Mission, and the reason why I am here on Earth."

For Further Reading

Most, though not all, of the following resources are written from a Judaic-Christian viewpoint, but they should be suggestive and helpful for people of any faith, as you mentally translate these texts into your own thought-forms and concepts of your faith:

Buford, Bob, *Half-Time: Changing Your Game Plan from Success to Significance.* 1994. Zondervan Publishing House., Grand Rapids, MI 49530.

Blanchard, Ken, *We Are the Beloved: A Spiritual Journey.* 1994. Zondervan Publishing House, Grand Rapids, MI 49530. By the co-author of *The One Minute Manager.*

Lewis, Roy, *Choosing Your Career, Finding Your Vocation: A Step by Step Guide for Adults and Counselors.* 1990. Integration Books, Paulist Press, 997 Macarthur Blvd., Mahwah, NJ 07430. Particularly helpful for mid-life issues.

Blanchard, Tim, *A Practical Guide to Finding and Using Your Spiritual Gifts.* 1983. Tyndale House Publishers, Inc., Box 80, Wheaton, IL 60189.

Edwards, Lloyd, *Discerning Your Spiritual Gifts.* 1988. Cowley Publications, 28 Temple Place, Boston, MA 02111.

Roskind, Robert, *In The Spirit of Business: Applying the Principles of* A Course in Miracles *to Business.* 1992. Celestial Arts, P.O. Box 7123, Berkeley, CA 94707.

A Center for the Practice of Zen Buddhist Meditation, *That Which You Are Seeking Is Causing You to Seek.* Available from the Center, P.O. Box 91, Mountain View, CA 94042. 1990. A *great* title, and a very interesting book, written -- of course -- from the Buddhist point of view, with one of the contributors being a woman who was at that time dying from cancer. (She has passed away, since.)

Mattson, Ralph, and Miller, Arthur, *Finding a Job You Can Love.* 1982. Thomas Nelson Publishers, Nelson Place at Elm Hill Pike, Nashville, TN 37214. The most useful, I think, of all the books in this section. It is out-of-print at the moment, but (while copies last) you can procure a copy directly from Arthur Miller, at 203-868-0317.

Kreinberg, Luke, *The Book of Goals.* 1994. First Step Publishing, P.O. Box 1092, Mill Valley, CA 94942. I know a woman who was able to turn her life around by taking large goals for her life, and breaking them down into smaller, more manageable projects or tasks. Soon she -- who had told herself she wasn't accomplishing anything with her life -- was deriving a great deal of benefit from a new-found sense of accomplishment. This book aims to help you with a number of journal pages, where you can take the same steps that she took: breaking larger life goals down into simpler *steps*.

For Counseling

All counselors in these centers are sincere; many are also very skilled. If you run into a clerical counselor who is sincere but inept, you will probably discover that the ineptness consists in an inadequate understanding of the distinction I often point out, namely, the distinction between career **assessment** -- roughly comparable to taking a snapshot of people as they are in one frozen moment of time -- vs. career **development** -- which is roughly comparable to teaching people how to take their own motion pictures of themselves, from here on out.

Having issued this caution, however, I will go on to add that at some of these centers, listed below, are some simply *excellent* counselors who fully understand this distinction, and are well trained in that empowering of the client, which is what career *development* is all about.

We begin with counseling centers founded primarily to help **clergy** (though in most cases not restricted just to them). No profession has developed, or had developed for it, so many resources to aid in career assessment as has this profession.

THE OFFICIAL INTERDENOMINATIONAL
CAREER DEVELOPMENT CENTERS

The Career and Personal
Counseling Service
St. Andrew's Presbyterian
College, Laurinburg,
NC 28352
919-276-3162
Also at: 4108 Park Rd.,
Suite 200,
Charlotte, NC 28209
704-523-7751
Elbert R. Patton, Director

The Career and Personal
Counseling Center
Eckerd College
St. Petersburg, FL 33733
813-864-8356, Ext. 356
John R. Sims, Director

The Center for Ministry
8393 Capwell Dr., Suite 220
Oakland, CA 94621-2123
510-635-4246
Robert L. Charpentier, Director

Lancaster Career
Development Center
561 College Ave.
Lancaster, PA 17603
717-397-7451
L. Guy Mehl, Director

North Central Career
Development Center
516 Mission House Lane
New Brighton, MN 55112
612-636-5120
Kenneth J. McFayden, Ph.D.,
Director

Northeast Career Center
407 Nassau Street
Princeton, NJ 08540
609-924-9408
Roy Lewis, Director

Career Development
Center of the Southeast
531 Kirk Rd.
Decatur, GA 30030
404-371-0336
Robert M. Urie, Director

Midwest Career
Development Service
1840 Westchester Blvd.,
Westchester, IL 60154
708-343-6268
Also at: 1520 Old Henderson Rd.,
Suite 102B,
Columbus, OH 43221-3616
614-442-8822
Also at: 754 N. 31st St.,
Kansas City, KS 66110-0816.
Ronald Brushwyler, Director

Southwest Career
Development Center
Box 5923
Arlington, TX 76005
817-640-5181
Jerry D. Overton
Director-Counselor

Center for Career
Development and Ministry
70 Chase St.
Newton Center, MA 02159
617-969-7750
Stephen Ott, Director.

Clergy wishing to stay within the parish ministry, but wanting help with the search, will want to know about:

Mead, Loren B., and Miller, Arthur F., and Ayers, Russell C., and Bolles, Richard N., *Your Next Pastorate: Starting the Search.* Order #AL122 from The Alban Institute, Inc., 4125 Nebraska Ave., N.W., Washington, DC 20016.

And now, on to centers which are open to anyone, and do career counseling from a spiritual point of view:

ALSO DOING CAREER COUNSELING FROM A RELIGIOUS POINT OF VIEW

(*These are listed by general geographical location, from West Coast to East Coast, North to South*)

People Management Group International, 924 First Street, Suite A, Snohomish, WA 98290. 206-563-0105. Arthur F. Miller, Jr., Chairman.

Bernard Haldane, 2821 2nd Ave., Suite 1002, Seattle, WA 98121. 206-448-0881. A pioneer in the clergy career management and assessment field, Bernard teaches (*totally independently of the agency which bears his name*) seminars and training of volunteers (particularly in churches) to do job-search counseling.

Career Development and Vocational Testing Services, 2515 Park Marina, Suite 203-B, **Redding, CA** 96001. 916-246-2871.

Lifework Design, 448 S. Marengo Ave., **Pasadena, CA** 91101, 818-577-2705. Kevin Brennfleck, M.A., and Kay Marie Brennfleck, M.A., Directors.

Harlan H. Shippy, M.Div., Ph.D., Counseling Ministries, 8035 La Mesa Blvd., **La Mesa, CA** 91941-6434. 619-462-2277.

Occupational and Career Services, Inc., 3311 N. 44th St., Suite 120, **Phoenix, AZ** 85018. 602-840-9084. Julie A. Schwartz, M.S., C.R.C.

Olson Counseling Services, 8720 Frederick, Suite 105, **Omaha, NE** 68124, 402-390-2342. Gail A. Olson, P.A.C.

Ministry of Counseling and Enrichment, 1333 N. 2nd St., **Abilene, TX** 79601, 915-675-8131. Mary Stedham, Director.

New Life Institute, Box 1666, **Austin, TX** 78767, 512-469-9447. Bob Breihan, Director.

Institute of Worklife Ministry, 2650 Fountainview Drive, Suite 444, **Houston, TX** 77057, 713-266-2456. Diana C. Dale, Director.

Life/Career Planning Center for Religious, 10526 W. Cermak Rd., Suite 111, **Westchester, IL** 60153, 708-531-9228. Dolores Linhart, Director. Doing work with Roman Catholics.

Life Stewardship Associates, 6918 Glen Creek Dr., SE, **Dutton, MI** 49316, 616-698-3125. Ken Soper, M.Div., M.A., Director.

Career Resources, 2323 Hillsboro Rd., Suite 508, **Nashville TN** 37212. 615-297-0404. Jane C. Hardy, Principal.

RHM Group, P.O.Box 271135, **Nashville, TN** 37227, 615-391-5000. Robert H. McKown.

Career Achievement, NiS International Services, 1321 Murfreesboro Road., Suite 610, **Nashville, TN** 37217, 615-367-5000. William L. (Bill) Karlson, Harry McClure, Manager.

Mid-South Career Development Center, 2315 Fisher Place, **Knoxville, TN** 37920, 615-573-1340. W. Scott Root, Director.

Dan Miller, The Business Source, 7100 Executive Center Drive, Suite 110, **Brentwood, TN** 37027. 615-373-7771.

Career and Personal Counseling Center, 1904 Mt. Vernon St., **Waynesboro, VA** 22980, 703-943-9997. Lillian Pennell, Director.

Center for Growth & Change, Inc., 6991 Peachtree Ind. Blvd., Suite 310, **Norcross, GA** 30092, 404-441-9580. James P. Hicks, Ph.D., L.P.C., Director.

Career Pathways, 601 Broad St., **Gainesville, GA** 30501, 800-722-1976. Lee Ellis, Director. Offers career-guidance from a Christian point of view, through the mails -- based on questionnaires and various instruments or inventories which they send you.

Call to Career, 8720 Georgia Ave., Suite 802, **Silver Spring, MD** 20910. 301-961-1017. Cheryl Palmer, M.Ed., NCC, NCCC, President.

Judith Gerberg Associates, 250 West 57th St., **New York, NY** 10107, 212-315-2322. Judith Gerberg.

VI. What To Do If Your Job-Hunt Drags On and On

How to Deal with Rejection and Depression

"I don't have a parachute of any color."

What To Do
If Your Job-Hunt
Drags
On and On

Dealing with Rejection
and Depression

WHY WE
GET DEPRESSED
WHEN UNEMPLOYED

Most of us are good at doing difficult things, as long as we only have to do them for a short time.

We can walk (quickly) through an area with a bad stench. We can put up with a three-day cold.

We can stand to miss one meal.

We can hold our breath for thirty seconds.

We can run a hundred-yard dash.

We can endure a bad relationship, as long as it doesn't last more than one week.

But we really don't like it when things go on for too long. That starts to get us down.

That, of course, is our situation when we are unemployed. A period of unemployment that lasts only two weeks -- hey, *no problem!* But if it drags on and on and on, many of us start to get depressed.

And how likely is it, that it will drag on and on?

Well, let's look at some statistics.

U.S. Statistics

Unemployment is pretty much the same the world around. But the U.S. keeps *statistics* about it all.

And so we know that in the U.S. one out of every five or six workers is unemployed at *some* time during each year. Of those who are unemployed in any given month:

35 out of every 100 of them have been out of work less than five weeks;

28 out of every 100 have been out of work between five and fourteen weeks;

13 out of every 100 have been out of work between fifteen and twenty-six weeks; and

24 out of every 100 have been out of work twenty-seven weeks or longer; and/or have stopped looking altogether.[1]

Which means, of course, that if you were 'downsized,' 'made redundant,' 'laid off,' 'fired,' or quit, there is a 35% chance that you will find work within five weeks.

But, the odds are twice as great -- 65% -- that your job-hunt will take longer, maybe *much* longer. (It can range up to two years, in worst-case scenarios.)

If it drags on for any length of time, it can put us into a real depression.

FOR TRULY DEEP DEPRESSIONS

Now what do we mean by *depression*? Well, the word is commonly used in two different senses: the *diagnostic* sense, as used by psychiatrists or therapists; and the looser, everyday meaning, as it is used out there on the streets.

Thus, when we are unemployed and we meet somebody out on the streets and say, *"I feel depressed,"* we usually mean: *'I've got the blues.'* We mean: *"I feel sad."* We mean: *"I'm not my usual self."* We mean: *"I feel down, because it's hard to stay upbeat or optimistic in this situation."* We mean: *"I'm in a funk."* This feeling of being *depressed* is our emotional response to *this one particular situation.* Once we have found a job, it lifts, and we start feeling happy and upbeat once again.

Psychiatrists and therapists, however, see a very different kind of depression, daily, in their offices.

---

1. Statistics based, in part, on the February 1992 issue of the Monthly Labor Review, published by the U.S. Department of Labor, Bureau of Labor Statistics; and, in part, on the figures for discouraged workers for that same time period; and, in part, on a paper by the late Bob Wegmann, entitled, "How Long Does Unemployment Last?"

This is an *illness,* which the person has usually lived with for a long time. It varies in its force and weight, sometimes seeming on a par with a cold, sometimes seeming on a par with double-pneumonia. It does not go away just because our life gets 'better.' When *this* kind of depression is upon us, it often feels like it is going to totally crush our spirit, and extinguish our life. Feelings of utter worthlessness, thoughts of suicide, often attend it. It is what has often been called 'the dark night of the soul.'[2]

Many brave souls have endured this 'dark night of the soul' for years, with astounding courage -- through sheer guts, through faith, through therapeutic treatments and medicines that hold the illness partly, or mostly, or completely, at bay.

It is estimated by experts that in the U.S. alone some 10 million Americans are experiencing this illness during a typical year.[3] And of course some of them are unemployed. But if we are subject to *this* kind of depression, it usually has antedated our period of unemployment, and is something we have wrestled with for years -- though our unemployment may turn it into a 'visitation' that is much deeper than usual.

If we go into *this* kind of a deep depression at the time of our unemployment, it is important to keep in mind that such an illness is not a character defect, something we could shrug off 'if only we were stronger characters.' No, no. Measles are not a character defect; neither is *this* illness.

---

de•pres•sion \di-'presh-ən\ n (1): a state of feeling sad : DEJECTION (2): a psychoneurotic or psychotic disorder marked esp. by sadness, inactivity, difficulty in thinking and concentration, a significant increase or decrease in appetite and time spent sleeping, feelings of dejection and hopelessness, and sometimes suicidal tendencies (3): a reduction in activity, amount, quality, or force (4): a lowering of vitality or functional activity.

Webster's

---

2. This term is sometimes used by mystics to mean something slightly different: when the soul feels, falsely, as though it had been abandoned by God. This is, however, not that different from *depression*, where false feelings (like, *worthlessness*) abound.

3. A patient's guide to Depression is available from Depression, P.O. Box 8547, Silver Spring, MD 20907, free. You may also call 1-800-358-9295, to ask for it. For further reading, I refer you to: *The Good News About Depression: New Medical Cures & Treatments That Can Work for You.*, by Mark S. Gold, M.D. 1988. Bantam Books, 1540 Broadway, New York, NY 10036. There is also: *Depression, the Mood Disease,* by Francis Mark Mondimore, M.D. rev. ed. 1993. Available from the Johns Hopkins University Press, 2715 N. Charles St.,, Baltimore, MD 21218, 1-800-537-5487.

There is also 'computer-aided psychotherapy,' as discussed in Julian Simon's book, *Good Mood,* 1993, Open Court Publishing Co., Carus Publishing, Suite 2000, 332 S. Michigan Ave., Chicago, IL 60604-9968. The software program, *Overcoming Depression,* can be obtained from Malibu Artificial Intelligence Works, 25307 Malibu Rd., Malibu, CA 90265. 800-497-6889.

To begin with, depression may have a physical basis.

It can be caused or made worse by such physical causes as a thyroid disorder, or a lack of serotonin in our brain, or the side-effects of medications we may be taking for other ailments, etc.

So, if your depression feels very deep, it is your first duty to yourself and your loved ones to check out this possibility, by getting yourself immediately to a qualified physician and asking them to do blood tests on you, to see if something physical is causing this, or making it worse.

> If you are depressed *and* feeling suicidal, you need to go see a psychiatrist, therapist, or doctor *today*. Suicidal thoughts, or intentions, indicate that your depression has become a medical emergency, *akin to* a heart attack; *don't* mess around with such thoughts, thinking, "Oh, it'll go away." Act! Go report it to someone who can give you some medicine or help, immediately. Many areas now have a 'Suicide Hot-Line.' Your local hospital should be able to give you the number. Call. Also, look in *The Yellow Pages* of your local telephone directory, under "Suicide Prevention Counselors."

If your depression is of lesser degree, but still numbing, and if investigation doesn't turn up any physical basis for it, then you need to consider the possibility that it is caused by factors in your situation, present or past, and the feelings they engendered -- particularly feelings of anger.

This, again, is not a character defect, but is rooted in our very nature as human beings. I think of it as comparable to a clogged drainage pipe. We human beings, like a pipe, are meant to have experiences, feel the emotions they engender, and then let those feelings drain out of us, as through a clear-running pipe.

But if the emotions don't drain off, if they get stored up, then things start to back up in our system, as in a clogged pipe. I think of *some kinds* of depression as the results of that backup.

The remedy is clear. We need to unclog that pipe, so that we may get on with our life, victoriously. And, *talking* about our experiences, present or past, plus the feelings they aroused within us, is the way we go about unclogging that pipe.

So, if you are depressed, *start talking*. Talk about anything that is bothering you, past or present, and talk about it first of all with your partner, mate, family, or friends. If that doesn't help, then you ought to get yourself to an experienced therapist, and I'd say preferably one who has had therapy themselves. *(Ask.)*

Now, having said this about the illness, I want to return to the *unlearned* sense in which we, when unemployed, use the term, in common everyday street talk. As I said, this is more about the situation we find ourselves in, for a time. It's when we're unemployed, and we wake up one morning thinking, "I feel *blue*," or "I'm in a *funk*," or "I'm *really* not enjoying life just now."

As I said, I think of this as *unemployment depression*.

THE FOUR ROOTS OF
'UNEMPLOYMENT DEPRESSION'

There are four roots to unemployment depression, as it seems to me. These are: (1) emotional; (2) mental; (3) spiritual; and (4) physical. Each of the four *contributes* toward the feelings of depression. In this sense, depression is like a river, fed by these four tributaries.

Hence, we need remedies which deal with these four.

THE EMOTIONAL ROOT
OF UNEMPLOYMENT DEPRESSION

We get depressed because we feel angry. If we are out of work because we were 'let go,' and especially if it came out of the blue, or was done in a shabby way, we may justifiably feel a great deal of anger about the whole thing.

It's rejection, and we hate it.

If we go looking for work, and can't find anything, after getting turned down at the 307th place, we may feel very angry.

Again, it's rejection, and we hate it.

And if, above all, we didn't expect any of this, then we're suffering from what I call:

Nobody likes to be rejected. Not at work. Not during the job-hunt. We *hate* it.

All of this anger, unresolved, doesn't just fade away with time; it often turns into depression, as I mentioned above.

Need I mention that we would probably drop our anger quickly if it were relatively easy to find another job, doing basically the thing we love at the same level of responsibility and at the same salary, or greater, in the same town, with an even better boss. But, given our Neanderthal job-hunting system, it is not. It is not easy to find such jobs even when they exist.

Hence, much of the blame for our anger should lie at the door of this so-called job-hunting '*system*'-- which leaves us feeling devalued and discarded by our society for weeks, months, and sometimes years. Our anger is justified and understandable, in the beginning.

But if it keeps on and on, then that's another story. And if our anger is directed not against the job-hunting system in this country, but against our ex-employers, that's the beginning of trouble. I see this often, as people who have been let go discuss the place where they used to work: *'I'll never forgive them. They've ruined the rest of my life.'*

Of course, the only way our former employers can actually ruin the rest of our lives is if *we* help them out, by holding on to our anger forever. This *will* wreck the rest of our lives. I have seen it happen many many times in the lives of the unemployed.

We forget an ancient truth: that when anger becomes a burning fire within us, that fire gradually consumes not its object, but its host. Certainly it doesn't achieve its desired effect upon the objects of our anger. They are sleeping soundly, while it is we who are lying awake at night. No, anger consumes its host not its object, and it does this by giving birth within us to irritability, withdrawal, loneliness, broken relationships, divorce (often), and sometimes (rarely) suicide. After a period of time, this anger commonly segues into depression.

Remedies

- *Your basic need is to face forward, toward your future, not backward, toward your past. Staying rooted in your anger keeps you facing toward the past.*
- *Talk out the anger with someone who is a good listener, understanding, and compassionate: partner, mate, friend, or therapist.*
- *If you have a lot of anger still left, so you feel you'd like to punch someone (your ex-employer comes to mind),* don't. *Punch a pillow instead. A big pillow. Or your mattress. Punch it hard.*
- *If you are a man or woman of faith, hand over your anger to God. Then set your face toward the future.*

THE MENTAL ROOT
OF UNEMPLOYMENT DEPRESSION

We get depressed because we feel powerless. For months, years, maybe decades, we have thought of ourselves in terms of *that job* at *that place*. It gave our life its coherence, it gave us our daily routine, it gave us our identity. *"Who are you?"* "Oh, I'm a foreman at the General Motors plant down the road." We may have been saying *that* for years. But when we are let go, that era comes to an end. What do we say now? *"Who are you?"* "Well, I don't really know, any more." Of course, we get depressed.

This often spirals into our spending much of our time each day, every day, brooding about what is *wrong*. What is wrong with people, what is wrong with our life, what is wrong with our situation, what is wrong with anything and everything. In our conversation with friends or family, we focus our attention on what we didn't like about the conversation...or *them*. In a movie or play, we focus on what we didn't like about it. When we travel, we focus on what we didn't like about each place we visited. This habit of mind focusses always on other people's failings, on what is not the way we want it to be, on what is (from our point of view) missing. We get more depressed.

We always get more depressed when we feel powerless. Obsessing on what's wrong with everything, is a good way to feel more and more powerless.

Remedies

• *Remember this simple truth: you always have power -- the power to change how you view your situation, and thus to alter your situation, in the days ahead.*

• *Spend time learning to think about yourself in a new way.* Do the Workbook in this book, called The Quick Job-Hunting Map, *so as to learn to think of yourself -- not in terms of a job-title, but in terms of gifts. "I am a person who. . . ."*

• *Spend time thinking about what you'd like to do with the rest of your life. Make it a time of philosophical and spiritual renewal for you.*

• *If you would avoid staying depressed, it is crucial to focus your attention on happy things.*[4] *Adopt a more lenient view of the world as it is, not as you would have it. And, as Baltasar Gracián said,*[5] *"Get used to the failings of your friends, family, and acquaintances . . ." And your bosses. And your co-workers.*

• *Don't stay by yourself all the time. Spend time with friends and loved ones, in conversation, cuddling, drives in the country, exercise, taking walks, singing, listening to beautiful music, sitting in front of the fireplace (hopefully with a fire burning in it). If you have no fireplace, sit in front of a burning candle, with your loved one.*

THE SPIRITUAL ROOT
OF UNEMPLOYMENT DEPRESSION

We get depressed because we feel life is meaningless. You will likely feel depressed while unemployed if you view this experience of being laid-off, and having to spend a long time finding a new job, as essentially a random, senseless and meaningless event in your life.

At a medical symposium which I attended many years ago, a doctor was reviewing the puzzle of healing. Two patients, he said, of the same age and with the same medical history, would undergo the same operation. Yet, one would heal rapidly, while the other's healing was long delayed. Doctors had no idea why this was so. They set up a study at a major New York hospital, to see if they could identify what factors explained this difference.[6] Using a computer, they decided to compare *everything* about the patients who healed quickly, with those same factors -- or to be more exact, the *absence* of those same factors -- in the patients who healed slowly. And so they began to ask the computer their questions.

---

4. Especially helpful is Barbara Ann Kipfer's *14,000 things to be happy about.* Workman Publishing Company, 708 Broadway, New York, NY 10003. 1990.

5. Baltazar Gracián, *The Art of Worldly Wisdom: A Pocket Oracle.* Doubleday/Currency, Publishers. 1992. Baltazar was a Spanish writer who lived in the 1600s.

6. I have, incidentally, tried to go back and identify that study, with the help of others as well; but we have been basically unsuccessful in this search. I am left only with a clear memory of *the findings,* as they were reported by that doctor at that symposium.

Were those who healed quickly characterized by *optimism*, while those who healed slowly were not? No, said the computer; that wasn't the answer.

Were those who healed quickly characterized by *some kind of religious faith*, while those who healed slowly were not? No, said the computer; that wasn't the answer.

And so it went.

What the answer finally turned out to be was this: those who healed quickly felt there was some meaning to every event that happened to them in their lives, even if they did not understand what that meaning was, at the present time; while those who healed slowly felt that most events which happened to them had no meaning; they were merely random or senseless. Hence, if both patients were being operated on for cancer, the one who viewed the cancer as having some meaning in the larger scheme of things, for their life, healed quickly; while the one who viewed the cancer as a senseless and meaningless interruption in their life, healed slowly.

We may apply all of this to being let go, at work. Being fired or terminated is rarely the outrageous, meaningless event that it at first seems to be. The last time I was fired, the firing occurred shortly before noon, and at 3 o'clock that same afternoon I had an appointment with my dentist, to have some drilling done on my teeth. '*What a wonderful day this is turning out to be!*' I thought, with rich irony.

Anyway, my dentist was a wise man, quite a bit older than I, and when I told him of my plight, he said some words I have never forgotten: "Someday," he said, "you will say this was the best thing that ever happened to you. I don't expect you to believe a word I am saying now, but wait and see. I have seen this happen in so many people's lives, that I know it will come true for you."

Of course, he was absolutely right. I now indeed say, that firing was the best thing that ever happened to me, for it caused me to rethink my whole life and what I wanted to contribute to the world. It caused *Parachute* to be born. Light was born out of darkness.

According to Gallup Polls since 1960, about 94% of the population in the U.S. believe in *some* concept of God.[7] When they find themselves summarily dismissed from a job that they may have held for *years,* many find their faith in God a bulwark of strength that helps them through this very difficult period, daily.

But, if you are a man or woman of faith, you must rest assured also of this truth: nothing which happens to you is meaningless. If unemployment drags on and on, there is a meaning to it, even if you can't figure out what it is, at this time.

To feel there is no rhyme or reason to anything that happens to you in life, will leave you feeling depressed.

7. Reported in George Gallup's *The People's Religion: American Faith in the 90s*. Macmillan & Co., Order Dept., 201 W. 103rd St., Indianapolis, IN 46290. 1989. In addition to reporting that 94% of us believe in God, the Gallup polls also discovered that 90% of us pray, 88% of us believe God loves us, and 33% of us report we have had a life-changing religious experience; and these figures have remained pretty unvarying during the last thirty years of opinion polls conducted by the Gallup Organization.

Remedies

- *If your job-hunt is dragging on and on, change your job-hunting strategy. Read, and devour Chapters 5, 6, 7 in* Parachute. *Try some new job-hunting behaviors, and methods.*
- *Think of your life as like a tapestry, being woven by God on an enchanted loom.[8] Every bobble of the shuttle has intention, every thread is important, every event in your life has meaning.*
- *Sit down and write out stories about your past years, when you were going through dark times. Write down what meaning you now see in those events.*
- *Don't feel abandoned by God, just because this happened to you. Hold high the truth that God does not save the believer from hard times. Hard times come to believer and non-believer alike. Above all, avoid the plaintive plea, "Why me?"*
- *Search for a higher concept of God. Consider this parable. Imagine that you have, in your dining room, a fine wooden chair, which one day has its back broken off completely -- I mean, into smithereens -- by someone in the house. You run down the street, to call a carpenter who lives nearby. He comes and examines the chair. He pronounces the back unrepairable. "But," he says, "I think I could make a fine wooden stool out of the remainder of the chair, for you." And so he spends much time, shaping, polishing and sanding it, and fashioning out of the former chair a fine stool, more resplendent than anything you have ever dreamed. He inlays it with gold, and soon it is the treasure of your house.*
- *Let me underline a couple of key points in this parable. First of all, the carpenter did not break the chair. Someone else did that. But the carpenter came quickly, and with all his art and powers, to see if he could not only repair it, but make of it something even finer than it had been before. And, he labored mightily, to that end.*
- *And so, a higher concept of God holds that God does not create our unemployment or any of the calamities in our life. God gives us all free-will, and it is our fellow human beings who misuse that free will and thus create our calamities. But though God has given freedom of choice to us all, yet He steps in as soon as someone else has misused their freedom of will in our lives. Like the carpenter, the Lord comes instantly, with all His art and powers, to not only repair our life, but to make of it something even finer than it had been before -- not a physical thing, like the stool inlaid with gold, but a work on the spiritual level that corresponds to the stool, in splendor. And thus no event in our lives remains meaningless. Some higher purpose is always worked out, therein.*
- *Do not limit your faith only to what you can feel. If you can't feel God's presence during these hard times, that does not mean a thing. Feelings often fail to correspond to reality. We can be in a fog that obscures our vision. Walk by faith.*

---

8. The reference to the *loom*, which follows, comes by analogy to Sir Charles Sherrington's description of the brain: *"It is as if the Milky Way entered upon some cosmic dance. Swiftly the brain becomes an enchanted loom where millions of flashing shuttles weave a dissolving pattern, always a meaningful pattern though never an abiding one; a shifting harmony of subpatterns."*

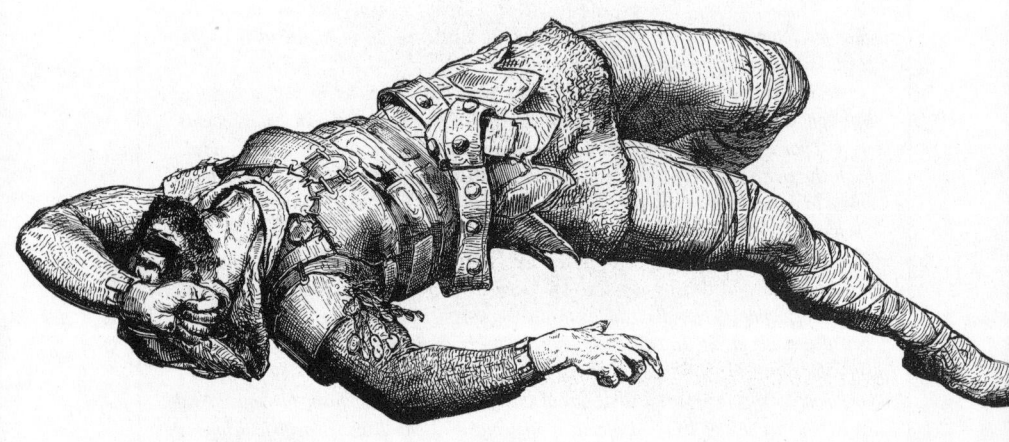

THE PHYSICAL ROOT
OF UNEMPLOYMENT DEPRESSION

We get depressed because we are physical creatures. You will feel depressed if you are short on your sleep, or your body is otherwise run-down.

The world never looks bright or happy to people who are *very short of sleep*.

The world never looks bright or happy to people who are *feeling depressed*.

It is therefore easy to confuse the two feeling-states. What you may imagine is depression may in fact be simply the feelings that come from sleep-deprivation.

I said we get depressed because we are physical creatures. This involves other things, as well.

As physical creatures, we need to keep a roof over our heads, food on the table, and clothes on our back. In the U.S. over 30% of *all adults* describe their financial situation as typically 'shaky' anyway -- whether they are working or not. And naturally, when we become unemployed a much higher percentage of us would describe our financial situation as 'shaky' -- inasmuch as many of us just live from paycheck to paycheck. The longer this 'hand-to-mouth' existence goes on, the more depressed you are likely to feel.

Remedies

- *It has been amazing to me, in the past, to see very-depressed job-hunters turn into happier, more upbeat people, just by catching up on their sleep. Turn off the TV by 10 o'clock, and go to bed! You'll soon feel better; sometimes,* much *better.*
- *Try to keep regular hours, going to bed at the same time every night.*
- *Avoid things that can keep you awake, like caffeine, once dinner is finished. Reduce alcohol consumption to one drink at most, per day.*
- *If you lie awake for more than 30 minutes,* get up *and read, write, or meditate until you get sleepy. Don't do this in bed. Use the bed only for sleeping and love-making.*
- *In addition to the sleep thing, there are other things that need to be done to keep yourself physically fit while unemployed.[9] When I was myself unemployed I found it important to:*
- *Get out in sunlight as much as possible, or sit under bright lights in one's apartment or house, especially during the winter (it is a well-known fact that many people get particularly depressed during winter, because they need light, and especially sunlight; the affliction is called S.A.D.);*
- *Get regular exercise, involving a daily walk;*
- *Drink plenty of water each day (I try for at least eight glasses of water a day -- this seems silly, but it is often very important);*
- *Eat balanced meals, with plenty of fiber. One must not pig out just on junk food in front of the telly; if ever one has thought about cutting down on fats (meats, dairy products), sugar, baked goods, and caffeine, now is an excellent time to do it;*
- *Eliminate sugar as much as possible from the diet;[10]*
- *Take supplementary vitamins daily (no matter how often doctors and nutritionists may tell us that we already get plenty, just from our daily food);*
- *And all that other stuff that our mothers always told us to do.*
- *If you're real short of money, take a 'stop-gap' job -- any honest work, whatsoever, that brings in some money while you continue your job-hunt. Look at 'temp agencies,' in particular, to see if there is one in your town or city that specializes in temporarily placing people with your background and skills. They're in the Yellow Pages, under "Employment Agencies." Look for the word 'temporary' in their title, or ad.*
- *Finally, you may want to use this time to think about what your essential needs are in life, and perhaps embrace a simpler life with less 'things' and more time spent with loved ones and friends. This 'voluntary simplicity' may be just what your soul is craving.*

---

9. Of course, these principles make sense equally when one has found a job.

10. The sugar/depression connection is a matter that has been well-established, and were I feeling depressed the first thing I would eliminate from my diet would be sugar. See *Sugar Blues*, by William Dufty. Warner Books, Inc., 1271 Avenue of the Americas, New York, NY 10020. 1993. Available in bookstores, health-food stores, and your local library.

PERSPECTIVE

When all these things are said and done, all roots diagnosed, all remedies pursued, unemployment depression may still remain -- especially if your job-hunt just keeps draggin' on and on. You've tried everything, you've done *The Map*, you've devoured the chapter on "The Determined Job-Hunter." You've prayed. You've done it all. What then?

The key at such a time, it seems to me, is to keep some kind of perspective about it all. You know, like when you're in the middle of a thunderstorm, and it looks like it will never let up. But you know it will, and you draw cheer from that thought.

Even so, while we are unemployed I think it is important to realize that life, by its very nature, consists in a series of *alternating* periods:

Life is sometimes somber; life is sometimes joyous.
Life is sometimes difficult; life is sometimes easy.
Life is sometimes tawdry; life is sometimes beautiful.
Life is sometimes worse; life is sometimes better.
Life finds us sometimes struggling; life finds us sometimes well off.
Life is sometimes sickness; life is sometimes health.
Life is sometimes depressing; life is sometimes elating.
Life is sometimes sorrow; life is sometimes happiness.
Life is sometimes death; life is sometimes resurrection.
Life sometimes casts us down; life sometimes exalts us.
Life is sometimes a battle; life is sometimes glorious.

It's an alternating rhythm -- a sort of *death and resurrection, death and resurrection.* Over and over again.

Hence this period, when you've been fired or let go, when you've been treated badly, when you're having a hard time with the job-hunt, is one of the periods we inevitably go through in life.

But life is an alternating rhythm. This difficult depressing time will eventually yield to the contrasting theme of joy and happiness, in due time. You need to know this, and thus put this period of your life in perspective.

After three months, do some other things besides your job-hunt. Seek out a career counselor for help. Go out, get active, volunteer someplace, take a college course, be a blessing to this Earth even though you don't yet have a job. In good time, the alternating rhythm will come.

VII. If You Decide
You Need
A Career Counselor

Some Universal Principles
A Sampler of U.S. Resources
Other Resources Around the World

Epilogue: Resources for Career Counselors
Books, Videos, CD-ROMs, and Newsletters
Workshops for Career Counselors (and Others)
Our Annual August Two-Week Workshop

How to Choose a Career Counselor,

LOOK BEFORE YOU LEAP:

There are two basic types of career counselors.

One type's primary expertise is in the area called 'career development' or 'career assessment.' They help people figure out what they want to do with their lives, by way of career choice, etc. They *may* know very little about the actual job-hunting process.

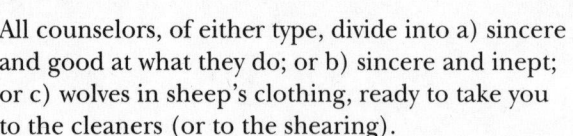

The other type almost always also knows something about 'career development' or 'career assessment,' but their *primary* expertise is in the job-search process.

Some of these follow the *traditional* approach: resumes and interviewing. If you have already given up on that traditional approach, then this is not the counselor for you.

Others follow the *creative* process of job-hunting, described in Chapter 5, in this book. This is the one you want.

All counselors, of either type, divide into a) sincere and good at what they do; or b) sincere and inept; or c) wolves in sheep's clothing, ready to take you to the cleaners (or to the shearing).

No one has a list of counselors who are sincere and good at what they do, either in this country or in any other part of the world.

if you decide you need one

You have to go find them yourself, and this is particularly true if you live outside a major city or you live outside the United States. You *can* do it. It's just going to take some work. And before you begin, you need to keep some principles in mind:

What you're looking for in them, besides a firm grasp of the whole job-hunting process at its most creative and effective level, is that they be someone you feel true *rapport* with. You *like* them. You *trust* them.

You've got to do your own homework, or research, here, and your own interviewing, in your own geographical area, or you will deserve what you get.

No one but you knows whether or not you're going to get along with a particular career counselor. Maybe he's a wonderful man, but unhappily he reminds you of your Uncle Harry. You've always **hated** your Uncle Harry. No one knows that, but you. Or maybe the counselor is a wonderful woman, but unhappily . . . *well, you get the point.*

No one can do this research for you. Because the real question is not "Who is best?" but "Who is best **for you**?" Those last two words demand that it be you who 'makes the call.'

Now, what do you want? First of all, you want **names**.

You want to find the names of at least **three** career counselors in your community.

Where do you find names?

First, from your friends: ask if any of them have ever used a career counselor. And if so, what is that counselor's name; and what did they think of them.

Secondly, from the *Sampler* toward the rear of this section of *The Resource Guide*. See if there are any names near you. They may know how you find out the other names in your community.

Try also your telephone book's local Yellow Pages, under such headings as: *Aptitude and Employment Testing, Career and Vocational Counseling, Personnel Consultants* and (if you are a woman) *Women's Organizations and Services*. You will discover that even the Yellow Pages can't keep up with the additional groups that spring up daily, weekly, and monthly -- including job clubs and other group activities. The most comprehensive list of these, in the U.S., is to be found in the *National Business Employment Weekly*, on its pages called "Calendar of Career Events." It is an extensive listing. Available on newsstands, $3.95 per issue; or, order an issue directly from: National Business Employment Weekly, P.O. Box 300, Princeton, NJ 08543. Their phone is: 800-JOB-HUNT, or 800-562-4868.

Then you want **talk**.

You want to go talk with all three of them, and decide which of the three (if any) you want to hook up with.

You're going to be doing comparison shopping.

You visit in person each of the three places you have chosen.
Don't try to do this over the telephone, *please!* There is so much
more you can tell, when you're looking the person straight in
the eyes.

When face-to-face, you ask *each* of the three
places the same questions. Keep a little
pad or notebook with you that looks like this
form below.

MY SEARCH FOR A GOOD CAREER COUNSELOR			
Questions I will Ask Them	Answer from counselor #1	Answer from counselor #2	Answer from counselor #3
1. What is your program?			
2. Who will be doing it? And how long have you been doing it?			
3. What is your success rate?			
4. What is the cost of your services?			
5. Is there a contract?			

Remember, you don't have to choose any of the three counselors,
if you didn't really care for any of them. If that is the case, then
choose three new counselors, dust off the notebook, and go out
again. It may take a few more hours to find what you want. But the
wallet, the purse, the job-hunt, the life, you save will be your own.

Back home now, after visiting the three places you chose for your comparison shopping, you have to decide: a) whether you want none of the three, or b) one of the three (and if so, which one). Look over your notes on all three places. Compare those places. The simple fact is: there is no definitive way for you to determine a career counselor's expertise. It's something you'll have to smell out, as you go along. But here are some clues:

BAD ANSWERS

• If they give you the feeling that everything will be done for you, by them (including interpretation of tests, and decision making about what this means you should do, or where you should do it) -- rather than you having to do all the work, with their basically assuming the role of coach,
  (15 bad points)
  You want to learn how to do this for yourself; you're going to be job-hunting again, you know.

• If they say they are not the person who will be doing the program with you, but deny you any chance to meet the counselor you would be working with,
  (75 bad points)
  You're talking to a salesperson. Avoid any firm that has a salesperson.

• If you do get a chance to meet the counselor, but you don't like the counselor as a person,
  (150 bad points)
  I don't care what their expertise is, if you don't like them, you're going to have a rough time getting what you want. I guarantee it. Rapport is everything.

• If you ask how long the counselor has been doing this, and they get huffy or give a double-barreled answer, such as: "I've had eighteen years' experience in the business and career counseling world,"
  (20 bad points)
  What that may mean is: seventeen and a half years as a fertilizer salesman, and one-half year doing career counseling. Persist. "How long have you been with this firm, and how long have you been doing formal career counseling, as you are here?"

You might be interested to know that some executive or career counseling firms hire yesterday's clients as today's new staff. Such new staff are sometimes given training only after they're "on-the-job." They are practicing on you.

- If they try to answer the question of their experience by pointing to their degrees or credentials,
  (3 bad points)
  Degrees or credentials tell you they've passed certain tests of their qualifications, but often these tests bear more on their expertise at career assessment than on their knowledge of creative job-hunting.

- If, when you ask about their success rate, they say they have never had a client that failed to find a job, no matter what,
  (15 bad points)
  They're lying. I have studied career counseling programs for over twenty years, have attended many, have studied records at State and Federal offices, and I have hardly ever seen a program that placed more than 86% of their clients, tops, in their best years. And it goes downhill from there. A prominent executive counseling firm was reported by the Attorney General's Office of New York State to have placed only 38 out of 550 clients (a 93% failure rate).[1] If they make it clear that they have had a good success rate, but if you fail to work hard at the whole process, then there is no guarantee you are going to find a job, give them three stars.

- If they show you letters from ecstatically-happy former clients, but when you ask to talk to some of those clients, you get stone-walled.
  (45 bad points)
  I quote from one job-hunter's letter to me: "I asked to speak to a former client or clients. You would of thought I asked to speak to Elvis. The Counselor stammered and stuttered and gave me a million excuses why I couldn't talk to some of these 'satisfied' former clients. None of the excuses sounded legitimate to me. We went back and forth for about thirty minutes. Finally, he excused himself and went to speak to his boss, the owner. The next thing I knew I was called into the owner's office for a more 'personal' sales pitch. We spoke for about 45 minutes as he tried to convince me to use his service. When I told him I was not ready to sign up, he became angry and asked my Counselor why I had been put before 'the committee' if I wasn't ready to commit? The Counselor claimed I had given a verbal commitment at our last meeting. The owner then turned to me and said I seemed to have a problem making a decision and that he did not want to do business with me. I was shocked. They had turned the whole story around to make it look like it was my fault. I felt humiliated. In retrospect, the whole process felt like dealing with a used car salesman. They used pressure tactics and intimidation to try to get what they wanted. As you have probably gathered, more than anything else this experience made me angry."

---

1. For further details, go to your local library and look up "Career Counselors: Will They Lead You Down The Primrose Path?" by Lee Guthrie, in the December 1981 issue of *Savvy* Magazine, pp. 60ff.

- If they claim they only accept 5 clients out of every hundred who apply, and your name will have to be put before 'The Committee' before you can be accepted.

  (**1000 bad points**)

  This is one of the oldest tricks in the book. You're supposed to feel 'special' before they lift those thousands of dollars out of your wallet. Personally, the minute I heard this at a particular agency or service, I would run for the door and never look back.

- If you ask what is the cost of their services, and they reply that it is a lump sum that must all be paid "up front" before you start or shortly after you start, either all at once or in installments,

  (**100 bad points**)

  For twenty-five years I've tried to avoid saying this, but I have grown weary of the tears of job-hunters who 'got taken.' So now I say it without reservation: if the firm charges a lump sum for their services, rather than allowing you to simply pay for each hour as you go, go elsewhere. Every insincere and inept counselor or firm charges a lump sum. So, of course, do a few sincere and good counselors and firms. Trouble is: you won't know which kind you've signed up with, until they've got all your money. The risk is too great, the cost is too high. If you really like to gamble that much, go to Las Vegas. They give better odds.

- If they asked you to bring in your partner or spouse with you,

  (**45 bad points**)

  This is a well-known tactic of some of the slickest salespeople in the world, who want your spouse or partner there so they can manipulate one or the other or both of you to reach a decision on the spot, while they have you in their 'grasp.'

- If they ask you to sign a contract,

  (**1000 bad points**)

  With insincere and inept firms or counselors, there is always a written contract. And you must sign it, before they will help you. (Often, your partner or spouse will be asked to sign it, too.) The fee normally ranges from $1000 on up to $10,000 or more. You may think the purpose of that firm's contract is that they are promising you something, that they can be held to. Uh-uh! More often, the main purpose of the contract is to get you to promise them something. Like, your money. Don't . . . do . . . it.

  You will sometimes be told that, "Of course, you can get your money back, or a portion of it, at any time, should you be dissatisfied with the career counselor's services." Nine times out of ten, however, you are told this verbally, and it is not in the written contract. Verbal promises, without witnesses, are difficult if not impossible for you to later try to enforce. The written contract is binding.

  Sometimes the written contract will claim to provide for a partial refund, at any time, until you reach a cut-off date in the program, which the contract specifies. Unfortunately, many crafty fraudulent firms bend over backwards to be extra nice, extra available, and extra helpful to you until that cut-off point is reached. So, when the cut-off point for getting a refund has been reached, you let it pass because you are very satisfied with their past services, and believe there will be many more weeks of the same. Only, there aren't. At fraudulent firms, once the cut-off point is passed, the career

counselor becomes virtually impossible for you to get ahold of. Call after call will not be returned. You will say to yourself "What happened?" Well, what happened, my friend, is that you paid up in full, they have all the money they're ever going to get out of you, and now they don't want to give you any more time.

You may think I am exaggerating: I mean, can there possibly be such mean men and women, who would prey on job-hunters, when they're down and out. Yes, ma'am, and yes, sir, there are. That's why you have to do this preliminary research so thoroughly.

I quote from the late Robert Wegmann, former director of the UHCL Center for Labor Market Studies: "One high-charging career counseling firm went bankrupt a few years ago. They left many of their materials behind in their former office. A box of what they abandoned has come into my possession. Going through the contents of the box has been fascinating.

"Particularly interesting are several scripts used to train their salespeople. The goal of the sales pitch is to convince the unemployed (or unhappily employed) person that he or she can't find a good job alone, but can do it with professional help. Hiring us, they argue, is just like hiring a lawyer . . .

"Then, at the end of the pitch, comes the 'takeaway.' The firm may not accept your money, you are warned! There will have to be a review board meeting at which your application is considered. Only a minority of applicants are accepted. The firm only wants the right kind of clients.

"That's the pitch. But the rest of the documents tell a very different story. In fact, the firm is running a series of sales contests with all the 'professionalism' of a used car lot . . .

"These salespeople were paid on commission. The higher the sales the higher the percentage of the customer's fee they got to keep.
"There are sales contests. The winner receives a handsome green Master's jacket. Each monthly winner qualifies for a Grand Master's Tournament, with large prizes. . .
"So take this one piece of advice. . . . If someone offers to help you find a great job as long as you'll pay several thousand dollars in advance, do as follows:
"A. Find door
"B. Walk out same
"C. Do not return. "

Over the last twenty years, I have had to listen to grown men and women cry over the telephone, all because they signed a contract. Most often they were executives, or senior managers, who never had to go job-hunting before, and unknowingly signed up with some executive counseling firm that was fraudulent, or at least on the edge of legality.
If you want to avoid their tears in your own job-search, don't sign anything-- ever.[2]

---

2. If you are dying to know more, and your local library has back files of magazines and newspapers (on microfiche, or otherwise) there was a period when bad firms and counselors came under heavy fire (1978-1982) and you can look up some of the articles of that period, as well as those articles which have appeared more recently, to wit:
   "A Consumer's Guide to Retail Job-Hunting Services," Special Report, reprinted from the *National Business Employment Weekly;* available from National Business Employment Weekly Reprint Service, P.O. Box 300, Princeton, NJ 08543-0300. 1-800-730-1111. $8 by mail; $12.95 by fax. A very thorough series of articles on the industry, and its frauds, which names names, and gives the addresses of Consumer protection agencies in each state, to whom you may complain. Required reading for anyone who wants to avoid getting 'burned.'
   " 'Employment counselors' costly, target of gripes," *The Arizona Republic,* 10/8/89.
   "Career-Counseling Industry Accused of Misrepresentation," *New York Times,* 9/30/82.
   "Consumer Law: Career Counselors and Employment Agencies" by Reed Brody, *New York Law Journal,* Feb. 26, 1982, p. 1. Reed was Assistant Attorney General of the State of New York, and more recently Deputy Chief of the Labor Bureau within that State's Department of Law; in this capacity he became the leading legal expert in the country, on career counseling malpractices, though unfortunately (for us) he now works overseas in Europe, in another profession.
   "Career Counselors: Will They Lead You Down the Primrose Path?" by Lee Guthrie, *Savvy* Magazine, 12/81, p. 60ff.
   "Franklin Career Search Is Accused of Fraud In New York State Suit," *Wall Street Journal,* 1/29/81, p. 50.
   "Job Counseling Firms Under Fire For Promising Much, Giving Little," *Wall Street Journal,* 1/27/81, p. 33.

Of course, you're tempted to skip over all this research and visiting and questioning, aren't you? *"Well, I'll just call up one place, and if I like the sound of them, I'll sign up. I'm a pretty good judge of character."* Right. I hear many a sad tale from people who had this over-confidence in their ability to detect a phony, and then found out too late that they had been *taken,* by slicker salespeople than they had ever run into before. As they tell me their stories, they *cry* over the telephone. My reply usually is, "I'm sorry indeed to hear that you had a very disappointing experience; that is very unfortunate, But -- as the Scots would say -- "Ya dinna do your homework. Often you could easily have discovered whether a particular counselor was competent or not, before you ever gave them any of your money, simply by asking the right questions during your preliminary research." [3]

Alternatively, people try to avoid all this research by saying, "Well, I'll just see who Bolles recommends." That takes a leap, because I never recommend *any* agency or counselors -- though some try to claim I do. *(Rockport Institute in Maryland is one example that comes to mind; I just read them, yesterday, claiming this on the Internet.)* In this book, now and in the past, all that I ever list are *'examples'* of the type of agencies out there, and I do this purely as a public service to my readers. But, such an inclusion in this book does *not* constitute an endorsement or recommendation by me -- as I have been at great pains to make clear for the past twenty-five years. Never has. Never will.

Faced with this silence on my part, some readers, then, have *tried to read between the lines.* I can give you an example. Because I allude to the wisdom of *the man* Bernard Haldane in this book, some readers have assumed that this means *the agency* which bears his name must be recommended by me. Nope. Nada. Never.

The man is the oldest figure in this field -- he is eighty-four -- and was the original fountainhead in the '40s and '50s of many ideas that help job-hunters today. He is justly venerated, and as I just said to him when we were together recently, I appreciate all that he has contributed over the past 50 years.

But *the agency* which bears his name is another kettle of fish, entirely. Bernard gave up ownership of that agency years ago. And, for my part, I have neither gone to that agency (as some have claimed) nor recommended them.

So, in sum: *don't* try to 'read between the lines.'

Go do your own homework.

Ask searching questions of *anyone* you are thinking of signing up with. And remember, my advice -- for what it's worth: don't sign up with *anyone* who offers you a contract, or charges other than by the hour.

---

3. If you are reading this too late, did pay some firm's fee all in advance, and feel you were ripped off, you will want to know about Mr. Stuart Alan Rado. Mr. Rado is a former victim of one of the career counseling agencies, and ever since he has been

GOOD ANSWERS

Fortunately there are career counselors who charge by the hour. With them, there is no written contract. You sign nothing. You pay only for each hour as you use it, according to their set rate. Each time you keep an appointment, you pay them at the end of that hour for their help, according to that rate. Period. Finis. You never owe them any money. You can stop seeing them at any time, if you feel you are not getting the help you wish.

What will they charge? You will find, these days, that the best career counselors (and some of the worst, too) will charge you whatever a really good therapist or marriage counselor charges per hour, in your geographical area. Currently, in large metropolitan areas, that runs around $100 an hour, sometimes more. In suburbia or rural areas, it may be much less -- $40 an hour, or so.

That fee is for individual time with the career counselor. If you can't afford that fee, ask whether they also run groups. If they do, the fee will be much less. And, in one of those delightful ironies of life, since you get a chance to listen to problems which other job-hunters in your group are having, the group will often give you more help than an individual session would. Not always; but often. It's always ironic when *cheaper* and *more helpful* go hand in hand.

If the career counselor in question does offer groups, there should (again) never be a contract. The charge should be payable at the end of each session, and you should be able to drop out at any time, without further cost, if you decide you are not getting the help you want.

There are, incidentally, some career counselors who run free (or almost free) job-hunting workshops through local churches, synagogues, chambers of commerce, community colleges, adult education programs, and the like, as their community service, or pro bono work (as it is technically called). I have had reports of such workshops from a number of places in the U.S. and Canada. They surely exist in other parts of the world as well. If money is a big problem for you, in getting help with your job-hunt, ask around to see if such workshops as these exist in your community. Your Chamber of Commerce will likely know, or your church or synagogue.

---

waging a sort of "one-man crusade" against career counseling firms which take advantage of the job-hunter. Send Mr. Rado your story, together with a self-addressed stamped envelope, and he will send you a one-page sheet of some actions you can take. It may not get your money back, but at least you'll feel better for having done something. His address is: 1500 23rd St., Sunset Island #3, Miami Beach, FL 33140. 305-532-2607.

A Sampler

This is not a complete directory of anything. It is exactly what its name implies: a **Sampler**. Were I to list all the career counselors *out there*, we would end up with an encyclopedia. Some states, in fact, have *encyclopedic* lists of counselors and businesses, in various books or directories, and your local bookstore or library should have these, in their *Job-Hunting Section*, under such titles as "How to Get A Job in . . ." or "Job-Hunting in . . ."

Most of the places listed in this **Sampler** are listed at their own request, simply as places for you to begin your investigation with -- nothing more.

Many truly *helpful* places are *not* listed here. If you discover such a place, which is very good at helping people with *Parachute* and creative job-hunting or career-change, do send us the pertinent information. We will ask them, as we do all the listings here, a few intelligent questions and if they sound okay, we will add that place to next year's edition.

We do ask a few questions because our readers want counselors and places which claim some expertise in helping them finish their job-hunt, *using this book*. So, if they've never even heard of *Parachute*, we don't list them. On the other hand, we can't measure a place's expertise at this long distance, no matter how many questions we ask.

Even if listed here, you must do your own sharp questioning before you decide to go with anyone. If you don't take time to research two or three places, before choosing a counselor, you will deserve whatever you get (or, more to the point, *don't* get). So, please, *do your research*. The purse or wallet you save, will be your own.

Yearly readers of this book will notice that we do remove people from this Sampler, over time. Specifically, we remove (without further notice or comment):

Places which have disconnected their telephone, or otherwise suggest that they have gone out of business.

Places which have moved, and don't bother to send us their new address; we have not the staff to try to track them down.

Places which our readers lodge complaints against, with us, as being either unhelpful or obnoxious. The complaints may be falsified, but we can't take that chance.

Places which change their personnel, and the new person has never even heard of *Parachute*, or creative job-search techniques.

Places which misuse their listing here, claiming in their brochures, ads, or interviews, that they have some kind of 'Parachute Seal of Approval' -- that we feature them in *Parachute*, or recommend them or endorse them. This is a big 'no-no.' A listing here is no more of a recommendation than is a listing in the phone book.

College services that we discover (belatedly) serve only '*Their Own.*" Counseling firms which employ salespeople as the initial 'in-take' person that a job-hunter meets.

If you discover that any of the places listed in this Sampler falls into any of the above categories, you would be doing a great service to our other readers by dropping us a line and telling us so. (P.O. Box 379, Walnut Creek, CA 94597.)

The listings which follow are alphabetical within each state, except that counselors listed by their name are in alphabetical order according to their *last* name. To make this clear, only their last name is in **bold** type.

What do the letters after their name mean? Well, B.A., M.A. and Ph.D. you know. However, don't assume the degree is in career counseling. Ask. N.C.C. means "Nationally certified counselor." There are about 20,000 such in the U.S. This can mean *general counseling expertise*, not necessarily career counseling. On the other hand, N.C.C.C. does mean "Nationally certified career counselor." There are currently about 850 in the U.S. Other initials, such as L.P.C. -- "Licensed professional counselor" -- and the like, often refer to State licensing. There are a number of States, now, that have some sort of regulation of career counselors. In some States it is mandatory, in others it is optional. But, *mostly*, this field is unregulated.

Sharp-eyed readers (and professional proofreaders) will note that there is no uniform *form* to the degrees, or to the addresses below (sometimes, for example, you will see *Avenue*, sometimes *Ave.*) This is because we have tried to list their degrees and addresses the way *they* want them to be listed, rather than imposing one uniform style upon all.

Incidentally, the places listed offer a variety of services, which we have not space to list: for example, some offer group career counseling, some offer testing, some offer access to job-banks, etc. Ask.

Generally speaking, these places counsel *anybody*. A few, however, take only women as clients, or have other restrictions unknown to us. So you must ask if they will take you. If they aren't able to help you, your phone call wasn't wasted, *so long as* you then go on to ask them "who else in the area can you tell me about, who helps with job-search, and are there any (among them) that you think are particularly effective?"

If you are looking for places which specialize in doing career counseling from a religious point of view, these are listed separately on page 232. However, many of the counselors listed below are also people of faith.

ALABAMA

(There is a new area code in Alabama, 334, which may affect some of the numbers below.)

Enterprise State Junior College, P.O. Box 1300, Enterprise, AL 36331. 205-347-2623 or 393-ESJC. Nancy Smith, Director of Guidance Services.

Interchange, 2 Perimeter Park S., Suite 200W, Birmingham, AL 35243. 205-324-5030. Michael Tate, Vice-President.

Joseph G. **Law,** Jr., Ed.D., L.P.C., 900 Western America Circle, Suite 501, Executive Center 1, Mobile, AL 36609. 205-341-0600.

ALASKA

Career Transitions, 2221 East Northern Lights Boulevard, Suite 207, Anchorage, AL 99508. 907-278-7350. Deeta Lonergan, Director.

ARIZONA

(There is a new area code in Arizona, 520, which may affect some of the numbers below.)

Career/Life Planning Services, SummerSmith Inc., 4740 E.Sunrise Dr., #323, Tucson, AZ 85718. 520-529-1565. Janet Summers, MEd., President.

College PLUS Career Connections, 4540 S. Rural Rd., #P-8, Tempe, AZ 85282. 602-730-5246. Dr. Warren D. Robb, Director.

Debra Davenport Associates, Eldorado Square, 6619 N. Scottsdale Rd., Scottsdale, AZ 85250. 602-391-2802. Debra Davenport, M.A., L.C.C., Peter Tornich, MBA, MC.

Occupational and Career Services, Inc., 3311 N. 44th St., Suite 120, Phoenix, AZ 85018. 602-840-9084. Julie A. Schwartz, M.S., C.R.C.

Southwest Institute of Life Management, 11122 E. Gunshot Circle, Tucson, AZ 85749. 602-749-2290. Theodore Donald Risch, Director.

Tucson/Pima County Job Club, 110 E. Pennington, Lower Level, Tucson, AZ 85701. 602-884-8280. *(Their mailing address, should you need it, is 2510 North Winstel Boulevard, #184, Tucson, AZ 85716-2350.)* Stuart R. Thomas, President/Founder.

ARKANSAS

Donald **McKinney**, Ed.D., Career Counselor, Rt. 1, Box 351-A, DeQueen, AR 71832. 501-642-5628.

CALIFORNIA

(Note: some 310 area codes, listed below, will change to 562 no later than February 1, 1997.)

Alumnae Resources, 120 Montgomery St., Suite 1080, San Francisco, CA 94104. 415-274-4700.

Judy Kaplan **Baron Associates,** 6046 Cornerstone Ct. West, Suite 208, San Diego, CA 92121. 619-558-7400. Judy Kaplan Baron, Director.

Astrid **Berg**, M.S., Career and Life Planning, P.O. Box 1686, Capitola, CA 95010. 408-462-4626.

Dwayne **Berrett**, M.A., RPCC, Berrett & Associates, 1551 E. Shaw, Suite 103, Fresno, CA 93710. 209-221-6543.

Beverly **Brown**, M.A., N.C.C.C., N.C.C. 809 So. Bundy Drive, #105, Los Angeles, CA 90049. 310-447-7093.

Career Action Center, 445 Sherman Ave., Palo Alto, CA 94306. 415-324-1710. Betsy Collard, Program Director, Linda Surrell, Manager, Counseling Services. *A tremendously impressive career center, one of the most comprehensive in the U.S., with a large number of job listings (81,000) and other resources, including individual counseling, workshops, books, videos, etc.*

Career and Personal Development Institute, 690 Market St., Suite 402, San Francisco, CA 94104. 415-982-2636. Bob Chope.

Career Decisions, 760 Market St., Suite 962, San Francisco CA 94102-2304. 415-296-7373. Mark Pope, Ed.D., NCC, NCCC.

Career Development Center, John F. Kennedy University, 1250 Arroyo Way, Walnut Creek, CA 94596. 510-295-0610. Susan Geifman, Director. *Open to the public. Membership or fee.*

Career Development Life Planning, 3585 Maple St., Suite 237, Ventura, CA 93003. 805-656-6220. Norma Zuber, N.C.C.C., M.S.C., & Associates.

Career Dimensions, Box 7402, Stockton, CA 95267. 209-473-8255. Fran Abbott.

Career Directions, 215 Witham Road, Encinitas CA 92024. 619-436-3994. Virginia Byrd, M.Ed., Work/Life Specialist, Career Management.

Career Planning Center/Business Action Center, 1623 S. La Cienega Blvd., Los Angeles, CA 90035. 310-273-6633.

Career Strategy Associates, 1100 Quail Street, Suite 201, Newport Beach, CA 92660. 714-252-0515. Betty Fisher.

Center for Career Growth and Development, P.O. Box 283, Los Gatos, CA 95031. 408-354-7150. Steven E. Beasley.

Center for Creative Change, 2222 "F" St., San Diego, CA 92102. 619-231-3716. Nancy Helgeson, M.A., MFCC.

The **Center for Life and Work Planning**, 1133 Second St., Encinitas, CA 92024. 619-943-0747. Mary C. McIsaac, Executive Director.

Stephen **Cheney-Rice**, M.S., 2113 Westboro Ave., Alhambra, CA 91803-3720. 818-281-6066, or 213-740-9112.

Constructive Leisure, Patsy B. Edwards, 511 N. La Cienega Blvd., Los Angeles, CA 90048. 310-652-7389.

Consultants in Career Development, 2017 Palo Verde Ave., Suite 201B, Long Beach, CA 90815. 310-598-6412. Dean Porter and Mary Claire Gildon.

Criket Consultants, 502 Natoma St., P.O. Box 6191, Folsom, CA 95763-6191. 916-985-3211.

Cypress College, Career Planning Center, 9200 Valley View St., Cypress, CA 90630. 714-826-2220, Ext. 120.

Margaret L. **Eadie**, M.A., A.M.Ed. Career Consultant, 1000 Sage Pl., Pacific Grove, CA 93950. 408-373-7400.

Experience Unlimited Job Club. There are 35 Experience Unlimited Clubs in California, found at the Employment Development Department in the following locations: Anaheim, Corona, El Cajon, Escondido, Fremont, Fresno, Hemet, Hollywood, Lancaster, Monterey, North Hollywood, Oakland, Ontario, Pasadena, Pleasant Hill, Redlands, Ridgecrest, Riverside, Sacramento (Midtown and South), San Bernardino, San Diego (also East and South), San Francisco, San Mateo, San Rafael, Santa Ana, Santa Cruz, Santa Maria, Simi Valley, Sunnyvale, Torrance, Victorville, and West Covina. Contact the club nearest to you through your local Employment Development Department (E.D.D.).

Mary Alice **Floyd,** M.A., N.C.C., Career Counselor/ Consultant, Career Life Transitions. 3233 Lucinda Lane, Santa Barbara, CA 93105. 805-687-5462.

Futures . . . , 103 Calvin Place, Santa Cruz, CA 95060. 408-425-0332. Joseph Reimuller.

Marvin F. **Galper,** Ph.D., 3939 Third Ave., Suite 204, San Diego, CA 92103. 619-295-4450.

Judith **Grutter,** M.S., N.C.C.C., G/S Consultants, P.O. Box 7855, South Lake Tahoe, CA 96158. 916-541-8587.

The Guidance Center, 1150 Yale St., Suite One, Santa Monica, CA 90403. 310-829-4429. Anne Salzman, Career Counselor and Psychologist.

H.R. Solutions, Human Resources Consulting, 390 South Sepulveda Blvd., Suite 104, Los Angeles, CA 90049. 310-471-2536. Nancy Mann, President/Consultant.

Patrick L. **Kerwin,** Kerwin & Associates, Career Counseling, 1347 N.Allen Avenue, Glendale, CA 91201. 818-840-0366.

Life's Decisions, 1917 Lowland Ct., Carmichael CA 95608. 916-486-0677. Joan E. Belshin, M.S., N.C.C.C.

Peller **Marion,** 388 Market St., Suite 500, San Francisco, CA 94111. 415-296-2559.

Susan W. **Miller,** M.A., 6363 Wilshire Blvd., Suite 210, Los Angeles CA 90048. 213-651-5514.

M. Robert **Morrison,** Ph.D., C.R.C., California Counselors, 327 Laurel Street, San Diego, CA 92101. 619-544-0844.

New Ways to Work, 785 Market St., Suite 950, San Francisco CA 94103-2016. 415-995-9860 fax: 415-995-9867. Primarily publishes job-hunting aids these days, rather than seeing clients: Looking for Work: A Bay Area Guide to Employment Resources. $5.00 plus tax.

Sacramento Women's Center, Women's Employment Services and Training (WEST) for income-eligible women, 1924 "T" St.,Sacramento, CA 95814. 916-736-6942.

Saddleback College, Counseling Services and Special Programs, 28000 Marguerite Pkwy., Mission Viejo, CA 92692. 714-582-4571. Jan Fritsen, Counselor.

George H. **Schofield,** 1529 Hearst Ave., Berkeley, CA 94703. 510-704-9406. Specializes in working with people who are 'stuck.'

Olivia Keith **Slaughter,** LEP, Sunshine Plaza, 71 301 Highway 111, Suite 1, Rancho Mirage, CA 92270. 619-568-1544.

Stoodley & Associates, 1434 Willowmont Ave., San Jose, CA 95118. 408-448-3691. Martha Stoodley, M.S., M.F.C.C., President.

Transitions Counseling Center, 171 N. Van Ness, Fresno, CA 93701. 209-233-7250. Margot E. Tepperman, L.C.S.W.

Turning Point Career Center, University YWCA, 2600 Bancroft Way, Berkeley, CA 94704. 510-848-6370. Winnie Froehlich, M.S., Director.

Caroline **Voorsanger,** Career Counselor for Women, 1650 Jackson St., #608, San Francisco, CA 94115. 415-567-0890.

Patti **Wilson,** P.O. Box 35633, Los Gatos, CA 95030. 408-354-1964.

Women at Work, 50 N. Hill Ave., Pasadena, CA 91106. 818-796-6870.

COLORADO

(There is a new area code in Colorado, 970, which may affect some of the numbers below:)

Accelerated Job Search, 4490 Squires Circle, Boulder, CO 80303. 303-494-2467. Leigh Olsen, Counselor.

CRS Consulting, 425 W. Mulberry, Suite 108, Fort Collins, CO 80521. 303-484-9810. Marilyn Pultz.

Patricia **O'Keefe,** M.A., 359 Cook St., Denver, CO 80206. 303-393-8747.

Life Work Planning, 4306 19th St., Boulder, CO 80304. 303-449-9603. Lauren T. Murphy, Career Development Counselor.

Betsy C. **McGee,** The McGee Group, 5866 South Lupine Drive, Suite 203, Littleton, CO 80123. 303-794-4749.

Resource Center, Arapahoe Community College, 2500 West College Dr., P.O. Box 9002, Littleton, CO 80160-9002. 303-797-5805.

Women's Resource Agency, 1018 N. Weber, Colorado Springs, CO 80903. 719-471-3170.

YWCA of Boulder County Career Center, 2222 14th St., Boulder, CO 80302. 303-443-0419. A full-service career center, fees on a sliding scale. Counseling, testing, support groups, workshops. Natalie Parker, NCCC, Career Services Manager.

CONNECTICUT

(There is a new area code in Connecticut, 860, which may affect some of the numbers below:)

Accord Career Services, The Exchange, Suite 305, 270 Farmington Ave., Farmington, CT 06032. 860-674-9654. Tod Gerardo, M.S., Director.

Associated Counseling Professionals, Career Development Division, 415 Silas Deane Hwy., Suite 224, Wethersfield, CT 06109-2119. 203-296-5523 or toll-free in CT, 1-800-654-4320. John H. Wiedenheft, M.A., Clinical Director.

Career Choices/RFP Associates, 141 Durham Rd., Suite 24, Madison, CT 06443. 203-245-4123.

Career Services Inc., 94 Rambling Rd., Vernon, CT 06066. 203-871-7832. Jim Cohen, Ph.D., C.R.C.

Fairfield Academic and Career Center, Fairfield University, Dolan House, Fairfield, CT 06430. 203-254-4220.

Jamieson Associates, 61 South Main Street, Suite 101, West Hartford, CT 06107-2403. 860-521-2373. Less Jamieson, Principal.

Bob **Pannone**, M.A., N.C.C.C., Career Specialist, 768 Saw Mill Road, West Haven, CT 06516. 203-933-6383.

People Management International Ltd., Ltd., 8B North Shore Rd., New Preston CT 06777. 203 868 0317 fax: 203 868 9776. Arthur Miller, founder and principal.

Releasing Your Original Genius™, The Center for Healing, 805 Farmington Ave., West Hartford, CT 06119. Lorraine P. Holden, MSW, Career/Life Planning Consultant.

The Offerjost-Westcott Group, 263 Main St., Old Saybrook, CT 06475. 203-388-6094. Russ Westcott.

Vocational and Academic Counseling for Adults (VOCA), 115 Berrian Rd., Stamford, CT 06905. 203-322-8353. Ruth A. Polster.

DELAWARE

Brandywine Psychotherapy Center, 2500 Grubb Road, Suite 240, Wilmington, DE 19810. 302-475-1880. Also at J-27 Omega Professional Center, Newark, DE 19713. 302-454-7650. Kris Bronson, Ph.D.

YWCA of New Castle County, Women's Center for Economic Options, 233 King St., Wilmington, DE 19801. 302-658-7161.

DISTRICT OF COLUMBIA

Community Vocational Counseling Service, The George Washington University Counseling Center, 718 21st St. NW, Washington, DC 20052. 202-994-4860. Robert J. Wilson, M.S., Asst. Director for Educational Services.

George Washington University, Center for Career Education, 2020 K Street, Washington, DC 20052. 202-994-5299. Abigail Pereira, Director.

Horizons Unlimited Inc., 1133 15th St. N.W., Suite 1200, Washington, DC 20005. 202-296-7224. Located also at 17501 McDade Court, Rockville, MD 20855. 301-258-9338. Marilyn Goldman, NCCC.

FLORIDA

(There is a new area code in Tampa, 941, and a new area code in Miami, 954, plus a new area code in northern Florida, 352, which may affect some of the numbers below:)

Barbara **Adler**, Ed.D., Career Consulting, 203 North Shadow Bay Dr., Orlando, FL 32825-3766. 407-249-2189.

The **Career and Personal Counseling Center**, Eckerd College, 4200 54th Ave. South, St. Petersburg, FL 33711. 813-864-8356. John R. Sims.

Career Moves, Inc., 5300 North Federal Highway, Fort Lauderdale, FL 33308. 305-772-6857. Mary Jane Ward, M.Ed., NCC, NCCC.

Center for Career Decisions, 980 N. Federal Hwy., Suite 203, Boca Raton, FL 33432. 407-394-3399. Linda Friedman, M.A., N.C.C., N.C.C.C., Director.

Chabon & Associates, 1665 Palm Beach Lakes Blvd., Suite 402, West Palm Beach, FL 33401. 407-640-8443. Toby G. Chabon, M.Ed., N.C.C., President.

The Challenge: Program for Displaced Homemakers, Florida Community College at Jacksonville, 101 W. State St., Jacksonville, FL 32202. 904-633-8316. Rita Patrick, Project Coordinator.

Colonial Clinic, 1155 South Semoran Boulevard, Suite 1139, Building 3, Winter Park, FL 32792. 407-657-8488. Neal A. Carter, Ph.D., Career/Life Specialist.

Crossroads, Palm Beach Community College, 4200 Congress Ave., Lake Worth, FL 33461-4796. 407-433-5995. Pat Jablonski, Program Manager.

Focus on the Future: Displaced Homemaker Program, Santa Fe Community College, 3000 N.W. 83rd St., Gainesville, FL 32606. 904-395-5047. Nancy Griffin, Program Coordinator. Classes are free.

Larry **Harmon**, Ph.D., Career Counseling Center, Inc., 2000 South Dixie Highway, Suite 103, Miami, FL 33133. 305-858-8557.

Ellen O. **Jonassen**, Ph.D., 10785 Ulmerton Rd., Largo, FL 34648. 813-581-8526.

Life Designs, Inc., 7860 SW 55th Ave. #A, South Miami, FL 33143. 305-665-3212. Dulce Muccio and Deborah Tyson, co-founders.

New Beginnings, Polk Community College, Station 71, 999 Avenue H, NE, Winter Haven, FL 33881-4299 (Lakeland Campus). 813-297-1029.

PEN (Professional Employment Network, Inc.), sponsored by Job Service (The Florida Department of Labor). Helps job-hunters who either have a four year college degree and/or have a salary history of $25,000 per year. 3421 Lawton Rd., Orlando, FL 32803. 407-897-2886.

Resource Center for Women, formerly FACE Learning Center, Inc., 12945 Seminole Blvd., Bldg. II, Suite 6, Largo, FL 34648. 813-585-8155 or 586-1110.

The Women's Center, Valencia Community College, 1010 N. Orlando Ave., Winter Park, FL 32789. 407-628-1976.

WINGS Program, Broward Community College, 1000 Coconut Creek Blvd., Coconut Creek, FL 33066. 305-973-2398.

GEORGIA

(There is a new area code in Atlanta, 770, which may affect some of the numbers below:)

Atlanta Outplacement and Career Consulting, 1150 Lake Hearn Drive, N.E., Suite 200, Atlanta, GA 30342. 404-250-3232. Harvey Brickley, Consultant.

Emmette H. **Albea,** Jr., M.S., LPC, NCCC, 2706 Melrose Drive, Valdosta, GA 31602. 912-241-0908.

Career Quest/Job search Workshop, St. Ann, 4905 Roswell Rd., N.E., Marietta, GA 30062-6240. 770-552-6402. Tom Chernetsky.

D & B Consulting, 1175 Peachtree St., 100 Colony Square, Suite 840, Atlanta, GA 30361. 404-874-9379. Deborah R. Brown, MSM, MSW, Career Consultant.

Jewish Vocational Service, Inc., 4549 Chamblee Dunwoody Road, Dunwoody GA 30338-6210, 770-677-9440, Anna Blau, Director.

St. Jude's Job Network, St. Jude's Catholic Church, 7171 Glenridge Dr., Sandy Springs, GA 30328. 404-393-4578.

Mark **Satterfield,** 720 Rio Grand Dr., Alpharetta, GA 30202. 770-640-8393.

HAWAII

Career Discovery, 1441 Kapiolani Blvd., Suite 2003, Honolulu, HI 96814. 808-739-9494. Nancy Hanson, M.A., NCCC.

IDAHO

Transitions, 1970 Parkside Dr., Boise, ID 83712. 208-368-0499. Elaine Simmons, M.Ed.

ILLINOIS

(There is a new area code in Chicago: 630.)

Alumni Career Center, University of Illinois Alumni Association, 322 South Green St., Suite 204, Chicago, IL 60607-3544. 312-996-6350. Barbara S. Hundley, Director; Claudia M. Delestowicz, Associate Director. Full Service Career Center open to the community.

Axis Mobility, Inc., Career Counseling Services, 519 North Cass, Suite 2SE, Westmont. IL 60559. 708-663-0301. William P. Henning, Counselor.

Career Path, 3033 Ogden Ave., Suite 203, Lisle, IL 60532. 708-369-3390. Donna Sandberg, M.A., Owner/Counselor.

Career Workshops, 5431 W. Roscoe St., Chicago, IL 60641. 312-282-6859. Patricia Dietze.

Jean **Davis,** Adult Career Transitions, 1405 Elmwood Ave., Evanston, IL 60201. 708-492-1002.

The **Dolan Agency,** 2745 East Broadway, Suite 102, Alton, IL 62002. 618-474-5328. J. Stephen Dolan, M.A., C.R.C., Rehabilitation and Career Consultant.

Barbara Kabcenell **Grauer,** M.A., N.C.C., 1370 Sheridan Road, Highland Park, IL 60035. 708-432-4479.

Grimard Wilson Consulting, 111 N. Wabash Ave., Suite 1006, Chicago, IL 60602. 312-201-1142. Diane Grimard Wilson, M.A.

Harper College Career Transition Center, Building A, Room 124, Palatine, IL 60067. 708-459-8233. Mary Ann Jirak, Coordinator.

David P. **Helfand,** Ed.D., N.C.C.C., 250 Ridge, Evanston, IL 60202. 708-328-2787. David, incidentally, is the author of a book entitled *Career Change: Everything You Need to Know to Meet New Challenges and Take Control of Your Career.*

Lansky Career Consultants, 500 N. Michigan Ave., Suite 430, Chicago, IL 60611. 312-494-0022. Judi Lansky, President.

Midwest Women's Center, 828 S. Wabash, Suite 200, Chicago, IL 60605. 312-922-8530.

Moraine Valley Community College, Job Placement Center, 10900 S. 88th Ave., Palos Hills, IL 60465. 708-974-5737.

Right Livelyhood$, 23 W. 402 Green Briar Drive, Naperville, IL 60540. 708-369-9066. Marti Beddoe, Career/ Life Counselor; or 312-281-7274, Peter LeBrun.

Jane **Shuman,** Career Management Consultant, 1S 283 Danby, Villa Park, IL 60181. 708-916-7754.

The Summit Group, P.O. Box 3702, Peoria, IL 61612-3702. 309-274-4100. John R. Throop, D. Min., President.

Widmer & Associates, 1510 W. Sunnyview Dr., Peoria, IL 61614. 309-691-3312. Mary F. Widmer, President.

INDIANA

Axis Mobility, Inc., Career Counseling Services, 312 Iroquois Trail, Suite 2S, Burns Harbor, IN 46304-9742. 219-787-9216. William P. Henning, Counselor.

Career Consultants, 107 N. Pennsylvania St., Suite 400, Indianapolis, IN 46204. 317-639-5601. Al Milburn, Career Management Consultant.

Cynthia **Compton,** Ph.D., 3021 E. 98th St., Suite 140, Indianapolis, IN 46280. 317-580-9994.

Sally **Jones,** Program Coordinator/Developer, Indiana University, School of Continuing Studies, Owen Hall, Room 202, Bloomington IN 47405. 812-855-4991.

KCDM Associates, 10401 N. Meridian St., Suite 300, Indianapolis, IN 46290. 317-581-6230. Mike Kenney.

John D. **King & Associates,** Career Counseling and Consulting, 205 N. College, Suite 614, Bloomington, IN 47404. 812-332-3888.

William R. **Lesch,** M.S., Career & Life Planning, Health Associates, 9240 N. Meridian St., Suite 292, Indianapolis, IN 46260. 317-844-7489.

IOWA

Rosanne **Beers,** Beers Consulting, 5505 Boulder Dr., West Des Moines, Iowa 50266. 515-225-1245.

Jill **Sudak-Allison,** 3219 SE 19th Court, Des Moines, IA 50320. 515-282-5040.

University of Iowa, Center for Career Development and Cooperative Education, 315 Calvin Hall, Iowa City, IA 52242. 319-335-3201.

Gloria **Wendroff,** Secrets to Successful Job Search, 703 E. Burlington Ave., Fairfield, IA 52556. 515-472-4529.

Suzanne **Zilber,** 801 Crystal St., Ames, IA 50010. 515-232-9379.

KANSAS

Leigh **Branham,** Right Associates, 6201 College Blvd., Suite 360, Overland Park, KS 66211. 913-451-1100.

KENTUCKY

OI/Ronniger, Career Consultants, The Summit II, 4360 Brownsboro Rd., Louisville, KY 40207. 502-894-9400. Phillip Ronniger.

LOUISIANA

Career Planning and Assessment Center, Metropolitan College, University of New Orleans, New Orleans, LA 70148. 504-286-7100.

MAINE

Susan L. **Arledge,** Life-Planning /Career Consultant, 50 Exeter St., Portland, ME 04102. 207-761-7755.

Career Perspectives, 75 Pearl Street, Suite 204, Portland, ME 04101. 207-775-4487. Deborah L. Gallant.

Heart at Work, 78 Main St., Yarmouth, ME 04096. 207-846-0644. Barbara Sirois Babkirk, M.Ed., N.C.C., L.C.P.C., Licensed Counselor and Consultant.

Johnson Career Services, 34 Congress St., Portland ME 04101. 207-773-3921. R. Ernest Johnson.

Women's Worth Career Counseling, 18 Woodland Rd., Gorham, ME 04038. 207-892-0000. Jacqueline Murphy, Counselor.

MARYLAND

Career Perspectives, 510 Sixth St., Annapolis, MD 21403. 410-280-2299. Jeanne H. Slawson, Career Consultant.

Careerscope, Inc., One Mall North, Suite 216, 1025 Governor Warfield Pkwy., Columbia, MD 21044. 410-992-5042 or 301-596-1866. Constantine Bitsas, Executive Director.

Career Transition Services, 3126 Berkshire Rd., Baltimore MD 21214-3404. 410-444-5857. Michael Bryant.

College of Notre Dame of Maryland, Continuing Education Center, 4701 N. Charles St., Baltimore, MD 21210. 410-532-5303.

Goucher College, Goucher Center for Continuing Studies, 1021 Dulaney Valley Rd., Baltimore, MD 21204. 410-337-6200. Carole B. Ellin, Career/Job-Search Counselor.

Anne S. **Headley,** M.A., 7100 Baltimore Ave., Suite 208, College Park, MD 20740. 301-779-1917.

Maryland New Directions, Inc., 2220 N. Charles St., Baltimore, MD 21218. 410-235-8800. Rose Marie Coughlin, Director.

Irene N. **Mendelson,** NCCC, BEMW, Inc., Counseling and Training for the Workplace, 7984 D Old Georgetown Rd., Bethesda, MD 20814-2440. 301-657-8922.

Prince George's Community College, Career Assessment and Planning Center, 301 Largo Rd., Largo, MD 20772. 301-322-0886. Margaret Taibi, Ph.D., Director.

TransitionWorks, 10964 Bloomingdale Dr., Rockville, MD 20852-5550. 301-770-4277. Stephanie Kay, M.A., A.G.S., Principal. Nancy K. Schlossberg, Ed.D., Principal.

MASSACHUSETTS

Changes, 29 Leicester St., P.O. Box 35697, Brighton, MA 02135. 617-783-1717. Carl Schneider. Career counseling and job hunt training services. Individual or group therapy for job hunters.

Career Link, Career Information Center, Kingston Public Library, 6 Green Street, Kingston, MA 02364. 617 585 0517. Free videos, audiocassettes, and books on job search, plus computerized career guidance (SIGI), public access computer, and workshops. Sia Stewart, Director of the Library.

Career Management Consultants, Thirty Park Ave., Worcester, MA 01605. 508-853-8669. Patricia M. Stepanski, President.

Career Resource Center, Worcester YWCA, 1 Salem Square, Worcester, MA 01608. 508-791-3181.

Center for Career Development & Ministry, 70 Chase St., Newton Center, MA 02159. 617-969-7750. Stephen Ott, Director.

Center for Careers, Jewish Vocational Service, 105 Chauncy St., 6th Fl., Boston, MA 02111. 617-451-8147. Lee Ann Bennett, Coordinator, Core Services.

Jewish Vocational Service, Mature Worker Programs, 333 Nahanton St., Newton, MA 02159. 617-965-7940.

Wynne W. **Miller,** 785 Centre St., Newton, MA 02158-2599. 617-527-4848.

Linkage, Inc., 110 Hartwell Ave., Lexington MA 02173. 617-862-4030. David J. Giber, Ph.D.

Murray Associates, P.O. Box 312, Westwood, MA 02090. 617-329-1287. Robert Murray, Ed.D., Licensed Psychologist.

Neville Associates, Inc., 10 Tower Office Park, Suite 416, Woburn, MA 01801. 617-938-7870. Dr. Joseph Neville, Career Development Consultant.

Radcliffe Career Services (open to the general public), 77 Brattle St., Cambridge MA 02138. 617-495-8631.

Smith College Career Development Office, Drew Hall, 84 Elm Street, Northampton, MA 01063. 413-585-2570. Career counseling services to the community. Jane Sommer, Associate Director.

Suit Yourself International, Inc., 115 Shade St., Lexington, MA 02173-7723. 617-862-6006. Debra Spencer, President.

Wellness Center, 51 Mill St., Unit 8, Hanover, MA 02339. 617-829-4300. Janet Barr.

Women's Educational & Industrial Union, Career Services, 356 Boylston St., Boston, MA 02116. 617-536-5657.

MICHIGAN

New Options: Counseling for Women in Transition, 2311 E. Stadium, Suite B-2, Ann Arbor, MI 48104. 313-973-0003. Phyllis Perry, M.S.W.

Lansing Community College, 2020 Career and Employment Development Services, PO Box 40010, Lansing, MI 48901-7210. 517-483-1221 or 483-1172. James C. Osborn, Ph.D., L.P.C., Director, Career and Employment Services.

Oakland University, Continuum Center for Adult Counseling and Leadership Training, Rochester, MI 48309. 313-370-3033.

University of Michigan, Center for the Education of Women, 330 East Liberty, Ann Arbor, MI 48104. 313-998-7080.

Women's Resource Center, 252 State St. SE, Grand Rapids, MI 49503. 616-458-5443.

MINNESOTA

Richard E. **Andrea,** Ph.D., Titan Office Park, Suite 202A, 1399 Geneva Ave., Oakdale, MN 55119. 612-738-6600.

Associated Career Services, 3550 Lexington Ave. N., Suite 120, Shoreview, MN 55126. 612-787-0501.

Career Dynamics, Inc., 8400 Normandale Lake Blvd., Suite 1220, Bloomington, MN 55437. 612-921-2378. Joan Strewler, Psychologist.

Human Dynamics, 3036 Ontario Rd., Little Canada, MN 55117. 612-484-8299. Greg J. Cylkowski, M.A., founder.

Stanley J. **Sizen,** Vocational Services, P.O.Box 363, Anoka, MN 55303. 612-441-8053.

Working Opportunities for Women, 2700 University Ave., #120, St. Paul, MN 55114. 612-647-9961.

MISSISSIPPI

Mississippi State University, Career Services Center, P.O. Box P, Colvard Union, Suite 316, Mississippi State, MS 39762-5515. 601-325-3344.

Mississippi Gulf Coast Community College, Jackson County Campus, Career Development Center, P.O. Box 100, Gautier, MS 39553. 601-497-9602. Rebecca Williams, Manager.

MISSOURI

Career Center, Community Career Services, 110 Noyes Hall, University of Missouri, Columbia, MO 65211. 314-882-6803.

Career Management Center, 8301 State Line Rd., Suite 202, Kansas City, MO 64114. 816-363-1500. Janice Y. Benjamin, President. Janice is also co-author of *How to Be Happily Employed in Kansas City, 4th ed.*

Women's Center, University of Missouri-Kansas City, 5100 Rockhill Rd., 104 Scofield Hall, Kansas City, MO 64110. 816-235-1638.

MONTANA

Career Transitions, 321 E. Main, Suite 215, Bozeman, MT 59715. 406-587-1721. Estella Villasenor, Executive Director. Darla Joyner, Assistant Director.

NEBRASKA

Career Management Services, 5000 Central Park Dr., Suite 204, Lincoln, NE 68504. 402-466-8427. Vaughn L. Carter, President.

Olson Counseling Services, 8720 Frederick, Suite 105, Omaha, NE 68128. 402-390-2342. Gail A. Olson, P.A.C.

Student Success Center, Central Community College, Hastings Campus, Hastings, NE 68902. 402-461-2424.

NEVADA

Greener Pastures Institute, 6301 S. Squaw Valley Rd., Suite 1383, Pahrump, NV 89048-7949, 800 688 6352. Bill Seavey.

NEW HAMPSHIRE

Individual Employment Services, 90-A Sixth St., P.O. 917, Dover, NH 03820. 603-742-5616. James Otis, Employment Counselor.

NEW JERSEY

Adult Advisory Service, Kean College of New Jersey. Administration Bldg., Union, NJ 07083. 908-527-2210.

Adult Resource Center, 100 Horseneck Road, Montville, NJ 07045. 201-335-6910.

Arista Concepts Career Development Service, P.O. Box 2436, Princeton, NJ 08540. 609-921-0308. Kera Greene, M.Ed.

Beverly **Baskin**, M.A., Baskin Business & Career Services, 6 Alberta Drive, Marlboro, NJ 07746-1202. 800-300-4079. Offices also in Woodbridge, and Princeton.

Behavior Dynamics Associates, Inc., 34 Cambridge Terrace, Springfield, NJ 07081. 201-912-0136. Roy Hirschfeld.

Career Options Center, YWCA Tribute to Women and Industry (TWIN) Program, 232 E. Front St., Plainfield, NJ 07060. 908-756-3836, or 908-273-4242. Janet M. Korba, Program Director.

Jerry **Cohen**, M.A., NCC, NCCC, Chester Professional Bldg., P.O. Box 235, Chester, NJ 07930. 908-979-4404.

Loree **Collins**, 3 Beechwood Rd., Summit, NJ 07901. 908-273-9219.

Douglass College, Douglass Advisory Services for Women, Rutgers Women's Center, 132 George St., New Brunswick, NJ 08903. 908-932-9603.

Juditha **Dowd**, 179 County Road 517, Califon, NJ 07830; *and* 180 Township Line Road, Belle Mead, NJ 08502. 908-439-2091.

Sandra **Grundfest**, Ed.D., Princeton Professional Park, 601 Ewing St., Suite C-1, Princeton, NJ 08540. 609-921-8401. Also at 11 Clyde Rd., Suite 103, Somerset, NJ 08873. 908-873-1212.

Job Seekers of Montclair, St. Luke's Episcopal Church, 73 S. Fullerton Ave., Montclair NJ. 201-783-3442. Meets Thursdays 7:30-9:30 p.m.

Lester **Minsuk & Associates**, 29 Exeter Rd., East Windsor, NJ 08520. 609-448-4600.

W.L. **Nikel & Associates**, Career Development and Outplacement, 28 Harper Terrace, Cedar Grove, NJ 07009. 201-239-7460. William L. Nikel, M.B.A., Founder.

Resource Center for Women, 31 Woodland Ave., Summit, NJ 07901. 908-273-7253. Juditha Dowd, Coordinator of the Career Division.

NEW MEXICO

Young Women's Christian Association, YWCA Career Services Center, 7201 Paseo Del Norte NE, Albuquerque, NM 87113. 505-822-9922.

NEW YORK

Alan B. **Bernstein** CSW, PC, 122 East 82nd St., N.Y., NY 10028. 212-288-4881.

Career Agenda, Inc., 560 West 43rd St.,, New York, NY 10036. 212-595-9226, or 268-0564. Carol Allen, President.

Career Development Center, Long Island University, C.W. Post Campus, Brookville, NY 11548. 516-299-2251. Pamela Lennox, Ph.D., Director.

Career Development Services, 706 East Avenue, Rochester, NY 14607. 716-244-0570. Karen S. Kral, Director, Information and Resources.

Career Resource Center, Bethlehem Public Library, 451 Delaware Ave., Delmar, NY 12054. 518-439-9314. Denise L. Coblish, Career Resources Librarian.

Career Strategies, Inc., 350 West 24th Street, New York, NY 10011. 212-807-1340. "CB" Bowman, President.

Career 101 Associates, 230 West 55th St., Suite 17F, New York, NY 10019. L. Michelle Tullier, Ph.D., Director. 212-333-4013.

The John C. **Crystal Center**, 152 Madison Ave., 23rd fl., New York, NY 10016. 212-889-8500, or 1-800-333-9003. Nella G. Barkley, President. *(John died in 1988; Nella was his business partner, for many years preceding his death, and now carries on his work. The Center also has offices in Chicago and Los Angeles, run under the aegis of The Crystal-Barkley Corporation. The 800 number above will work for reaching all three centers.)*

Hofstra University, Career Counseling Center, Room 120, Saltzman Community Center, 131 Hofstra, Hempstead, NY 11550. 516-463-6788.

Kingsborough Community College, Office of Career Counseling and Placement, 2001 Oriental Blvd., Rm. C102, Brooklyn, NY 11235. 718-368-5115.

Janice **La Rouche** Assoc., 333 Central Park W., New York, NY 10025. 212-663-0970.

Livelihood Job Search Center, 301 Madison Ave., 3rd Floor, New York, NY 10017. 212-687-2411. John Aigner, Director.

James E. **McPherson**, 101 Ives Hall, Cornell University, Ithaca, NY 14853-3901

New Options, 960 Park Ave., New York, NY 10028. 212-535-1444.

Onondaga County Public Library, The Galleries of Syracuse, 447 South Salina St., Syracuse, NY 13202-2494. 315-435-1900. Karen A. Pitoniak, Librarian, Information Services. Has InfoTrac, a computerized index and directory of over 100,000 companies, plus other job-hunting resources.

Orange County Community College, Counseling Center, 115 South St., Middletown, NY 10940. 914-341-4070.

Celia **Paul Associates**, 1776 Broadway, Suite 1806, New York, NY 10019. 212-397-1020.

Personnel Sciences Center, Inc. 276 Fifth Ave., Suite 704, New York, NY 10001. 212-683-3008. Dr. Jeffrey A. Goldberg.

Leslie B. **Prager**, M.A., The Prager-Bernstein Group, 441 Lexington Avenue, Suite 1404, New York, NY 10017. 212-697-0645.

Psychological Services Center, Career Services Unit, University at Albany, SUNY, Husted 167, 135 Western Ave., Albany, NY 12222. 518-442-4900. George B. Litchford, Ph.D., Director. Individual and group career counseling.

RLS Career Center, 3049 East Genesee St., Suite 211, Syracuse, NY 13224. 315-446-0500. Jerridith Wilson, Executive Director.

Allie **Roth**, 160 East 38th St., New York, NY 10016. 212-490-9158.

Schenectady Public Library, Job Information Center, 99 Clinton St., Schenectady, NY. Has weekly listings, including job search listings of companies nationwide.

Scientific Career Transitions, Stephen Rosen, Science & Technology Advisory Board, 575 Madison Ave., 22nd Fl., New York, NY 10022-2585. 212-891-7609. Works with unemployed and underemployed scientists, specializing in émigrés from the Soviet Union.

WIN Workshops (Women in Networking), Emily Koltnow, 1120 Avenue of the Americas, Fourth Floor, New York, NY 10036. 212-333-8788.

NORTH CAROLINA

Career Consulting Associates of Raleigh, P.O. Box 17653, Raleigh, NC 27619. 919-782-3252. Susan W. Simonds, President.

Career, Educational, Psychological Evaluations, 2915 Providence Rd., Suite 300, Charlotte, NC 28211. 704-362-1942.

Career Management Center, 3203 Woman's Club Drive, Suite 100, Raleigh, NC 27612. 919-787-1222, ext. 109. Temple G. Porter, Director.

Sally **Kochendofer**, Ph.D., P.O. Box 1180, Cornelius, NC 28031. 704-892-4976.

Diane E. **Lambeth**, M.S.W., Career Consultant. P.O. Box 18945, Raleigh, NC 27619. 919-571-7423.

Life Management Services, LC, 301 Gregson Dr., Cary, NC 27511. 919-481-4707. Marilyn and Hal Shook. The Shooks originally were trained by John Crystal, though they have evolved their own program since then.

Joyce **Richman & Associates, Ltd.**, 2911 Shady Lawn Dr., Greensboro, NC 27408. 910-288-1799.

Bonnie M. **Truax**, Ed.D., N.C.C.C., Career/Life Planning and Relocation Services, 2102 N. Elm St., Suite K1, Greensboro, NC 27408. 910-271-2050. Free support group.

Women's Center of Raleigh,128 E. Hargett St., Suite 10, Raleigh, NC 27601. 919-829-3711.

NORTH DAKOTA

Business & Life Resources Career Development Center, 17 - 7th Street South., Fargo, N.D. 58103. 701-234-9190.

OHIO

Adult Resource Center, The University of Akron, Buckingham Center for Continuing Education, Room 55, Akron, OH 44325-3102. 216-972-7448. Sandra B. Edwards, Director.

Career Initiatives Center, 1557 E. 27th St., Cleveland, OH 44114. 216-574-8998. Richard Hanscom, Director.

Career Point, Belden-Whipple Building, 4150 Belden Village Street, N.W., Suite 101, Canton, OH 44718. 216-492-1920. Victor W. Valli, Career Consultant.

Cuyahoga County Public Library InfoPLACE Service, Career, Education & Community Information Service, 5225 Library Lane, Maple Heights, OH 44137-1291. 216-475-2225.

Hill & Hill Consulting, Inc., 393 Hawthorne Lane N.E., Warren, OH 44484. 216-856-4440. Barbara H. Hill, President.

J&K Associates, Inc., 607 Otterbein Ave., Dayton, OH 45406-4507. 513-274-3630. Pat Kenney, Ph.D., President.

Judy **Kroger**, LPC, Career and Human Resources Counselor, 260 Northland Blvd., Suite 234, Cincinnati, OH 45246. 513-772-5839.

New Career, 328 Race St., Dover, OH 44622. 216-364-5557. Marshall Karp, M.A., N.C.C., L.P.C., Owner.

Pyramid Career Services, Inc., 2400 Cleveland Ave., NW, Canton, OH 44709. 216-453-3767. Zandra Bloom, Director.

OKLAHOMA

Career Development Services, 5314 S. Yale, Suite 600, Tulsa, OK 74135. 918-495-1788. William D. Young, Ed.D.

OREGON

Career Development, PO Box 850, Forest Grove, OR 97116. 503-357-9233. Edward H. Hosley, Ph.D., Director.

Joseph A. **Dubay**, 425 NW 18th Avenue, Portland, OR 97209. 503-226-2656.

Lansky Career Consultants, 9335 S.W. Capitol Highway, Portland OR 97219. 503-293-0245, 800-498-5247. Judi Lansky, M.A., President.

Marcia **Perkins-Reed & Associates**, New Work Directions, 14153 SW Daphne St., Beaverton, OR 97008. 503-641-3167.

Marion Bass **Stevens**, Ph.D., 2631 E. Congress Way, Medford, OR 97504. 541-773-3373.

Verk Consultants, Inc., 1441 Oak St., #7, P.O. Box 11277, Eugene, OR 97440. 541-687-9170. Larry H. Malmgren, M.S., C.R.C., President.

PENNSYLVANIA

Career by Design, 1011 Cathill Rd., Sellersville, PA 18960. 215-723-8413. Henry D. Landes, Career Consultant.

Career Development Center, Jewish Family & Children's Center, 5737 Darlington Road, Pittsburgh, PA 15217. 412-422-5627. Linda Ehrenreich, Director.

Career Management Consultants, Inc., 3207 N. Front St., Harrisburg, PA 17110. 717-233-2272. Louis F. Persico, Career Consultant.

Center for Adults in Transition, Bucks County Community College, Newtown, PA 18940. 215-968-8188.

Center for Career Services (CCS), 1845 Walnut Street, 7th floor, Philadelphia, PA 19103-4707. 215-854-1800. William A. Hyman, Director. Lucy Borosh, Aviva Gal, Tracey Tanenbaum, Career Counselors.

The **Creative Living Center**, 1388 Freeport Road, Pittsburgh, PA 15238. 412-963-8765. David R. Johnson, Director.

Carol **Eikleberry**, Ph.D., 1376 Freeport Rd., Suite 3A, Pittsburgh, PA 15238. 412-963-9008.

Jack **Kelly**, Career Counselor. Career Pro Resume Services, 251 DeKalb Pike, Suite E608, King of Prussia, PA 19406. 610-337-7187.

Options, Inc., 225 S. 15th St., Philadelphia, PA 19102. 215-735-2202. Marcia P. Kleiman, Director.

Priority Two, P.O. Box 343, Sewickley, PA 15143. 412-935-0252. *Five locations in the Pittsburgh area; call for addresses.* Pat Gottschalk, Administrative Assistant. No one is turned away for lack of funds.

RHODE ISLAND

Career Designs, 104 Rankin Ave., Providence, RI 02908-4216, 401-521-2323. Terence Duniho, Career Consultant.

SOUTH CAROLINA

(There is a new area code in South Carolina, 864, which may affect some of the numbers below:)

Career Counselor Services, Inc., 25 Woods Lake Road, Suite 324, Greenville, SC 29607. 803-370-9453. Al A. Hafer, Ed.D., N.C.C.C., N.C.C., L.P.C.

Greenville Technical College, Career Advancement Center, P.O. Box 5616, Greenville, SC 29606. 803-250-8281. F.M. Rogers, Director.

SOUTH DAKOTA

Career Concepts Planning Center, Inc., 1602 Mountain View Rd., Suite 102, Rapid City, SD 57702. 605-342-5177, toll free: 1-800-456-0832. Melvin M. Tuggle, Jr., President.

Sioux Falls College, The Center for Women, 1501 South Prairie, Glidden Hall, Sioux Falls, SD 57105. 605-331-6697.

TENNESSEE

(There is a new area code in Tennessee, 423, which may affect some of the numbers below:)

Career Resources, 2323 Hillsboro Rd., Suite 508, Nashville TN 37212. 615-297-0404. Jane C. Hardy, Principal.

Mid-South Career Development Center, 2315 Fisher Place, Knoxville, TN 37920. 615-573-1340. W. Scott Root, President/ Counselor.

Dan **Miller**, The Business Source, 7100 Executive Center Drive, Suite 110, Brentwood, TN 37027. 615-373-7771.

World Career Transition, P.O. Box 1423, Brentwood, TN 37027-1423. 1-800-366-0945. Bill Karlson, Executive Vice-President.

TEXAS

(There is a new area code in Houston, 281, which may affect some of the numbers below:)

Austin Career Associates, 4501 Spicewood Springs Rd., Suite 1007, Austin, TX 78759. 512-343-0526. Maydelle Fason, Career Consultant.

Career Action Associates, 12655 N. Central Expressway, Suite 821, Dallas, TX 75243. 214-392-7337. Joyce Shoop, L.P.C. Office also at 1325 8th Avenue, Ft. Worth, TX 76112. 817-926-9941. Rebecca Hayes, L.P.C.

Career Management Resources, 222 W. Las Colinas, Suite #2114, Irving, TX 75039. 214-556-0786. Mary Holdcroft, M.Ed., L.P.C., N.C.C.

Career and Recovery Resources, Inc., 2525 San Jacinto, Houston, TX 77002, 713-754-7000. Beverley Marks, Director.

Richard S. **Citrin**, Ph.D., Psychologist, Iatreia Institute, 1152 Country Club Ln., Ft. Worth, TX 76112. 817-654-9600.

Counseling Services of Houston, 1964 W. Gray, Suite 204, Houston, TX 77019. 713-521-9391. Rosemary C. Vienot, M.S., Licensed Professional Counselor, Director.

Employment/Career Information Resource Center, Corpus Christi Public Library, 805 Comanche, Corpus Christi, TX 78401. 512-880-7004. Lynda F. Whitton-Henley, Career Information Specialist.

Maydelle **Fason**, Employment Consultant, 1607 Poquonock Road, Austin, TX 78703. 512-474-1185.

New Directions Counseling Center, 8140 North Mopac, Bldg. II, Suite 230, Austin, TX 78759. 512-343-9496. Jeanne Quereau, M.A., Licensed Professional Counselor.

New Life Institute, 1203 Lavaca St., Austin, TX 78701-1831. 512-469-9447. Bob Breihan, Director.

Chuck **Ragland**, Transformational Consultancy, 2504 Briargrove Drive, Austin, TX 78704-2704. 512-440-1200.

San Antonio Psychological Services, 6800 Park Ten Blvd., Suite 208 North, San Antonio, TX 78213. 210-737-2039.

Mary **Stedham**, Counseling/Consulting Services, 2434 S. 10th, Abilene, TX 79605. 915-672-4044.

VGS, Inc. (Vocational Guidance Service), 2600 S.W. Freeway, Suite 800, Houston, TX 77098. 713-535-7104. Beverley K. Finn, Director.

UTAH

University of Utah, Center for Adult Development, 1195 Annex Bldg., Salt Lake City, UT 84112. 801-581-3228.

VERMONT

Career Networks, 7 Kilburn St., Burlington, VT 05401. 800-918-WORK. Tim King, President.

VIRGINIA

(There is a new area code in Virginia, 540, which may affect some of the numbers below:)

Tanya **Bodzin**, NCCC, Career Consultant, 9215 Santayana Drive, Fairfax, VA 22031. 703-273-6040.

Change & Growth Consulting, 1334 G Street, Woodbridge, VA 22191. 703-494-8271; also: 2136-A Gallows Road, Dunn Loring (Tyson's Corner area), VA 22027. 703-569-2029. Barbara S. Woods, M.Ed., NCC, LPC, Counselor.

Educational Opportunity Center, 7010-M Auburn Ave., Norfolk, VA 23513. 804-855-7468. Agatha A. Peterson, Director.

Fairfax County Office for Women, The Government Center, 12000 Government Center Pkwy., Suite 38, Fairfax, VA 22035. 703-324-5735. Elizabeth Lee McManus, Program Manager.

Golden Handshakes, Church of the Epiphany, 11000 Smoketree Dr., Richmond, VA 23236. 804-794-0222. Jim Dunn, Chairperson; also at Winfree Memorial Baptist Church, 13617 Midlothian Turnpike, Midlothian, VA 23113. 804-794-5031. Phil Tibbs, Volunteer Coordinator.

Hollins College, Women's Center, P.O. Box 9628, Roanoke, VA 24020. 703-362-6269. Tina Rolen, Career Counselor.

Life Management Services, Inc., 6849 Old Dominion Dr., McLean, VA 22101. 703-356-2630. Buz Rollins. (See North Carolina listings also for this firm.)

Mary Baldwin College, Rosemarie Sena Center for Career and Life Planning, Kable House, Staunton, VA 24401. 703-887-7221.

McCarthy & Company, Career Transition Management, 3908 Terry Place, Alexandria, VA 22304. 703-823-4018. Peter McCarthy, President.

Office for Women, The Government Center, 12000 Government Center Parkway, Suite 318, Fairfax, VA 22035. 703-324-5730. Betty McManus, Director.

Psychological Consultants, Inc., 6724 Patterson Ave., Richmond, VA 23226. 804-288-4125.

Virginia Commonwealth University, University Career Center, 907 Floyd Ave., Room 2007, Richmond, VA 23284-2007. 804-367-1645.

The Women's Center, 133 Park St., NE, Vienna, VA 22180. 703-281-2657. Conda Blackmon.

Working From The Heart, 1309 Merchant Lane, McLean, VA 22101. Jacqueline McMakin and Susan Gardiner, Co-Directors.

WASHINGTON

Career Management Institute, 8404 27th St. West, Tacoma, WA 98466. 206-565-8818. Ruthann Reim, M.A., N.C.C., President.

Diane **Churchill**, 508 W. Sixth, Suite 202, Spokane, WA 99204. 509-458-0962.

The Individual Development Center, Inc. (I.D. Center), 1020 E. John, Seattle, WA 98102. 206-329-0600. Mary Lou Hunt, N.C.C., M.A., President.

People Management Group International, 924 First Street, Suite A, Snohomish, WA 98290. 206-563-0105. Arthur F. Miller, Jr., Chairman.

University of Washington Extension, GH-21, Career Development Services, 5025 25th Ave. NE, Suite 205, Seattle, WA 98195. 206-543-3900.

Centerpoint Institute for Life and Career Renewal, Career Consultants, 624 Skinner Bldg., 1326 Fifth Ave., Seattle, WA 98101. 206-622-8070. Carol Vecchio, Career Counselor. *A multifaceted center, with various workshops, lectures, retreats, as well as individual counseling.*

WEST VIRGINIA

Ed **Jepson**, 2 Hazlett Court, Wheeling, WV 26003. 304-232-2375.

WISCONSIN

Making Alternative Plans, Career Development Center, Alverno College, 3401 S. 39th St., P.O. Box 343922, Milwaukee, WI 53234-3922. 414-382-6010.

David **Swanson,** Career Seminars and Workshops, 7235 West Wells Street, Wauwatosa, WI 53213-3607. 414-774-4755, 414-259-0265.

WYOMING

Barbara W. **Gray**, Career Consulting, P.O. Box 912, Jackson, WY 83001. 307-733-6544.

National Education Service Center, P.O. Box 1279, Riverton, WY 82501-1279. 307-856-0170.

University of Wyoming, Career Planning and Placement Center PO Box 3195/Knight Hall 228, Laramie, WY 82071-3195. 307-766-2398.

U.S.A. - - NATIONWIDE

Forty Plus Clubs. A nationwide network of voluntary, autonomous nonprofit clubs, manned by its unemployed members, paying no salaries, supported by initiation fees and monthly dues. At this writing, there are clubs in the following cities (listed alphabetically by States): California: Laguna Hills, Los Angeles, Oakland, San Diego, San Jose; Colorado: Colorado Springs, Fort Collins, Lakewood; District of Columbia: Washington; Hawaii: Honolulu; Illinois: Chicago; Minnesota: St. Paul; New York: New York, Buffalo; Ohio: Columbus; Pennsylvania: Philadelphia; Texas: Houston, Dallas; Utah: Murray, Ogden, Provo; Washington: Bellevue; and in Canada: Toronto. If you live in or near any of these cities, you can check the white pages of your Phone Book for their address and phone number; also you can call Forty Plus of New York, 15 Park Row, New York, NY 10038. 212-233-6086 to get current information about any of the nationwide locations - - to see if the club is still there, or if there is a new club nearer where you live - - and what their current address and phone number are.

CANADA

(These are listed by Provinces, from East Coast to West Coast, rather than in alphabetical order)

Sue **Landry**, Enhancing Your Horizons Consulting, 25 Birchwood Terr., Dartmouth, Nova Scotia B3A 3W2. 902-464-9110.

careerguide, Ryan Bldg., 3rd Floor, 57 Carleton Street, Fredericton, New Brunswick 506-459-4185. Elspeth (Beth) Leroux, B.A., B.Ed., M.Ed.

Kenneth **Des Roches**, André Filion & Associates, Inc., 259 St. Joseph Blvd., Suite 305, Hull, Québec J8Y 6T1. 819-770-8474.

Jewish Vocational Service, Centre Juif D'Orientation et de L'Emploi, 5151, ch. de la Côte Ste-Catherine, Montréal, Québec, H3W 1M6. 514-345-2625. Alta Abramowitz, Director, Employment Development Services. *Uses both French and English versions of* Parachute.

After Graduation Career Counseling, 73 Roxborough St. West, Toronto, Ontario M5R 1T9. 416-923-8319. Teresa Snelgrove, Ph.D., Director.

Donner & Wheeler and Associates, Career Development Consultants, Health and Social Services Sector, 307 Richview Ave., Toronto, Ontario M5P 3G4. 905-949-5954. Offers workshops particularly for those in the health and social services sector. Mary W. Wheeler.

Hazell & Associates, 60 St. Clair Avenue East, Seventh Floor, Toronto, Ontario M4T 1N5. 416-961-3700.

Mid-Life Transitions, 2 Slade Ave., Toronto, Ontario M6G 3A1, 416-653-0563. Marilyn Melville.

YMCA Career Planning & Development, 15 Breadalbane St., Toronto, Canada M4Y 2V5. 416-324-4121.

Changes by Choice, 190 Burndale Ave., North York, Ontario M2N 1T2. 416-590-9939. Patti Davie.

Susan **Steinberg**, M.Ed., 74 Denlow Blvd., Don Mills, Ontario M3B 1P9. 416-449-6936.

Harold **Harder**, B.Sc.,B.Admin.St. The Precision Group, 400 Matheson Blvd. East, Unit 18, Mississauga, Ontario L4Z 1N8. 905-507-8696.

Human Achievement Associates, 22 Cottonwood Crescent, London, Ontario N6G 2Y8. 519-657-3000. Mr. Kerry A. Hill.

David H. **Wenn**, B.A., M.Ed. Career Counseling. 9 Lindbrook Court, London, Ontario N5X 2L4. 519-660-0622.

Job-Finding Club, 516-294 Portage Ave., Winnipeg, Manitoba R3C 0B9. 204-947-1948.

People Focus, 712 10th St. East, Saskatoon, Saskatchewan S7H OH1. 306-933-4956. Carol Stevenson Seller.

Susan Curtis, M.Ed., 4513 West 13th Ave., Vancouver, British Columbia V6R 2V5. 604-228-9618.

Alice Caldwell, P.B. #19009, 4th Avenue Postal Outlet, Vancouver, British Columbia V6K 4R8. 604-737-7842.

OVERSEAS

(Listed by country and city, in bold type.)

Cabinet Daniel Porot, 1, rue Verdaine, CH-1204 Geneve, Switzerland. phone 41 22 311 04 38. Daniel Porot, Founder. *Daniel is co-lecturer with me each summer at our international workshop.*

Kessler-Laufbahnberatung, Alpenblickstr. 33, CH-8645, Jona b. Rapperswil, Switzerland. phone 055 210.46.48. Peter Kessler, Counselor.

Castle Consultants International, 140 Battersea Park Road, London England SW11 4NB. phone 44-171 798 5688. Walt Hopkins, Founder and Director.

Anne Radford, Warriner House, 140 Battersea Park Road, London England SW11 4NB. 44-171-622-7011.

The Chaney Partnership, Hillier House, 509 Upper Richmond Rd. West, London, England SW14 7EE. phone 081 878 3227. Isabel Chaney, B.A.

Jane Bartlett, Bridgeway Associates Ltd., Career Consultants, Bradford Ct., Bradford Street, Birmingham, England B12 0NS. phone: 0121-773-8770.

Philip Houghton, Career Development. 10 York Pl., Brandon Hill, Bristol, England BS1 5UT. phone: 0117-9254363.

Adigo Consultores, Av. Doria 164, Sao Paulo SP, 04635-070 Brazil. phone 55 11 530 0330. Alberto M.Barros, Director.

Centre for WorkLife Counselling, Suite 3, 5 Earl St., Mosman, P.O. Box 407, Spit Junction, (Sydney area) Australia 2088. phone 61 2 968 1588. Paul Stevens, Director. Paul is the dean of career counseling in Australia.

Imogen Wareing & Associates Pty Ltd, 105 Mowbray Road, Willoughby NSW, Australia 2068. phone 61 2 967 2300. Imogen Wareing, Director.

Career Action, 5 Ivo Whitten St.,, Kambah ACT 2902, Australia. 61 2 319 138, fax: 61 2 316 656. Narelle Milligan.

Judith Bailey, Designing Your Life, 10 Nepean Pl., Macquarie Australia, ACT 2614. phone 61 6 253 2231.

Robert J. Bisdee & Associates, 22 Allenby Ave., Malvern E., Victoria, Australia 3145. phone 61 3 885 4716. Dr. Bob Bisdee, Director.

New Zealand Creative Career Centre, Ltd., 4th Floor, Braemar House, 32 The Terrace, P.O. Box 3058, Wellington, New Zealand. phone 64 4 499 8414. Felicity McLennan,

Max Palmer, Life Work Career Counselling, P.O. Box 2223, Christchurch, New Zealand. phone 64 03 379 2781.

Readers often contact us to ask which of these overseas counselors are familiar with my approach to job-hunting and career-changing. The answer is: everyone of the overseas counselors listed above has attended my two-week workshop, and therefore know my approach well.

Other counselors overseas:

Judy Feierstein, M.A., 46/2 Derech Bet Lechem, Jerusalem 93504, Israel, phone (02) 71 06 73.

Lori Mendel, 14/3 Zui Bruk, Tel Aviv 63423, Israel, phone (03) 29 28 30.

Johan Veeninga, Careers by Design, Business Park "De Molenzoom," P.O. Box 143, NL-3990 DC, Houten/Utrecht, The Netherlands. phone 31 (0) 3403-75153.

Epilogue

Resources for Career Counselors

Books of Particular Interest to Career Counselors:

Just since 1990, 3,100 books have been published on the subject of job-hunting and careers, according to *Fortune* Magazine.[1]

When I first came into this field, that number was only 14.

My pathetic attempts, over the past twenty-five years, to list a decent number of the new job-hunting books that come out each year has obviously succumbed under sheer weight of numbers.

Therefore, from now on I am simply listing *the ten* books published in the past year that I stumbled across, and liked the best -- often for very idiosyncratic reasons.

I know, of course, as you do, that there are *hundreds* of other excellent books out there, which I just have no space to list.

Anyway, here are my ten favorite books for 1995–1996, in no particular order, with a few words in each case as to *why*:

The PIE Method for Career Success: A Unique Way to Find Your Ideal Job, by Daniel Porot. JIST Works, Inc., 720 North Park Avenue, Indianapolis, IN 46202. 1996. Daniel and I have taught together for two weeks every summer but one, since 1979. He is a Frenchman, who lives in Geneva, Switzerland.

---

1. *Fortune*, 1/15/96.

This book, like its author, is brilliantly helpful. No career counselor should fail to read and memorize this book. It is profusely illustrated, and a marvelous 'read.' (For the worried, it *is* in English.)

The Guide to Internet Job Searching, by Margaret Riley, Frances Roehm, and Steve Oserman. VGM Career Horizons, a division of NTC Publishing Group, 4255 West Touhy Avenue, Lincolnwood (Chicago), IL 60646-1975. 1996. Known on the Web as 'the Riley guide,' I like this book the best of all those which have been coming out about job-hunting and the Internet. The table of contents includes such topics as "Jobs in Business," "Jobs in the Social Sciences," "International Opportunities," etc. An impressive work, representing hundreds of hours of research on 'the Net.'

Live the Life You Love, in ten easy step-by-step lessons, by Barbara Sher. Delacorte Press, 1540 Broadway, New York, NY 10036. 1996. I love Barbara. She is smart, witty, caring, and helpful. She is also the author of one of my favorite books, *Wishcraft.* She helps people define, and then get, their dreams. Here we have her latest thinking, and exercises.

Career Satisfaction and Success: A Guide to Job and Personal Freedom, by Bernard Haldane. JIST Works, Inc., 720 North Park Avenue, Indianapolis, IN 46202. 1996. Bernard has been a leading figure in the career field for fifty years now, having begun in 1946. This is a re-issue, revised and enlarged, of his most important book. I am glad to see this book available to us all, once again; I always learn something new, and refresh my knowledge of basic principles, when I hear or read Bernard's thoughts. *(Incidentally, this is not a recommendation of the executive counseling agency which he founded and then sold some years ago, though it still bears his name.)*

Now, to a bunch of very useful new books about the various instruments or *schema* that career counselors like myself so dearly love:

The Whole Brain Business Book: Unlocking the Power of Whole Brain Thinking in Organizations and Individuals, by Ned Herrmann. McGraw-Hill, 11 West 19th Street, New York, NY 10011. 1996. Ned is one of the world's authorities on the two sides of the brain, and this is his application of his theory about the four 'quadrants' of 'the whole brain' as it applies to careers. Beginning on page 72 in his book, he shows the dominant brain pattern for a number of occupations. The rest of the book is equally fascinating, as it discusses skills, work styles, etc.

7 Kinds of Smart: Identifying and Developing Your Many Intelligences, by Thomas Armstrong. A Plume Book, published by Penguin Books USA Inc., 375 Hudson Street, New York, NY 10014. 1993. Well, sure, it's been out for a while. I'm just a little slow. Saw this mentioned on the Internet, went and got it, found it fascinating. A whole different way of looking at skills, based on Howard Gardner's *Frames of Mind.* Daniel Goleman's current best-seller, *Emotional Intelligence: Why it can matter more than IQ,* is also based on Gardner's theory. Both books should be profoundly useful to career counselors.

The Career Guide for Creative and Unconventional People, by Carol Eikleberry. Ten Speed Press, Box 7123, Berkeley, CA 94707. 1995. Carol here gives a brilliant exposition of the "A" corner in John Holland's hexagon. I learned a tremendous amount by reading this. Chapter Two alone is worth the price of the book. It lists 215 jobs that creative, "A"-type people might consider. Another book about Holland's theory also was published recently, and is very useful. It's called *Real People, Real Jobs: Reflecting Your Interests in the World of Work,* by David H. Montross, Christopher J. Shinkman, and the late Zandy B. Leibowitz. Davies-Black, a division of Consulting Psychologists Press, 3803 E. Bayshore Road, Palo Alto, CA 94303. 1995. Interviews with real people, illustrating each of the corners in Holland's hexagon.

Give Yourself the Unfair Advantage! by William D. G. Murray, illustrations by Ashleigh Brilliant. Type and Temperament, Inc., PO Box 200, Gladwyne, PA 19035-0200. 1995. The description of the Myers-Brigg Type Indicator that I find the most appealing among all the books about the MBTI that are out there. Plus, Ashleigh Brilliant is my favorite wit; has been for years.

Benchmark Tasks for Job Analysis: A Guide for Functional Job Analysis (FJA) Scales, by Sidney A. Fine and Maury Getkate, of the Royal Canadian Mounted Police. Lawrence Erlbaum Associates, Inc., Publishers, 10 Industrial Avenue, Mahwah, NJ 07430. 1995. Every counselor who is familiar with the *Dictionary of Occupational Titles* knows Sidney's hierarchy of skills, ranked according to those used with Things, Data, and People. Here he explains his skill charts in detail, and gives sample/benchmark tasks for each skill. A tremendously useful work for everyone who helps people analyze their skills.

Catalogs of Job-Hunting Materials

If you want to know what other career books are out there, I recommend you browse a very big book store, *or* write and ask for various publishers' career catalogs.

Here is a *sampling* (only) of some of them, which you can write and ask for -- no matter where you are, in the world. Some of these catalogs feature not only books, but also software, film, videotape, audiotape, and assessment instruments. I have tried to indicate the range of the catalog, in the listing:

The Whole Work Catalog: Career Resources. The New Careers Center, Inc., P.O. Box 339-AJ, Boulder, CO 80306. Books and videos from over 175 different sources. A comprehensive listing.

Career Development Resources Catalog. Career Research & Testing, 2005 Hamilton Ave., San Jose, CA 95125. Lists books, reference books, journals, workbooks, assessment instruments, audiotapes, videos, computer software, and workshops. Has the computerized *D.O.T.*

Career Planning and Job Search Catalog. JIST Works, Inc., 720 North Park Avenue, Indianapolis, IN 46202.

Masterco Career Catalog, Masterco, P.O. Box 7382, Ann Arbor, MI 48107. Books.

Catalog, Careers, Inc., 1211 10th St., SW, P.O. Box 135, Largo, FL 34649-0135.

Catalog. Reed Reference Publishing, 121 Chanlon Road, New Providence, NJ 07974. R.R. Bowker and other publishers' reference books, plus CD-ROMs, computer software, and online services.

the official publication of the National Employment Counseling Association, a division of the American Counseling Association (ACA)[2], 5999 Stevenson Ave., Alexandria, VA 22304. $20/yr.

Career Savvy: The Career Resources and Media Up-Date Newsletter. A four page newsletter, issued monthly, which informs career counselors of the latest directories, software, online resources, etc. A service of: Developing Executives, Inc., 32580 Grand River, Farmington, MI 48336. 810-615-1811. $24/yr. Kathryn R. Diggs, President.

> *All the above periodicals or newsletters have a subscription fee, as noted. To be sure the newsletter meets your particular needs or interests, I recommend you ask for a sample issue, prior to putting down your money on a subscription.*

Computer Software, Film, Audiotape, Videotape:

For those who wish to explore the *non-print arena*, there are catalogs which you can order, such as:

The 1995-1996 Personnel Software Census, Richard B. Frantzreb, Editor. Advanced Personnel Systems, P.O. Box 1438, Roseville, CA 95678. A dictionary of over 1,200 software programs for human resource management.

650 Career Videos: Ratings Reviews and Descriptions. 1994. Rich Feller, Clearinghouse on Video Usage, Colorado State University, School of Occupational and Educational Studies, Fort Collins, CO 80523. 303-491-6879.

Additional Software Programs *(not in the catalogs above)*

Most of these are for the IBM computer family; rarely, the Macintosh. A listing here is for supplemental information only, and does not constitute a recommendation or endorsement on my part:

Jackson, Tom, *The Perfect Resume.* Davidsons. CD-ROM. Assists in preparing resumes, based on Tom's very popular book. Enables the user to prepare customized, target resumes. For Macintosh as well as Windows 95 computers and compatibles.

Parker, Yana, *Ready-To-Go-Resumes (Self-Teaching Resume Templates).* 1995. Ten Speed Press, Box 7123, Berkeley, CA 94707. This includes three computer disks and manual, for both Macintosh and IBM compatible computers. It is based on her very popular book.

Visual Resume™. Heapsort Software, P.O. Box 324, Holly, MI 48442-0324. 1994. Gives the user who is interested in preparing a chronological resume, the ability to produce such a resume in a very unusual visual layout format (an 8½ × 11″ page, lying on its side, with a time bar at the bottom); also

---

2. Previously known as the American Association for Counseling and Development (AACD), and -- before that -- as the American Personnel and Guidance Association (APGA).

does cover letters, and labels. $19.95 when ordered directly from the publisher (Michigan residents add 6% sales tax). For IBM computers and compatibles.

Easy Working Resume Kit™. Spinnaker Software Corporation, 201 Broadway, Cambridge, MA 02139. 1992. Written only for IBM computers and compatibles. The merits of this software aside, the program has an *excellent* manual, including a long, helpful, and realistic section called *"Beyond Resumes"* -- obviously written by someone who knows what she is talking about, and who is wise and witty to boot. This company also publishes *PFS: Resume and Job Search Pro,* for IBM computers and compatibles. A *Windows* version is available.

Course Syllabi:

If you are interested in course syllabi from courses in career development, career counseling and/or career planning, there is a clearinghouse for such materials, maintained by Dr. Stan Cramer, Dept. of Counseling & Educational Psychology, Faculty of Educational Studies, 409 Christopher Baldy Hall, SUNY Buffalo, Amherst, NY 14260.

Career Assessment Instruments:

This, of course, is a wide world. There are a *million* assessment instruments out there: the Strong Interest Inventory, the Holland SDS, the Myers-Briggs, and a host of others -- plus some quasi-instruments, such as my own *Quick Job-Hunting (and Career-Changing) Map: How to Create A Picture of Your Ideal Job or Next Career.*

If you want to know about instruments available to you, see: Kopes, Jerome T., and Mastice, Marjorie Moran, eds., *A Counselor's Guide to Career Assessment Instruments.* 1988 ed. Published by the American Counseling Association, 5999 Stevenson Ave., Alexandria, VA 22304.

Counselor Training:

By Others: There are countless training opportunities for career counselors in the U.S. and abroad. *Career Planning & Adult Development Newsletter,* mentioned earlier (published monthly by the Career Planning and Adult Development Network, 4965 Sierra Rd., San Jose, CA 95132) maintains a *very good* calendar of these events, and anyone interested in further training would be well advised to be receiving this *Newsletter.*

By Me: Whenever the subject of training comes up, I am asked (endlessly) whether or not I do any teaching. We receive hundreds of letters and phone calls each year asking this. Since I would like to cut down on the mail and phone calls, and also save you some trouble, I will give you the desired information, right here.

I rarely speak, and I do not do any training except once a year -- in August, when I go up to Bend, Oregon, and teach nonstop for fourteen days at a resort there, along with my esteemed colleague from Geneva, Switzerland, Daniel Porot, whose insights you can see frequently throughout *Parachute.* We call this workshop:

Two Weeks of
LIFE/Work Planning
at the Inn of the Seventh Mountain

This is not, as its name might suggest, held in the Orient. The Inn of the Seventh Mountain is a beautiful and popular resort on the outskirts of **Bend, Oregon**, which -- as everyone knows -- is in the center of the United States (Honolulu is 3,000 miles to the West, New York City is 3,000 miles to the East).

The workshop is always in August, always the first Friday through the third Friday. In 1997, the dates are August 1–15. In 1998, August 7–21. In 1999, August 6–20.

Since two weeks is a long time, and people who attend usually do so in lieu of their regular summer vacation, we have deliberately put this workshop at a first-class vacation resort, which past participants have delighted in -- as they can 'have their cake and eat it, too.' The Inn has two swimming pools, waterslide, hot baths/saunas, hiking trails, tennis, whitewater rafting, horseback riding, moped rental, bicycle rental, roller-skating, ski-lifts to the top of Mount Bachelor, and other vacation amenities, outdoor eating -- with *wonderful* food -- all in a lovely pine-forest setting near the foot of a large mountain topped with snow even in the summertime. To enjoy all these amenities, you should plan to come early and/or stay late, particularly if you are coming from a long way away.

The total training at this workshop exceeds 100 hours, and is limited to the first 55 people who apply, each year. In age, participants have ranged from 17–74, have embraced all ethnic groups, and have come from all parts of the world in addition to the U.S.: Scandinavia, England, Wales, The Netherlands, France, Switzerland, Germany, Gabon, Zimbabwe, Brazil, Venezuela, Costa Rica, Panama, Canada, New Zealand, Australia, Singapore, and Japan. Year after year people say that this was close to the most enjoyable fifteen days of their entire life. *Be sure to bring your playful self.*

Our methodology at this workshop is to have you master the principles of life/work planning by rigorously applying them to *your own life* during the two weeks, rather than discussing the problems of clients or their case histories, etc., as is often the fashion these days.

Because of this methodology, **the workshop is useful to anyone, and each year over half the people who attend are not career counselors** -- but job-hunters of all ages, career-changers, homemakers, union organizers, CEOs, teachers, people facing a move, people facing retirement, the recently divorced, college students, clergy and so forth.

The cost of these fourteen days is $3600, double occupancy, all expenses included except breakfasts (tuition, fourteen days room and board and all materials and handouts for the daily sessions).

As this workshop is our one annual fundraiser, to underwrite our worldwide work throughout the rest of the year, there are neither discounts for early registration, nor any kind of scholarships available. However we do have a piece called "How to Find Your Own Scholarship," which you may request.

The workshop is filled strictly on a first come, first served, basis.

How early registration closes, varies from year to year. It closes as soon as we are full. This has ranged from nine days ahead of August to 9 months ahead of August. You never know.

There are usually some last-minute cancellations, in any case, so always write or call to inquire, rather than simply concluding that it is already filled.

For a brochure and registration blank, write to:
    Norma Wong, Workshop Registrar
    What Color Is Your Parachute?
    P.O. Box 379
    Walnut Creek, CA 94597-0379

Phone No.: 1-510-837-3002
    (9:30 a.m.–12 noon. Monday thru Friday, Pacific Coast Time)
    Fax No.: 1-510-837-5120 (twenty-four hours a day)

Index

Outdoor jobs, *158, 180*
Outlook, occupational, *119, 162*
Overseas jobs, *111–14*
  back-up strategies, *113*
  beginning at home, *111–12*
  career counselors, *274*
  directories of, *189*
  in government, *112–13*
  listings of, *112–13, 181*
  resources for, *113–14*
  for teachers, *114*

P

Part-time work, 221. *See also*
  Temporary employment
  agencies
Party Exercise, *23–24, 80, 81, 84,
  159*
Pay. *See* Salary
People. *See also* Contacts; Family;
  Friends
  favorite to work with, *44–49*
  researching, *125*
  skills dealing with, 109, 110–11,
  34–35
  as sources of career information, 136–43
  as sources of salary information,
  217–19
Personality types, 110, *160. See also*
  Holland codes; Myers-Briggs
  Type Indicator; Style of working
Personal traits. *See* Style of working
Personnel departments. *See* Human
  resources departments
Person-who-has-the-power-to-hire-
  you. *See also* Employers
  contacts with, 173
  explaining what makes you different to, 118
  fears of, 189–90, 194–97
  identifying, 170, 173, 176–78
  impossible to see, 175
  problems identifying, 180
  rescuing, 179–80

Perspective, maintaining, *248*
Petals. *See* Flower Diagram
Philosophy of life, *19. See also*
  Mission in life
Physical sciences, resources for, *121*
Physical setting, ideal, *10–15, 16, 19*
PIE Method, 125, 159–65, *126–27,
  275–76*
*Places Rated Almanac, 103, 104,
  109–10, 198*
Pleasure interviews. *See* Practice
  interviews
Porot, Daniel, 64, 125, 159, 162,
  221, *126–27, 275–76, 281*
Portfolios, 66
Practice interviews
  length of, 160
  number of, 165
  people for, 160
  purpose of, 159, 160, 162
  questions for, 160–61, 164
  thank-you notes after, 161
  topics for, 162–64
Prejudice. *See* Discrimination
Prioritizing
  grids, *17, 18*
  method, *16*
  software, *16*
Prison, job-hunting after, *208–9*
Procrastination, overcoming,
  120
Professional societies, *162*
Promotions
  employers' view of, 67
  summarizing accomplishments
  for, 222
  for women, *192*
Psychological types, 110, *160.
  See also* Holland codes;
  Myers-Briggs Type Indicator;
  Style of working
Public service careers, *121–22*

Q

Quick Job-Hunting Map. *See* Flower
  Diagram

NOTES

NOTES

NOTES